Heritage, Nostalgia and Modern British Theatre

Staging the Victorians

Benjamin Poore
University of York, UK

First published 2012 by
PALGRAVE MACMILLAN

Palgrave Macmillan in the UK is an imprint of Macmillan Publishers Limited,
registered in England, company number 785998, of Houndmills, Basingstoke,
Hampshire RG21 6XS.

Palgrave Macmillan in the US is a division of St Martin's Press LLC,
175 Fifth Avenue, New York, NY 10010.

Palgrave Macmillan is the global academic imprint of the above companies
and has companies and representatives throughout the world.

Palgrave® and Macmillan® are registered trademarks in the United States,
the United Kingdom, Europe and other countries.

ISBN 978-0-230-29889-7

This book is printed on paper suitable for recycling and made from fully
managed and sustained forest sources. Logging, pulping and manufacturing
processes are expected to conform to the environmental regulations of the
country of origin.

A catalogue record for this book is available from the British Library.

A catalog record for this book is available from the Library of Congress.

10   9   8   7   6   5   4   3   2   1
21   20   19   18   17   16   15   14   13   12

Printed and bound in Great Britain by
CPI Antony Rowe, Chippenham and Eastbourne

To Mum and Dad

Contents

Illustrations

Acknowledgements

I gratefully acknowledge the support of the Arts and Humanities Research Council, which has enabled me to undertake the research for this book.

I would also like to thank my doctoral supervisor, Professor Dan Rebellato, who has given an extraordinary degree of thought, encouragement and attention to my work as it has developed. I am grateful to Frances Babbage and Aoife Monks for their kind, encouraging and insightful comments on my doctoral thesis. Thanks to Nigel Morris at the University of Lincoln for his stimulating thoughts on *The Prestige*, and to the publisher's anonymous reader for their encouraging feedback. Also, thanks to Elizabeth Mansfield and Nao Nagai for their kind permission to use a photograph from *Marie*. Thanks are also due to Louise LePage and Rachel Clements for their insights and engagement with my research in its various stages of deliberation and delivery. Particular thanks to Kelly Jones for her constant support and painstaking organizational help and for pointing me in the direction of so much useful material.

Heritage, Nostalgia and Modern British Theatre is funded by

Arts & Humanities
Research Council

Introduction: Staging the Victorians – 'Angry Ghosts'?

Bankable Victorians

A glance at the listings for West End theatre or regional theatre season brochures across the UK will confirm the ongoing significance to the theatre industry of drama based on the Victorians. In 2010–11, for instance, there were adaptations and re-imaginings of Dickens's novels (such as Deborah McAndrew's *David Copperfield* at the Bolton Octagon, and Tanika Gupta's re-imagining of *Great Expectations* on tour), alongside the familiar onslaught of seasonal productions of *A Christmas Carol*.[1] There were revivals of twentieth-century adaptations of late Victorian adventure stories, like *Dracula* and *The Invisible Man*.[2] Sherlock Holmes was enjoying a series of stage revivals, which could well be connected to the recent Guy Ritchie film and modernized BBC series,[3] and the television success of *Lark Rise to Candleford*, based on Flora Thompson's books, led to a touring revival of Keith Dewhurst's 1978 play of the same name. Revivals of Victorian plays like Bernard Shaw's *Mrs Warren's Profession* (Comedy Theatre, 2010), Wilde's *An Ideal Husband* (Vaudeville Theatre, 2010–11) and Boucicault's *London Assurance* (National Theatre, 2010) continued to be popular. Edward Fox was touring his one-man show about Anthony Trollope, *Trollope in Barsetshire* (Riverside Studios, 2010), Out of Joint produced a new play about Dickens at Hampstead Theatre and Shared Experience staged a revival of its biographical play *Brontë* at the Oxford Playhouse.[4]

How did productions like this – from inventive physical and ensemble approaches to Victorian classics to the fascination with Victorian writers' lives – become a fixture in British theatre? Film and, in particular, television certainly play a part in consolidating and perpetuating contemporary notions of the Victorian, but this book will argue that it was

1

the social and political upheavals of the later twentieth century, particularly from 1968 to 1990, that generated new theatrical forms with which to interrogate and reassess the Victorian past. Most of these forms are still with us, I will argue, even though our national relationship with the Victorians has undergone a series of radical transformations.

Hence, the overarching argument of this study is that the way in which we represent the past on stage tells us much about how we regard ourselves in the present. Often unwittingly, plays about the Victorians reflect modern concerns about the place of Britain, and the individual, in a post-imperial world of globalized capitalism. Theatre is a sensitive litmus-test for these anxieties because it is a shared, social, space-and-time bound experience in an increasingly individuated, material and private culture. Over the years, these concerns have changed, and from the standpoint of 40 years' distance, we can see profound theatrical differences in the way in which Britain has related to its 'glory years' of the nineteenth century. This book seeks to place British theatre about the Victorians in its broader cultural context, and in doing so will refer to trends in television, films, music, architecture, visual art and fashion over the last four decades. Although these are disciplines with their own vocabularies and perspectives for both audiences and critics, I have drawn on these fields here in order to pursue an argument centred on theatre studies, where fashions in other media and art forms feed into, and are in turn fed by, the theatre.

Why the Victorians?

One objection to this book's focus on heritage and nostalgia is that its ideas could be applied to the theatrical treatment of any period in British history. In this section, I want to propose some reasons for the Victorian period's long-standing and continuing importance to British theatre, to historical playwriting and to contemporary British culture in general.

First, the kinds of plays with historical settings performed on the British stage would have been quite different over the last 40 years had it not been for two plays, in particular, which draw on the Victorian period and our feelings towards it. Edward Bond's *Early Morning*, as Chapter 1 explores, was a provocation to the Lord Chamberlain's Office, a way of demonstrating that its antiquated function was irrelevant and insulting to British society in the 1960s; and the play chose to portray Queen Victoria, Florence Nightingale, Gladstone, Disraeli and others in a surreal and unflattering light in order to make this point. This had the effect that, when the Lord Chamberlain's Office was abolished by the Theatres Act of September 1968, not only was swearing and nudity in the theatre suddenly much more popular (most prominently, initially, in the musical *Hair*)[5] but also a series of plays examining the political, social and sexual mores of the Victorians went into production: Peter Barnes' *The Ruling Class* (1968); Edward Bond's *Narrow Road to the Deep North* (1968) and *Passion* (1968); Charles Wood's '*H*' (1969); Peter Terson's *The 1861 Whitby Lifeboat Disaster* (1970); John Spurling's *Shades of Heathcliff* (1971); and Snoo Wilson's *Vampire* (1973), for instance.

So, while it may well have been inevitable that swearing and nudity, say, would have been much more evident in the immediate aftermath of the Theatres Act, the outbreak of plays mocking or examining the Victorians' legacy was a less obvious consequence. This, I argue, stems in part from the way in which the Lord Chamberlain's pre-censorship applied to depictions even of dead monarchs, and in particular, it seems, frivolous or uncomplimentary representations of Queen Victoria.[6] Furthermore, the attempts by the Royal Court to turn *Early Morning* into a *cause célèbre* on Bond's behalf drew this anomaly to the attention of the theatre-makers and audiences.[7] The controversy seemed to underline the idea that, in the mindset of significant sections of the British establishment, Queen Victoria had only recently died.

The second play that, I believe, is well known and revered enough to have changed British theatrical practice is David Edgar's adaptation of Charles Dickens's *The Life and Adventures of Nicholas Nickleby* for the Royal Shakespeare Company (RSC) in 1980. Its popularity, and hence the length of its run in British theatres and on Broadway, helped greatly to popularize the adaptation of Victorian literature and the narrative techniques that it utilized: recent large-cast Dickens productions, such as the Giles Havergal adaptation of *David Copperfield* and the Declan Donnellan adaptation of *Great Expectations*, are obviously in its debt. The production has also come to be seen as epitomizing a popular reaction against Thatcherism,[8] and fed into the 'Victorian Values' public debate of the early 1980s (as Chapter 3 explains). Hence, for the second time in 15 years, characters from Victorian life and culture were being called up as national bogey figures, which inspired culturally and financially important follow-on activity in British theatre. This book takes as one of its starting points the question that if contemporary ideas of the Victorians were influencing British theatrical practice in such obvious ways, what are some of the more subtly pervasive ways in which our ideas of the Victorians might continue to be an influence?

The second reason for finding my argument drawn to the Victorians in particular is that British culture often seems preoccupied with the Victorian age. Partly, this may be because, as Martin Hewitt has affirmed with some qualification, the events and developments that took place during the reign of Queen Victoria can indeed be seen to have a distinctive character: 'British culture shared more common features between the later 1840s and the early 1890s than it did with British culture twenty years before the first date or after the second.'[9] Still, regardless of whether 'the Victorian period' has a discreet historical identity, the Victorians have often taken centre ground in the long-running 'history wars', fought over the content and teaching style of history in British education, in primary and secondary school in particular.[10] Was the Victorian age one of military and parliamentary heroes, or political and aesthetic rebels?[11] Of industrial might and empire, or exploitation and prejudice? And should it be studied through the absorption of facts and narrative, or through the interrogation of sources? Skirmishes in these history wars have reliably broken out in the media over the last three decades whenever there is a change of political leadership and new educational initiatives are announced.

However, a more important factor in this national preoccupation is the physical presence of Victorian building and infrastructure in the everyday lives of the British people. As Adam Hart-Davis puts it in his book accompanying the television series *What the Victorians Did for Us,* 'much of the world we live in is Victorian. I live in a Victorian house and cycle along Victorian roads, riding what is in essence a Victorian cycle; I travel to London on the Great Western Railway, built by Isambard Kingdom Brunel' – and, we might add, he presumably makes use of the Victorian sewage system within London, as well as the Victorian underground network.[12] Louisa Hadley, in a recent study of neo-Victorian fiction subtitled 'The Victorians and Us', makes a similar point, as does the writer and director Mike Leigh (of whom more we shall see in Chapter 6), who considers at length the influence of Manchester's Victorian architecture while reflecting on the making of his Gilbert and Sullivan film, *Topsy-Turvy*.[13] This Victorian structural inheritance often provokes a mixture of pride and exasperation; the common perception of the failings of Britain's Victorian rail network contrasts sharply with the prestige surrounding the opening of the refurbished St Pancras Station in London, which I explore further in Chapter 6.

Victorian and pre-1919 houses make up a substantial proportion of the UK's housing stock and, while many of these 'period' homes, in estate agents' language, command a price premium, others are associated with nineteenth-century slum living and can provide problems when it comes to modernization and refurbishment. The first and final chapters of this book discuss in more depth the psychological effects of 'slum-clearance' programmes in the 1960s, and the use of Victorian housing as modern dwellings in the 1990s and 2000s.

Culture and the neo-Victorian

A further reason for focusing on the stage representation of the Victorians in particular is that theatre has not been alone as an art form, over the last 40 years, in having a special fascination for this historical era, and for re-presenting it through modern creative works. In prose fiction, Sarah Waters' neo-Victorian[14] trilogy *Tipping the Velvet* (1998), *Affinity* (1999) and *Fingersmith* (2002) is perhaps the most well known, but there is a lineage stretching back to John Fowles's *The French Lieutenant's Woman* (1967), and later including A.S. Byatt's *Possession: A Romance* (1990), Peter Ackroyd's *Dan Leno and the Limehouse Golem* (1994), Michel Faber's *The Crimson Petal and the White* (2002), D.J. Taylor's *Kept: A Victorian Mystery* (2006) and Jane Harris's *The Observations* (2006), among many others. Some of the most highly regarded graphic novels in recent years, such as Alan Moore and Eddie Campbell's *From Hell* (2000) and the ongoing Alan Moore and Kevin O'Neill series, *The League of Extraordinary Gentlemen* (2002 on), are also neo-Victorian, and have each been adapted for the cinema, as has happened to the Byatt and Fowles novels mentioned above, along with Christopher Nolan's *The Prestige*, which I discuss in Chapter 4 on stage biography. In addition, we might consider the proliferation of versions of *Sweeney Todd: The Demon Barber of Fleet Street* as an indicator of the prevalence of a 'neo-Victorian' drama. The story began its modern life as a play by Christopher Bond, before being adapted as a musical by Stephen Sondheim and Hugh Wheeler in 1979, and it is now perhaps most well known as a 2008 film directed by Tim Burton and starring Johnny Depp.

Waters' *Tipping the Velvet*, *Fingersmith* and *Affinity* were adapted for television in 2002, 2005 and 2008, respectively, and indeed British television and its ongoing panoply of documentaries, adaptations and lifestyle programmes are one of the major ways in which the Victorians continue to occupy the British consciousness. To take a particularly striking example, on terrestrial television in the first week of June 2008, one could view the final show in the series *I'd Do Anything* on BBC1 on the Saturday night (a talent show where the winner plays

Nancy in the musical *Oliver!*, adapted from Dickens), a biographical drama about Florence Nightingale on the same channel on the Sunday (1 June), a drama-documentary on the Monday about Queen Victoria on Channel 4 as part of the 'Victorian Passions' series, and *The Supersizers Go... Victorian* on the Tuesday night, in which presenters Sue Perkins and Giles Coren attempt to eat the diet of wealthy Victorians for a week. It is the full range of interests in Victorian life, of which I have listed only a sample above, that Cora Kaplan has called 'Victoriana' and defined thus: 'Today "Victoriana" might usefully embrace the whole phenomenon, the astonishing range of representations and reproductions for which the Victorian – whether as the origin of late twentieth century modernity, its antithesis, or both at once – is the common referent... a kind of conceptual nomad, not so much lost as permanently restless and unsettled.'[15]

Re-presenting the Victorians

Despite all this cross-media activity around Victorian historical and fictional sources, to date there has been no monograph or history of the 'neo-Victorian' on the British stage, and I discuss in this section some of the difficulties in applying the neo-Victorian classification to theatre. Ann Heilmann and Mark Llewellyn's significant and wide-ranging study *Neo-Victorianism* (2010) defines its field thus: 'To be part of the neo-Victorianism we discuss in this book, texts (literary, filmic, audio/visual) must in some respect be *self-consciously engaged with the act of (re)interpretation, (re)discovery and (re)vision concerning the Victorians.*'[16] Furthermore, their book's introduction states that there is a distinction between 'contemporary literary and filmic neo-Victorian culture' and 'other aspects of contemporary culture which embrace historical settings but do not involve themselves to such a high degree in the self-analytic drive that accompanies "neo-Victorianism" '.[17] Hence, for example, the television series *Lark Rise to Candleford* 'did not constitute a neo-Victorian engagement as such with the nature of how to tell the Victorian story now' but rather was 'weekend entertainments'.[18] This pattern of aesthetic judgement, defining a neo-Victorian text as one that is distinct from texts that are merely naive or imitative, is one that is echoed in Louisa Hadley's *Neo-Victorian Fiction and Historical Narrative* (2010).[19] If the category of the 'neo-Victorian' has such entry requirements, then it is rather too exclusive for the range of cultural production that I intend to cover in this book. *Heritage, Nostalgia and Modern British Theatre*, as the title suggests, focuses on theatrical and cultural manifestations of the Victorians, even if they do, individually, constitute 'a purely nostalgic or aesthetic approach to the Victorian past', as Hadley puts it.[20] For, taken together and over time, I argue that these manifestations form a picture of how the UK has coped with the loss of international prestige, and of belief in progress, and how that has characterized the post-Victorian age (the last four decades in particular). It is a quantitative approach, investigating and drawing conclusions from the patterns of theatrical production, and discussing representative examples, rather than a qualitative approach, which would make fine judgements about the best and most seriously engaged drama about the Victorians.

This book's reading of patterns and trends is made possible by the sheer volume of new playwriting on the Victorian period since the 1960s. My research was drawn to the period on the basis of the differing perspectives of a handful of well-known plays with Victorian settings, such as *The Elephant Man*, *Nicholas Nickleby*, *The Ruling Class*, *Sweeney Todd*, *Poppy* and *Cloud Nine*. However, having consulted several sources to produce a working database (see the Section) 'Research methodologies' below, it became evident that there were at least 1200 'Victorian' productions in British theatres over the 40 years since 1968, including revivals of Victorian plays, adaptations and neo-Victorian drama.

I would also argue that while there are clearly lines of connection between the classic Victorian novel and its screen adaptation(s), and between the neo-Victorian novel and its screen adaptation(s), in considering representations of the Victorian there is much work to be done in connecting the practices of theatre, film and television. There are obvious cross-fertilizations, such as *Sweeney Todd* and *Lark Rise to Candleford*, where adaptations have influenced each other across media, and also historical points where styles of film or television can appear to influence playwriting (as examined in discussing the influence of 1960s satire in Chapter 1).[21] But it also makes sense to consider modern British theatre, film and television as post-Victorian entertainment forms, where the novel is not. A novel with a Victorian setting can pastiche the styles of the period and, as Hadley notes, can in some cases 'pass' as actually Victorian.[22] TV, cinema and theatre can never do so: the very nature of the presentational technology makes such sleight-of-hand impossible. The experience of watching theatre, film and television about the Victorians is also often socially negotiated; we are partly watching each other as well as of the production, aware of our group as well as of our individual engagement with a representation of the past, and gauging our responses as in accord with, or in opposition to, the general consensus.

Victorians and the birth of modernity

Kaplan's definition of 'Victoriana', quoted above, suggests that there is a widespread cultural habit of ascribing the birth of modernity to (particularly the latter years of) the Victorian period, a tendency that historiographers have called 'emergence theory'. As Matthew Rowlinson has pointed out, the development of the Victorian studies discipline in the 1950s and 1960s, and the establishment of the journal *Victorian Studies*, was founded in part on Michael Wolff's influential idea that 'to study the Victorian era is actually to study modernity itself'.[23] Kate Flint has echoed this concern more recently, stating that 'For me, the importance of our period lies in the extent to which it is still contiguous, in many recognizable ways, with the formation of our own world and in the development, which it witnessed, of a number of different modernities ... that ... draw from eighteenth-century projects and evolve into twentieth-century values and imperatives.'[24] My own theoretical approach, a 'presentist' (defined below) view from the early twenty-first century, attempts to look with a degree of objectivity at late twentieth-century theatrical assessments of the Victorians, and attempts a critique of the idea of 'emergence', and the behaviour and structures that have been attached to it since the 1960s.

Research methodologies

In this respect, and insofar as it has been influenced by new historicist techniques, this book draws considerably on the practice of Michel Foucault. His *History of Sexuality: 1* has been an important point of departure for this study, with its anatomization of the 'discourse on modern sexual repression', where we can erroneously blame the Victorians for the silence and secrecy surrounding sex.[25] This idea that we can be liberated if only we were to embark on 'this strange endeavour: to tell the truth of sex', and the way that this liberatory endeavour is doomed to failure when sex and sexuality are assumed to be the same thing, is an important part of my analysis of plays about empire in Chapter 2.[26] As Foucault discusses in 'Questions of Method', I look for 'a sort of multiplication or pluralisation of causes', as in my analysis of the emergence of empire plays (Chapter 2) or biodrama (Chapter 4), rather than straightforward causality; I investigate the problems of using the 'floating signifier' of 'the Victorians' in British theatre, rather than the subject of 'Victorian plays after 1968'; and I have tried not to overgeneralize these findings into other time periods, geographical areas and media, in the latter case examining points of difference rather than assuming similarity.[27]

However, I am wary of Foucault's tendency, despite the strategy outlined above, to attempt to place himself outside his own historical moment. This, as John M. Ellis has argued, has led to some of Foucault's followers assuming that they have access to a universal truth about 'the reality of sexism, racism, and oppression', a flaw that Mark Bauerlein also recognizes in what he calls 'social constructionism' and what Thomas Nagel labels an all-purpose postmodern 'unmasking' strategy.[28] Hence the use of some methods associated with new historicism, and the conscious adoption of a particular formulation of the 'presentist' approach, which I hope will obviate any tendencies towards universalism, or the denial of any political standpoint.

The new historicists, as characterized in Jonathan Gill Harris's useful summary, argue that we have no direct access to a history – be that Victorian or, more pertinently, one of the late twentieth century – that exists outside texts (a claim that, for Harris, stages a break between new historicism and cultural materialism, which posits the unproblematic existence of a reality outside language).[29] My own practice in this book does not go so far; certainly, I affirm that there is no access to history outside interpretation, but I do not conceive of everything as a 'text'. I have adopted, at several points in the argument, the classic new historicist strategy of placing a 'literary' and a 'non-literary' text side by side, in order to see whether the same discourse circulates in each.[30] Hence, the present study seeks to deepen an understanding of these theatrical texts by placing them alongside pop music and fashion in Chapter 1, or Stuart Hall's analysis of 'moral panics' in the 1970s in Chapter 2, or Margaret Thatcher's speeches in Chapters 3 and 4, or contemporary art and the refurbishment of public buildings in Chapter 6. Nevertheless, I consider this a 'borrowing' of the technique of viewing cultural artefacts as texts and do not wish to suggest that this is the only way to experience them.

I see the foregrounding of patterns of lesser known plays about the Victorians as adding a fresh dimension to histories of recent British theatre. However, I also hope, in the case of well-known plays like *Cloud Nine* and *Nicholas Nickleby*, to explore what Stephen Greenblatt has called 'resonance': 'By resonance I mean the power of the object displayed to reach out beyond its formal boundaries to a larger world, to evoke in the viewer the complex, dynamic cultural forces from which it has emerged.'[31] Greenblatt goes on to assert that new historicism's affinity with 'resonance'

> would call for an attempt to reduce the isolation of individual "masterpieces," to illuminate the conditions of their making, to disclose the history of their appropriation and the circumstances in which they come to be displayed, to restore the tangibility, the openness, the permeability of boundaries that enabled the objects to come to into being in the first place.[32]

This passage seems to make clear Greenblatt's debt to Foucault's notion of the contingency of historical events, and it is an important strategy for texts that we think we know. How far has *Cloud Nine*, for instance, been appropriated by the history of the Royal Court, or Joint Stock, or of studies of Churchill's development as a writer, rather than allowed to be seen out of periodic isolation, as a 1970s 'empire' play alongside those of Edward Bond, Charles Wood, Simon Gray and Tony Harrison?

However, the new historicist approach is not adopted exclusively, for there is some use of a cultural-materialist frame of reference. Jonathan Dollimore and Alan Sinfield famously defined cultural materialism in their 1985 introduction to *Political Shakespeares* as 'a combination of historical context, theoretical method, political commitment, and textual analysis', and Gill Harris has similarly described cultural materialists as being 'interested in the multiple ideological uses to which historical texts can be put in the critic's own moment, including the goal of effecting radical social change'.[33] This book makes no such claims for effecting radical social change, although a better understanding of the UK's ambivalent feelings towards its Victorian past may well inform the ongoing debates about citizenship and nationhood. Nevertheless, I do see the history of stage representations of the Victorians as including, and being influenced by, the present moment; in Gill Harris's schema, the individual chapters tend to look at theatre history as a new historicist 'synchronic moment', while the way in which the book overall is structured, and the conclusions drawn, tends to view history as 'a diachronic continuum that includes the present location of the critic'.[34]

Situating 'presentism'

Hugh Grady has labelled such an approach 'presentism', claiming that 'While only a few critics have consciously used this terminology, it refers in this context to any critical practice which takes as its point of origin the cultural present.'[35] In this sense, he argues, such movements as cultural materialism, feminism, postcolonial criticism and even performance studies can be seen as instances of 'presentist practice'.[36] Indeed, he continues, there is no historicism that does not imply a latent presentism: 'all reconstructions of the past are interested and motivated by our current history and situation'.[37] Hence my use of such present-day reference points, at the beginning of this introduction, as, television schedules, graphic novels, sewers and train stations: the aim is to start from the everyday, profoundly ambiguous weaving of the Victorian into British life, and use that to inform the themes being interrogated. Hadley's neo-Victorianism, by contrast, declares its suspicion of presentism, which, she states, 'implicitly validates the idea of universal values that transcend historical boundaries and, therefore, is prone to (mis)appropriation for political ends'.[38] I would contend that a self-aware presentism when analysing the appropriation of the Victorians is a vital tool, since all of us have some degree of presentist (and political) bias. After all, only time will tell which of our fictions – and our critical analyses of them – will be judged to have been hopelessly presentist in 50 or 100 years' time.

The adoption of presentist practice does not solve the chicken-and-egg problem of understanding one's own relation to history while still in a historical moment. To take one of Grady's examples above, cultural materialists in the 1970s may well have conceived their own historical moment very differently from the one that, in hindsight, it turned out to be. They may have been writing in the confident expectation of socialist revolution, intensely aware of their moment but unaware of the coming dominance of Thatcherite conservatism. All that can be offered is an open attempt to note the way in which my perspective is shaped by my place in, and relation to, the events described. Therefore, because it may well influence my 'presentist' standpoint, I believe it is worth declaring my position as part of that generation that came to political consciousness as a teenager during Margaret Thatcher's period as prime minister and achieved voting age shortly before John Major was elected; and the adulthood of whom has witnessed the marked convergence of the ideological ground of both major political parties in the UK, and the devolution of power to Northern Ireland, Scotland and Wales. Membership of this demographic group may well have influenced my perception of the importance of the 'Victorian values' debate in Chapters 3 and 4, for instance, or socialist fringe theatre groups of the 1970s in Chapter 4, or the suggestion of an English 'victimological narrative' in Chapter 6.

However, it is also worth stating some reasons why Britain in the early years of the twenty-first century is, in my view, a very useful standpoint from which to view the history of Victorian plays since the abolition of the Lord Chamberlain's Office. As the chapters that follow will make clear, Britain's relationship with the Victorians during the decades from the 1960s to the 1990s had much to do with concerns about the identity of modern Britain, and fears of national decline. This reflects, to a considerable degree, the strain placed on the post-war political consensus by the economic turbulence and union activism of the 1960s and 1970s, the introduction of monetarism in the early 1980s and the shift away from welfare-statism to a more individualistic, neo-liberal political economy that is now endorsed by all the major political parties. We in Britain now inhabit a political landscape where even the Labour Party has favoured, in its recent administrations, financial deregulation, tax cuts and private-sector, 'free-market' solutions to public needs,[39] and it is therefore inconceivable that a post-war-style socialist government will be returned to power in the near future.[40] Having crossed over into the territory of neo-liberal economics during the Thatcher and Major years, and having been kept there during Labour's thirteen years in power, now seems a good time to look back, with a degree of historical distance, on the conflicts and tensions in British society as it transformed into its current state.

Anecdotalism

The present study also makes use of the term 'anecdotalism', which I have used as a presentist strategy to explore the ways in which our culture packages ideas of who the Victorians were. The term borrows from Erin O'Connor's polemic against overly extended postcolonial critiques of the Victorian novel, 'Preface for a Post-Postcolonial Criticism', a practice that she terms 'Victorientalism', and which I refer to more fully in Chapter 5. O'Connor's 'Victorientalism', the term itself suggested of course by Edward Said's book *Orientalism*, is a presentist critique, I argue, in that it takes as its starting point what it perceives as the modern critical tendency to find evidence of imperialism in every Victorian novel, to make this the most important aspect of the work and thus to condemn the novel *in toto*. A similarly 'relentlessly synecdochal' approach to the Victorians is what I have found in researching the theatrical and wider cultural representations of the period.[41]

Put simply, people like to tell stories about the Victorians, to capture them 'in a nutshell', in order to reinforce the meanings of the widespread deployment of the word as an adjective. One such story is the idea that the Victorians covered the legs on their pianos, since the display of 'legs' of any kind was viewed as indecent. As Matthew Sweet has shown convincingly in his book *Inventing the Victorians*, the myth was used in Victorian times to mock American prudery and was popularized as a view of the Victorians themselves in 1947.[42] He concludes, 'the synecdochic relationship that now exists between Victorian sensibilities and the clothed piano leg is wholly fraudulent'.[43] In Chapter 3, I explore how competing versions of the Victorian era were used in the political battleground of the 1980s, each based on a massive oversimplification of how 'the Victorians' thought or behaved. In Chapter 5, I examine how unsubstantiated stories about Charlotte and Emily Brontë have been used to support ideas about the authors' respective talents, and their novels. In Chapter 6, I investigate how 'supernatural realist' plays dramatize the form of the anecdote or urban myth in order to make sweeping points about the relationships between the nineteenth and twentieth centuries.

Before deploying this critical apparatus, however, it is important to position my use of the term 'anecdote'. The use of the anecdote as research tool can be traced back to Stephen Greenblatt's 1990 introduction to his *Learning to Curse*. He refers to Joel Fineman's description of the anecdote as that which 'uniquely refers to the real', adding his own gloss, that the anecdote 'has at once something of the literary and something that exceeds the literary, a narrative form and a pointed, referential access to what lies beyond or beneath that form'.[44] This, I argue, is true of 'supernatural realist' plays, as discussed in Chapter 6: they tell us a surface story yet point to something going on beneath the surface, representative of a nation ill at ease with itself.

Greenblatt defines a further function of anecdote as its provision of 'the sense if not of a break then at least of a swerve in the ordinary and well-understood succession of events'.[45] When he declares himself the enemy of literary criticism and explication that seeks to disparage 'mere anecdote', he talks of how such an approach 'was brought in to lay contingency and disturbance to rest'.[46] By contrast, he states that he is 'committed to the project of making strange what has become familiar, of demonstrating that what seems an untroubling and untroubled part of ourselves (for example, Shakespeare) is actually part of something else, something different'.[47] In this light, the supernatural realist play might be read as an attempt to highlight contingency – the chance encounters through which we 'trip over' a history that is unofficial, private, strange and hidden – and disturbance, phenomenologically and psychologically felt. However, I see anecdotalism as essentially the opposite strategy to Greenblatt's, since his determination to take anecdote seriously involves using it as evidence to challenge the dominant version of history. By contrast, in my view of anecdotalism, the anecdote becomes one of the popular, dominant ways of thinking about the period, based not on evidence but on a widespread willingness to believe things that feel as if they ought to be true.

Jacky Bratton has further theorized the function of anecdote within theatre histories, and she makes a number of important points that must be adapted or refined if the idea of anecdote here is to retain its cohesion. First, it is important to note that although Bratton, apparently like Greenblatt above, sees anecdote as poised between fact and fiction, for her there is a claim to truth, but also a claim to a deeper truth, an 'ineffable "essence"' about the person.[48] This is much closer to my idea of anecdotalism regarding the Victorians, where the essence of Emily Brontë, or Rudyard Kipling, or (through 'emergence') of our own modernity, or of Victoria's entire reign, is being claimed.

The second relevant point from Bratton's discussion of anecdote that I want to bring in here is that 'the recounting of anecdotes, which are the building blocks of theatrical memoir and biography, may be understood not merely as the vehicle for more or less dubious or provable facts, but as a process of identity formation that extends beyond individuals to the group or community to which they belong'.[49] For the purposes of my argument, then, the play as anecdote functions not always to tell an individual's story but to form or propose group or community identity (the British and how they relate to their Victorian past). Thus, Victorian biodrama, as Chapter 4 shows, seeks to take us from 'the good old days' to modernity, presenting a version, channelled through one person, of what was gained and lost.

Thirdly, Bratton explores how the anecdote shields as much as it exposes, the anecdotes of Charles Mathews being a case in point; it provides a mask to hide behind, in the form of amusing stories and impersonations.[50] We might conjecture that in many cases, the nineteenth-century timeframe is being used as a way of sneaking in less historically specific concerns (patriarchy, say, or the treatment of madness) for which the Victorians, as scapegoats, stock characters in the national psyche, are expected to take the blame. Elizabeth Schafer, in the introduction to her biography of Lilian Baylis, makes a connected point: that the anecdotes about Baylis 'cumulatively suggest a tendency towards containment, as if the most effective way for many to deal with Baylis's unladylike, unorthodox but completely phenomenal success was to render her a joke'.[51] If, as Foucault pointed out, we can characterize the Victorians as repressed, bumbling sexual hypocrites, then this promises to contain our anxieties and characterize us as 'free'.

Another sense in which this familiar, comforting element of anecdotalism manifests itself is in its provision of a neat sense of closure. An anecdote would be felt to have failed if it did not deliver a punchline, or a conclusion, from which might be drawn one or more implied meanings. This is true of Dickens's happy endings, but also of the supernatural realist stories of Chapter 6, where the hauntings are all eventually explicable. Similarly, an oral ghost story, told in anecdotal or urban myth form, has to fit together neatly; the events (the hauntings) appear unexplained, but then someone does some research or has a chance conversation and it is revealed that the lady in question died on that road seven years before, or the house was built on an old plague pit, or the building used to contain a staircase right there, back when it was a convent.

This neatness and causality is one of the features of a story that the folklorist Bruce Jackson highlights in his wayward, ruminative volume *The Story Is True*. I will first explain what I believe he has to say that is relevant to the above discussion of anecdote, and then call into question his particular use of the term 'story'. First, as just mentioned, stories have a causality that real life tends to lack. Jackson recalls a fraught conversation with an MA creative-writing student where he tried to explain that 'narrative fiction usually has to make sense but real life is under no such obligation. One event may follow another in real life, but only once in a great while will the relationship between the two be causal.'[52] Furthermore, Jackson goes on to argue, 'People who live in what anthropologists used to call "primitive societies" believe the world is perfectly causal... The closest mindsets to that of primitive thinking are found, perhaps, in paranoid-schizophrenics and scientists.'[53] This does not, of course, mean that stories are wicked, immoral things because they bend and shape real life (Jackson quotes the Italian proverb, 'All stories are true... and some of them even happened'); rather that, in order to 'mean', stories have to have an artificial cut-off point and a causality that we accept as the price of admission.[54]

A second point of Jackson's argues a very similar point to what Bratton and Schafer have claimed above regarding anecdotes: that the 'rigid story doesn't only bring in information; it also keeps other information out. It's as much screen as it is window.'[55] Jackson also discusses the stories that circulate within families, and argues that 'they're at least as much of a story of our regard for the family now as they are a report of what happened then', a point that Bratton touches on when quoting Halbwachs on 'collective memory' and research by Bruner and Feldman.[56] Jackson's ideas about the place of stories in families set off an association, for me at least, with George Orwell's famous claim that England

> resembles a family, a rather stuffy Victorian family with not many black sheep in it but with all its cupboards bursting with skeletons. It has rich relations who have to be kow-towed to and poor relations who are horribly sat upon, and there is a deep conspiracy of silence about the source of the family income ... Still, it is a family ... A family with the wrong members in control.[57]

Jackson further asserts that

> To an outsider this myth or tale or anecdote [about a family] may make little or no sense, but that's how we know who's an outsider and who isn't: outsiders are the people to whom we have to explain the things that everybody who is one of us already knows.[58]

The shibboleth-like quality of the family anecdote is therefore a test of membership.

What if we apply this to the idea of Englishness as a form of family membership? Well, we might find that, as the following chapters will assert, the empire play functions as a reminder of the corrupt (even, we might say, perverted) nature of imperialism, serving as a consolation for narratives of national decline; that Dickens adaptations often portray a world in which we are saved from anonymity by family ties that protect us from the indifference of posterity; that British television in the 1970s used family narratives as a way of helping audiences come to terms with the discontents of modernity; and that the prevalence of Victorian hauntings in contemporary theatre is a way for the English to tell themselves another national story in which they can feature as the victims of their Victorian predecessors.[59]

Scope and limitations

Despite my earlier mention of Oscar Wilde's *An Ideal Husband*, and his clear importance as a late Victorian figure, I have decided not to base a chapter here on Wilde revivals, one-man shows or other plays of biographical conjecture about him, such as Terry Eagleton's *Saint Oscar*, Neil

Bartlett's *In Extremis* and David Hare's *The Judas Kiss*. Wilde has already featured since the early 1990s as a key figure in works of queer theory, such as Jonathan Dollimore's *Sexual Dissidence*, Ed Cohen's *Talk on the Wilde Side* and Eve Kosovsky Sedgwick's *Tendencies*. The representation of Wilde has also been comprehensively covered by Robert Tanitch's *Oscar Wilde on Stage and Screen* in 1999. Moreover, my own particular approach, of linking representations of the Victorians to the cultural, political and academic preoccupations of the age in which they were written, has already been successfully attempted by a number of critics. Most impressively, Shelton Waldrep has investigated the representation of Wilde in the 1990s, focusing on the film *Wilde* and Moises Kaufman's play *Gross Indecency*. Waldrep's argument that 'Wilde is made to represent the particular mood of the times that create him', his relation of 1990s versions of Wilde to 'gay martyr' and 'queer' academic interpretations and his conclusion that 'our representations of him betray our own anxieties about our origins and structures for knowing ourselves' represent precisely the approach that I would have taken in writing a chapter on Wilde for this book.[60]

With the exception of Wilde, then, the selection of themes and genres has been dictated, first, by those plays whose existence, as explained above, is linked to a change in the style, tone or patterns of theatre production in their wake. Chapters 1 and 2 are linked in this way, in that 1968's *Early Morning* and 1969's *'H'* and *Narrow Road to the Deep North* seem to have featured a style of performing imperialism that persisted into the early 1980s. Secondly, the selection has been decided on by the popularity of certain forms: it is force of numbers that dictates that the broad categories of Dickens and Brontë adaptations be covered rather than adaptations of the novels of Henry James or George Eliot, and similarly 'solo biodrama' as a category has been singled out because it has formed such a notable proportion of 'new work' in theatres during the 1980s.

Because much of the research for this book was conducted in London and based on searches of *Theatre Record* and items from the British Library and the V&A's Theatre Collections, it may be argued that this study favours England, and London in particular, over the other constituent parts of the UK. Nevertheless, Scottish and Welsh theatre appears to have produced its own examples of the trends covered in this book, such as Ranald Graham's 1968 agit-prop play for the Traverse Theatre, Edinburgh, *Aberfan*, linking the Welsh pit disaster of 1966 with the Victorian Tay Bridge disaster, or the Marie Lloyd biodrama at the Traverse in 1975, mentioned in Chapter 4, or the

Aberystwyth Arts Centre's commission of a Neil Bartlett adaptation of *Great Expectations* in 2007.[61] However, it is worth tentatively suggesting reasons why the notion of 'the Victorian' may hold sway in England more than, say, in Scotland or Wales. Scottish playwriting, for instance, seems to have been much more concerned with the early nineteenth century over the last few decades than the Victorian period itself. Hector MacMillan's *The Rising* addresses the Scottish Insurrection of 1820, while his *The Royal Visit* features Sir Walter Scott during the visit of George IV to Edinburgh in 1822.[62] Stewart Conn's *Thistlewood* (1975) concerns Arthur Thistlewood and the other participants in the 1820 Cato Street Conspiracy; *The Domination of Fancy* (1992) is about the 1825 theatrical wars between Alexander and Seymour in Glasgow.[63] James Kelman's *Hardie and Baird: The Last Days* (1990) is also about the 1820 Scottish Insurrection.[64] Ian Brown states in *Scottish Theatre since the Seventies* that

> very few [plays] indeed fit into the consolatory category [that is, revisiting the past to comfort the audience that a state of nationhood might exist or, conversely and paradoxically, no longer matters], perhaps the most nostalgic and potentially regressive of all, while almost all tend towards lively and forward-looking perspectives.[65]

There also appear to have been few Welsh-language plays about Wales during the Victorian period, although Nic Ros does mention Gruffydd Jones's 1985 play *Bedlam*, set in London in 1883 and addressing the hypocrisy of Victorian business and family values, while the theatre company Brith Gof made a film about Welsh emigration to Patagonia in 1865, and their performance *Tri Bywyd* [Three Lives] featured the story of a girl, Sarah Jacobs, who starved to death in the nineteenth century.[66] It may be that for Welsh theatre-makers, 'the Victorian' does not have the same resonance as for the English, since it is not necessarily regarded as distinct from the previous five centuries of being classified as a principality (or colonized, depending on one's position). Moreover, in the period leading up to, and since, the founding of the Welsh Assembly in 1999, the more important theatre task may well have been to represent Wales as it is now. Both Heike Roms and Lisa Lewis have used postcolonial theory, and Homi K. Bhabha in particular, to formulate their discussion of contemporary Welsh theatre, and it may be that a postcolonial fear of mimicry, and a striving, instead, to discover distinctively Welsh forms of performance, precludes the use of Victorian-based historical drama.[67] This latter form can, as we shall see in Chapter 6, produce a historical-determinist argument that suggests we are slaves to our Victorian inheritances in one way or another, not a message that is particularly useful to notions of post-devolution Welshness. And, as that chapter and others elaborate, it is a picture of the English as a nation, a 'family' victimized by, or struggling in the shadow of, its past – colonized, as it were, by its own history – that dominates the dramatic representations of the Victorians since 1968.

Chapter review

In Chapter 1, I investigate the circumstances surrounding Bond's *Early Morning* and the passing of the Theatres Act in 1968. The chapter argues that the play, although it seemed to be heralding a new age where the Victorian stranglehold on British society could be consigned to history, was in fact a 'last gasp' for the modernist outlook of the mid-1960s. I look at it alongside Peter Barnes's *The Ruling Class*, another work of the same year, which seems to invite condemnation of Victorian influences as anachronistic and dangerous. I then consider the backlash against modern architecture and the popularity of pop music drawing on music hall and variety as indicators of the full-blown nostalgia boom that was to be one of the strongest cultural forces of the 1970s.

Chapter 2 extends this analysis, taking into consideration plays over the longer period of 1968–82. It examines how the theme of empire (and its visual corollary, the vampire or cannibal) kept recurring in plays of the period, and places this phenomenon in the context of New Left thought, growing fears about youth crime (the 'folk-devil') and national decline, and the beginnings of black and Asian theatre in Britain. Simon Gray's *The Rear Column*, Tony Harrison's *Phaedra Britannica* and Caryl Churchill's *Cloud Nine* are considered as particular exemplars.

I begin Chapter 3 by examining, through David Edgar's *The Life and Adventures of Nicholas Nickleby* and the Dickensian adaptations that followed, how the early years of Margaret Thatcher's Conservative government brought about a switch in playwriting about the Victorians, as the focus changed from the imperial to the domestic during the years of recession and monetarism, and the Victorian phrases 'hard times' and 'self-help' were put to use to signify contrasting responses to poverty. The chapter goes on to consider the two main directions in which adaptations of Dickens have developed over the last 25 years (the 'studio psychodrama' and the 'world-on-a-stage'), and ends by exploring the continued popularity of particular kinds of Dickensian entertainment in British culture, and the reassurances that they offer.

The growth of biographical drama (biodrama) and monodrama about the Victorians during the 1980s is the focus of Chapter 4. Building on the previous chapter's analysis of Thatcherism, Chapter 4 looks at the artistic, ideological and financial pressures that may have brought this trend to prominence. The context behind Alec McCowen's successful 1984 West End solo show *Kipling: East and West* is investigated in the light of the then recent Falklands Conflict and notions of a resurgent nationalism as Margaret Thatcher began her second term as prime minister. The interest in biodramas about music hall performers – Marie Lloyd in particular – is then analysed, and interpreted as a development of the 1970s agit-prop theatre movement's interest in the Victorian age.

Developing the previous chapter's theme of biodrama, Chapter 5 considers the uses to which Charlotte Brontë's life story and her novel *Jane Eyre* have been put since the 1970s. I show how, through a series of theatrical adaptations, the life and the work have been entwined and conflated, and show how the increasing identification, in stage adaptations, with Bertha Mason, the so-called 'mad woman in the attic', has corresponded with a distancing from Jane (and Charlotte Brontë herself). I argue that the refiguring of *Jane Eyre* as 'Bertha's story', particularly in the Shared Experience 'Brontë trilogy' of *Jane Eyre*, *After Mrs Rochester* and *Brontë*, reflects a contemporary disposition to identify with the lost, the displaced and the underdog rather than the 'respectable' and the ambitious in Victorian culture.

The book's final chapter returns explicitly to Edward Bond's idea of being haunted by the restless dead of the Victorian period, but shows how this trope, revisited 30 or 40 years after the Bond and Barnes plays, has become much more domestic and individuated. It focuses on a trend within playwriting about the Victorians, evident since the late 1980s, of having modern-day characters haunted by the ghosts of the Victorians who previously inhabited that house or landscape. I coin the term 'supernatural realism' to describe this type of play, where a social-realist view of society is juxtaposed with a Victorian ghost story; in doing this, the implications for the plays' representation of 'the real' are further interrogated. I focus on two works with a similar subplot of a body hidden in a Victorian house – Kate Atkinson's *Abandonment* (2000) and Mike Leigh's *It's a Great Big Shame!* (1993) – exploring the ways in which their Victorian stories can be read as a key to the contemporary characters' behaviour. The chapter then broadens its scope to consider the feelings of alienation and rootlessness brought about by the postmodern condition, with reference to genealogy and the sociologists Berger, Berger and Kellner, Barber, and Bauman.

Looking back (and forth) in anger

This introductory chapter takes its title, 'Angry Ghosts', from Edward Bond's 'Author's Preface' to *Lear*, where the playwright describes the characters in *Early Morning* as 'angry, gleeful ghosts'.[68] Kaplan's notion of 'Victoriana' as being 'permanently restless and unsettled' in our culture, alluded to above, is an idea I wish to carry through each chapter of this study, connecting with the idea of the Victorians as 'angry ghosts', unable to rest and passing through the walls of our collective ideas of modernity and nationhood (Chapters 1 and 2), community (Chapters 3 and 4), fame and heroism (Chapter 4), and identity and home (Chapters 5 and 6). As Kaplan indicates, these ideas are often complex and contradictory, mixing nostalgia and condemnation. In this book, the ghosts range from the literal 'living dead' of *Early Morning* to the figurative folk-devils of the 1970s and their empire plays, the doubles and revenants of the Dickens, biodrama and Brontë chapters, and finally back to the literal ghosts in the haunted-house plays of 'supernatural realism' in the 1980s and 1990s. The ghosts may be 'gleeful' in Bond's 1968 play, but in subsequent decades their presence has been more mournful, elegiac, accusing and even comforting.

1
Staging the Bad Old Days

This chapter will explore how Edward Bond's *Early Morning*, and comparable works of theatre and performance from 1968 on, presented the Victorians as a 'dead hand', preventing society from progressing. The transformations for which these works seem to agitate, leading to a more enlightened, rational and equal future, had with hindsight begun to stall in this period. By the late 1960s a crisis of modernity had begun to take hold that led to an ever-growing fascination – a grieving, even – for the Victorians. The notion that theirs were exclusively the bad old days, to be subjected to the confident indictments of modernity, could no longer hold.

I will begin by investigating the circumstances surrounding Bond's *Early Morning* and the passing of the Theatres Act in September 1968. This chapter argues that the play, although it seemed to be heralding a new age where the Victorians could be seen in demystified terms and their icy grip evaded, can actually be seen as a 'last gasp' of the modernist outlook of the mid-1960s. I look at the play alongside Peter Barnes's *The Ruling Class*, another work of the same year in which the Victorians feature as unwelcome anachronisms haunting the present; and also one of the major film successes of 1968, Carol Reed's version of Lionel Bart's musical, *Oliver!* I place the progressivism of Bond and Barnes in the cultural context of the period, considering the backlash against modern architecture, the popularity of pop music drawing on music hall and variety, and costume drama on television from the late 1960s on, as 'co-texts' with which to assess *Early Morning*'s place as a work of theatre and as a public event.

In order to do this, the chapter develops some of the arguments found in Robert Hewison's book *The Heritage Industry*, which investigates the development of nostalgic feeling since the 1960s. Although first published in 1987, his point that 'The nostalgic impulse is an important agency in adjustment to crisis, it is a social emollient and reinforces national identity when confidence is weakened or threatened' still holds true with regard to this period.[1] These ideas are further investigated in a more wide-ranging way by Raphael Samuel in *Theatres of Memory*, published in 1994, which considers the growth of what Samuel calls 'retrochic' – the dressing-up of new items to give them the patina of age and inspire a sense of nostalgia and 'authenticity' – as it manifests itself in items such as the country kitchen, new Georgian-style traffic lights and car parks, and recreated Victorian streets in museums.[2] There is one statement in particular in Samuel's book that has influenced the methodology of this chapter, and the book in general. This is that 'history is not the prerogative of the historian . . . it is, rather, a social form of knowledge: the work, in any given instance, of a thousand different hands'.[3] I take this to mean that regardless of historical debates about what, say, the Victorian age 'really was like', the majority of the population will create their own vision of the past, and go to it for their own purposes – whether for a sense of personal origins and family roots (as explored in the Section "Genealogy and imaginary homelands", Chapter 6 section on genealogy), for escapist entertainment (films and novel adaptations, as discussed in the chapters on Dickens and the Brontës (Chapters 3 and 5)), or to reinforce or resituate ideas of nationhood. These re-creations, these generative acts, are worth studying in their own right, as ways of reading the cultural history of the 1960s, 1970s, 1980s and so on, rather than being interrogated in the aim of finding some kind of objective truth-value to them.

Miles Taylor has argued that, most importantly, 'the Victorian era offered to the 1960s' generation confirmation of its own modernity. The relaxation in the Wilson years of the laws relating to divorce, homosexuality, age of majority and censorship . . . made the Victorians seem very old, very different and, above all, very unenlightened.'[4] Such a claim, this chapter argues, may well fit in with the playfulness and radicalism of *Early Morning* and *The Ruling Class*, but it does not explain what came after the 1960s, the ongoing fascination with and resonances of the Victorian age, which extend far beyond Victorian historiography and into popular culture. To explain this, we need to look for cracks and contradictions in the notional modernity of the 1960s themselves.

Early Morning and censorship

We can usefully begin by investigating the circumstances surrounding the Theatres Act, which became law on 28 September 1968. This can be seen both as the successful liberalization of a Victorian institution (in that the 1843 Theatre Regulation Act established theatre licensing in the form it would preserve up to 1968), and as a reform that permitted and encouraged (in *Early Morning*, one of the 1968 Act's earliest beneficiaries) greater and broader onstage discussion of the Victorians. Nicholas de Jongh observes that 'If some satirist had been asked to dream up a theatrical scenario designed to outrage the Lord Chamberlain he would not have done better than... Bond's *Early Morning*', but it is also significant that campaigners for the ending of censorship wished to be free of the Victorians so that they could talk more about the Victorians.[5] William Gaskill, director of *Early Morning* and artistic director of the Royal Court between 1965 and 1969, recalls that 'we were fighting the censor and, in particular, we were fighting the censor on behalf of Edward Bond'.[6] The success of this battle was celebrated with a season of three Bond plays in early 1969, two of which feature Victorian figures (*Early Morning* and *Narrow Road to the Deep North*[7]).

Early Morning is a dark fantasy in which *quondam* Prime Minister Benjamin Disraeli and Prince Albert are plotting a military coup against Queen Victoria, while her son George, who is the Siamese twin of Arthur, is about to marry Florence Nightingale. Len, possibly the same character who features in Bond's earlier play *Saved*, is tried by Victoria for eating a man who pushed in front of him while he was queuing to see a film, *Policeman in Black Nylons*. Victoria rapes Florence, and as the coup begins, Victoria poisons and strangles Albert, and George is shot. William Gladstone has also joined the coup, and Victoria and her sons are placed before a firing squad, but are released when he dies. Although George has shot himself, Arthur continues to carry around the corpse of his conjoined twin. The conflict continues in heaven, where Victoria accuses Arthur of spoiling it for everyone, being desperate to die properly. He is eventually eaten, head and all, and placed in a coffin, from which he 'starts to rise in the air', unseen by the weeping Florence, who had tried to save his head by hiding it under her skirt.[8] The play ends with Victoria declaring that there is 'no dirt in heaven' and Len asking his girlfriend Joyce to 'Pass us that leg.'[9]

Clearly, then, Gaskill and the Royal Court were calling for the release of restrictions on the public performance of a play that attacked, or at the very least made absurd humorous capital out of, a number of sacred cows in the eyes of the conservative establishment. Opposition to censorship, and stage censorship in particular, was a popular rallying point for liberals and those aligned with the counterculture, as Nicholas de Jongh details in his history of stage censorship, *Politics,*

Prudery and Perversions. Kenneth Tynan's essay on censorship, 'The Royal Smut-Hound', accuses the West End theatres of colluding with the Lord Chamberlain's power in the belief that plays granted a licence would be immune from prosecution, and he says that because of such timidity 'our theatre skulks inside the nursery'.[10] De Jongh emphasizes that it was the 1843 Theatre Regulation Act that determined the Lord Chamberlain's discretionary role and established the censor's 'Victorian moral bias'.[11] Of course, the Lords Chamberlain defended their role with assurances such as Alexander Redford's statement (at the turn of the twentieth century) that 'I have no critical views of plays. I simply have to maintain standards.'[12]

All the same, Dominic Shellard, Steven Nicholson and Miriam Handley's history of censorship, *The Lord Chamberlain Regrets...*, which reproduces many reports on plays, letters and internal memos, shows how far the Lord Chamberlain's office went to maintain the pretence that it was refusing licences, or requesting cuts and changes, from a disinterested viewpoint. In fact, plays were censored on the grounds of personal taste and prejudice, annoyance or incomprehension. They relied on precedent in decreeing that a monarch could only appear in a serious work, in order to ban four post-war plays in which Queen Victoria appeared, but, as *The Lord Chamberlain Regrets...* points out, the Lord Chamberlain and his readers decided what was 'serious' or otherwise.[13] A play about Oscar Wilde was refused a licence because it was 'about perverts and perversion' and was 'not a masterpiece', making the perhaps disingenuous implication that a play that they found disgusting could simultaneously be recognized by the same readers as a masterpiece and so granted a licence.[14] The Lord Chamberlain's office had been notoriously intolerant of ambiguity, subtext and arousal: 'The theatre is an emotional place in which ugly things easily take on false glamour,' Lord Cobbold had reflected.[15]

Given the particular sensitivities of the Lords Chamberlain during the twentieth century, then, it seems clear that Bond was touching nearly every raw nerve possible, intentionally or otherwise, in *Early Morning*: monarchy, 'perverts and perversion', a good deal of sexual activity and an absurd, ambiguous narrative. *Early Morning* was scheduled to be performed at the Royal Court in April 1968, when the Theatres Act was on the statutes book but had yet to become law. The early rumour that the satirist John Bird would play the female lead, and the casting for the first production of Marianne Faithfull, Mick Jagger's then-girlfriend, as Florence Nightingale, indicates that the Royal Court wanted to ally the battle with censorship with the young and anti-establishment.[16]

On Lord Cobbold's (the then Lord Chamberlain) recommendation, the Director of Public Prosecutions considered legal action against the Royal Court, even though the production was a private club performance, and the Arts Council was concerned that the play might cause an amendment to be put into the Theatres Act disallowing references to any living person, the sovereign or her predecessors; it seems that a great deal was still at stake.[17] The play was attended by undercover police officers and vice squad members.[18] It had only one full performance in 1968 before the Royal Court's committee banned it; a Sunday afternoon 'dress rehearsal' performance followed, with the audience (all 'club members' so that the performance would not break the law by being classified as 'for hire') being led in by a side door.[19] After the Theatres Act had been passed, the Royal Court mounted another production in 1969, but the play never attracted as much interest in the reviews pages as it had in the news pages. One of the kinder comments is William Gaskill's 'you just have to live with it. It's one of the strangest experiences in the theatre' – and he directed it.[20] The *Evening Standard* said of the first night of the 1968 production, 'its reception was distinctly *sotto voce*... The audience, enthusiastic at first, seemed to lose contact as the play progressed.'[21]

The events and comments detailed above seem to indicate that *Early Morning* functioned more as a media event and a rallying point for 1960s progressives than a memorable theatrical entertainment in itself, but it is worth taking a closer look at the possible meanings of this highly complex work and how it might have resonated (or failed to resonate) with the wider culture. Although Bond has claimed that the play was inspired more by 'a consideration of the disasters of my own time than actual Victorian events', he did speak at the time in an interview with *The Times* of how he had chosen the Victorian period because 'Britain is still overwhelmed by nineteenth-century hypocrisy.'[22] That the play was mistakenly referred to in an *Evening Standard* article as 'Recent Morning Died Queen Victoria' suggests either that this was a working title, revealing the play's intention to expose a 1960s culture only just crawling out from under the weight of repressive Victorian ideals, or that the play was received as such by journalists.[23] The former explanation might be supported by a remark on a draft of the play in Bond's working notebooks from 1965: 'It sums up a dead society. It is the internment of Hamlet. And it is not dramatic, because, although a funeral can be very dramatic, it is not dramatic for the corpse. It closes the door on a society and an era.'[24]

Reading *Early Morning* as Marxist critique

However, how might the play have been received by theatre audiences in 1968–9? First, the play can be said to be amenable to a Marxist, or at least class-based, interpretation, attacking the present-day society of unbridled consumption (and presumably laying the blame for this at the feet of the Victorians). In this interpretation, Bond shows a society riven with conflict and competition, featuring the formation of secret pacts and a paranoiac fear of the enemy within, and the urge to possess more than everyone else, and possess it first. Queen Victoria is at the top of the tree, and is the most rapacious of the lot; she demands that her family line, which she claims began at Stonehenge, 'shall not fall till Stonehenge falls'.[25] She even requisitions her son George's proposed wife, Florence Nightingale, rapes her, dresses her up as John Brown and encourages her to put on a gruff Scottish accent.[26] Albert wants to kill Victoria and seize the throne. Disraeli is in league with Victoria to destroy her husband. Albert, a more sympathetic figure than his wife, repeats the capitalist mantra of progress: 'The people are strong. They want to be used – to build empires and railways and factories...I know there'll be crimes, but we can punish them.'[27] Victoria's son Arthur, the black sheep of the family, refuses to cut off his conjoined brother George, whom everyone insists is dead, and talks to him about his dream of the mill: 'they're grinding other people and cattle and children: they push each other in...They're sure they're reaching the horizon.'[28] The wrong-headedness of Albert's attempts at social good is made clear by Arthur's vision, and by the fact that Albert continues to eat human flesh, while Arthur refuses. Albert's philanthropic schemes are offering the people more of the same – work, obedience, punishment – where the play can be seen as arguing that this nightmarish cycle be broken altogether.

Cannibalism is *Early Morning*'s dominant image, complemented by the repeated event (once on earth, once in heaven) of a poisoned picnic.[29] The endless consumption of human flesh and poisoned wine and cake suggests the deadly pattern of consumption into which British society is locked. Arthur is the scapegoat: his refusal to eat people leads to him being wrongly accused of murder and placed on trial. His dissent is seen by Queen Victoria as simply that 'He hasn't got the gift of happiness. We must get rid of him.'[30] Arthur can be read as the rebel figure, the 1960s outsider seeking liberation. He finally finds happiness as a disembodied head in Florence Nightingale's lap, where he is no longer desperately hungry: 'They've cut off my body – but I'm alive. I could make love to you. Now. I can feel it. Hard. That's why I like it in your lap.'[31] His twin, George, whose hunger is never satisfied no matter how much he consumes, is finally sated when he eats Arthur's head, as if the consumption of his ideas about society will allow him – and us – to say, 'My pain's gone!...I'm free!'[32] Victoria confidently predicts that now Arthur cannot come back – and hammers in her own teeth to seal his coffin – but the ghost of Arthur, of those transcending needs beyond consumption, escapes from the box, unseen except by the audience.[33]

The view elaborated above is how the play has traditionally been read; for instance, the *Oxford Dictionary of Plays* states that 'The cannibalism that so shocked audiences is merely a metaphor for the behaviour of the capitalist who devours his own kind.'[34] Catherine Itzin follows the popular strategy of placing *Early Morning* within a putative trajectory for Bond as playwright, seeing *The Bundle* (a much less ambiguous 1978 rewrite of *Narrow Road to the Deep North*) as his 'most politically important play', and presenting a teleology that recuperates Bond's late 1960s strangeness: 'In retrospect, Bond can be seen to have been a "socialist" writing socialist plays long before these were common or in any fashion accommodated, indeed, before he himself recognised the full radical implications of his work.'[35] However, this chapter argues that *Early Morning* can be more interestingly seen in the context of cultural events and turns specific to the late 1960s.

Early Morning as Freudian dream-work

An alternative way of approaching the play, and one that may well have been popular with the late 1960s counterculture (as opposed to the more politically committed New Left, members of which might support the interpretation above), is in viewing it as a commentary on the sexual attitudes that the Victorians have bequeathed to us. In a Freudian reading of the play, Bond has rewritten the Victorian period as it would be if subjected to Freud's dream-work of condensation, displacement and disguise. Freud describes dreams as presenting 'reversals of relation...a "topsy-turvy" world', and this is extensively true of *Early Morning*.[36] If the historical myth is that Queen Victoria vetoed references to lesbians in the gross indecency laws because she refused to believe such people existed, then Bond reinvents Victoria as a lesbian who rapes Florence Nightingale.[37] Nightingale is remembered for raising nursing's reputation to that of a respectable profession, so here she describes running a brothel and sleeping with two prime ministers simultaneously.[38]

Other aspects of the play correspond to Freud's world of dreams and the unconscious, too. The play's confusing structure, with characters changing sides, or being eaten and then coming back to life or growing back limbs, is a regular feature of dreams, which are often inconsistent, and whose events are, according to Freud, *'timeless*, i.e., they are not ordered temporally'.[39] Similarly, as in dreams, speeches in *Early Morning* are often repetitive, incoherent or else made up of snippets of other conversations (as in Arthur's monologues, or the cries in the tug-of-war), just as Freud said our dream-dialogue is never a cohesive, structured speech or conversation.[40] During the grieving process, Freud says, it is very common to dream of the loved one being resurrected.[41] This is just what happens repeatedly in the play, as if we, as a nation, are still grieving for the Victorians and our lost status in the world.

Early Morning as 1960s topsy-turvydom

However – to refocus on the specific context of 1968 – the play's use of recurring actions and its dreamy, perpetual 'now-ness' can be seen as a very specific product of the late 1960s. This period's focus on spontaneity, impulsiveness and instantaneity has been explored by Ian MacDonald, and found public expression in free-form 'happenings' such as the International Festival of Poetry at the Albert Hall in 1965, Julian Beck and the Living Theatre's performance at the Roundhouse in June 1969, and the Royal Court's own Come Together festival in 1972, which Nicholas Wright recalls as 'a real, enjoyable fuck-you to tradition and a welcome to a new world', and which, according to William Gaskill, featured 'Stuart Brisley vomit[ing] from a scaffolding tower while the National Anthem was played backwards'.[42] In a country where, only a decade before, theatre audiences had had to stand for the playing of the national anthem each night, this must indeed have seemed like a new world.

Furthermore, it could equally be asserted that Bond's Victorian stage world is less inspired by psychoanalysis and more by the 'topsy-turvy' world of Gilbert and Sullivan's comic operas and Lewis Carroll's *Alice in Wonderland*. Bond's next play, *Narrow Road to the Deep North*, was to draw on Gilbert and Sullivan music and characters to satirize the imperial mission. *Alice in Wonderland*, whose vivid, polymorphous and unpredictable world could be said to have affinities with the late 1960s fashion for psychedelia (Carroll's imagery notably inspiring the Beatles' 'Lucy in the Sky with Diamonds'), had been made into a film by Jonathan Miller, broadcast on BBC television in 1966.[43] It starred such figures of

English comedy and satire as Peter Cook, Alan Bennett, Peter Sellers and John Bird.[44]

Hence, even in seeking to undermine or satirize the Victorian world-view and its influence on the twentieth century, one can end up quoting or using 'other Victorians' as a reference point. More generally, the idea that the public could still be potentially shocked by portrayals of public figures more than 60 years after their deaths, and that a play should take so seriously the idea of exploding their myth, suggests a continuing dependence on the Victorians for a sense of history and national identity, even as that influence is being angrily denied; it is not as easy as it may seem, in Bond's words, to '[close] the door on a society and an era'.

While, as is detailed below, *Early Morning* did not forestall the British public's enthusiasm for aspects of Victorian life and culture as the 1960s and 1970s wore on, it can be argued that one (presumably unintended) side effect of the furore in the media over the play was that it helped to popularize comic and satirical presentations of Queen Victoria. The relaunched *Private Eye* magazine, in February 1962, had already featured the Albert Memorial as a space rocket, complemented by a Willie Rushton sketch of Victoria saying 'Ho ho very satirical', but in the years that followed there was *Monty Python's Flying Circus*, the first series of which, broadcast in 1969, featured a mock-documentary called 'Our Whacky Queen', in which the monarch (played by Terry Jones) is seen indulging in silent-movie-style slapstick.[45] John McGrath's satirical revue for 7:84 Theatre Company, *The Cheviot, the Stag and the Black, Black Oil* (1974), featured Queen Victoria (in drag) singing, of the Scottish Highlands, 'These are our mountains/And this is our glen/The braes of your childhood/Are English again.'[46] A musical by Jay Allen, Charles Strouse and Lee Adams entitled *I and Albert* played briefly at the Piccadilly Theatre, London, in 1972, and in the Ron Pember and Denis DeMarne musical *Jack the Ripper* at the Players Theatre (1974), 'Queen Victoria keeps coming in comically with suggestions to help the police.'[47] What had been quite illegal six years earlier at the Royal Court was now thought of as mainstream fare for West End musical theatre.

The Ruling Class and anti-psychiatry

Most of the other plays produced at around the same time as the Theatres Act containing Victorian settings or characters were far less controversial. There were revivals of Leopold Lewis's *The Bells*, Boucicault's *The Shaughraun* and six Gilbert and Sullivan operettas at the Savoy in January 1968. Henry James appeared to be enjoying a dramatic revival, with *The Outcry*, *A Boston Story* (based on the tale 'Watch and Ward') and *The Other House* all receiving West End openings in 1969.[48] Hints of a more radical future for theatre were provided by Alan Plater's history of the miners, *Close the Coalhouse Door*, which had reached the Fortune Theatre, and Max Stafford-Clark was co-devising *Dracula*, 'a joint investigation...of man's preoccupation with evil' at the Traverse Workshop, Edinburgh.[49] Almost the only other recently written Victorian drama was William Douglas-Home's *The Queen's Highland Servant*, which had not troubled the Lord Chamberlain on its submission the previous year. In the light of the ongoing comparative conservatism of representations of the Victorians in the theatre in this period, then, *The Ruling Class* by Peter Barnes provides a useful point of comparison with *Early Morning*, having a similar irreverence towards chronology, but having been rather more commercially successful. It was originally staged at the Nottingham Playhouse in November 1968, transferred to the Piccadilly Theatre, London, in February 1969 and was subsequently made into a film starring Peter O'Toole.

Barnes's play concerns Jack, the 14th Earl of Gurney, who believes himself to be Jesus Christ. His family, eager to continue the family line and control the inheritance, try to marry him off to a young woman called Grace, while Dr Paul Herder attempts to cure Jack's madness. In the second act, Jack claims to be cured, but actually seems to be a reincarnation of Jack the Ripper, and goes back to 1888 to commit a Whitechapel murder. Nevertheless, he is certified sane and sent to the House of Lords, represented by rows of cobwebbed dummies.[50] In the epilogue, Jack gleefully continues his killing spree by murdering Grace.

Its focus on madness might encourage, as with *Early Morning*, a psychoanalytical reading, although this dimension probably leans less towards psychology and more towards anti-psychiatry, the then fashionable notion circulated by R.D. Laing, among others, that society itself was 'mad'; that the mental health services are 'divorced from reality, but they think they are sane'; and that western society in general 'presents more and more the appearance of total irrationality'.[51] Psychotherapy, in this analysis, does the opposite of its professed intentions, killing the individual with its cures and leading to 'the death of the soul'.[52] Schizophrenia, for example, was held to be a form of family scapegoating wherein a family member labelled a schizophrenic is 'made to take on the disturbance of each of the others and, in a sense, suffer for them'.[53] Laing and David Cooper, along with Leon Redler and Joseph Berke, organized the Dialectics of Liberation Congress of 1967, and in 1968 established the Anti-University of London, which aimed to continue 'the spirit of the Congress in what may be a permanent form'.[54]

In the play, as if reflecting these wider cultural resonances of the late 1960s, Dr Paul Herder's attempts to cure Jack are foiled by the vested interests of his relatives, so on one level Herder can be seen as a force for 'sanity' within the play (and Jack the scapegoated family member, conveniently labelled as mad). On the other hand, his own psychoanalytic methods are unorthodox: he presumably brings in the insane Scotsman, McKyle – who styles himself the High Voltage Messiah – in order to convince Jack of the wrongness of his own claims to be Jesus by confronting him with an even more delusional Christ-figure. Herder's suspicions that Jack is not cured in the second act are dismissed by the family when Jack is declared sane by the Master in Lunacy, who conveniently turns out to be a fellow old Etonian.[55] Beyond his psychoanalytical line of enquiry, Herder has more grandiose ambitions: he seems to wish, Nietzsche-like, not only to save Jack from his delusion but also to strip him of Christian belief, to convince him that the idea that 'God is Love' is the true delusion.[56] At the end, defeated in a duel, Herder is made to feel, as Laing would assert, that (as the representative of 'normal' psychiatry) he is the mad one.[57]

As with *Early Morning*, much of the humour stems from the shattering of taboos regarding sexuality and taste. The play opens with the 13th Earl of Gurney accidentally hanging himself, during some sexual misadventure, in a three-cornered hat and a ballet skirt, and ends with his son and heir, Jack, having overcome his Messiah-complex, taking his place in the House of Lords and then killing his wife, having acquired the belief that he is Jack the Ripper. Where the characters in *Early Morning* behave absurdly and yet act naturalistically (although the eating of human flesh and severed heads may well have drawn attention to their status as theatrical props), *The Ruling Class* seems to be more consciously playing with theatrical styles, breaking the illusion of naturalism with the butler Tucker's music hall asides and rendition of 'Gilbert the Filbert', and sight-gags such as the earl's terror being indicated by an instant smear of white make-up.[58] The conclusion subverts melodramatic narrative convention in that the 'hero' wins public approval in the House of Lords, only to be revealed as the 'heavy villain' who is just warming to his life of crime.[59]

And, where the theme of consumption is central, and made highly visible, in *Early Morning*, there seems to be no similarly consistent critique of capitalism in *The Ruling Class*, despite the invitation to think of the problem in class terms provided by the title and the jokey mentions of 'Bolshies'. Jack's platitudes about law and order, delivered from the House of Lords, could be read as Marx's superstructure protecting the rich, while the self-proclaimed communist butler, Tucker, is blamed for the murders committed by Jack.[60] On the other hand, as Brian Woolland argues, Tucker's claim to be 'a [revolutionary] cell' lacks credibility, both in his somewhat contradictory claims to be an 'Anarchist – Trotskyist – Communist', and in the methods of resistance to which he lays claim (spitting in soup and urinating on dinner plates).[61] Woolland sees Tucker's claim to be a revolutionary as a 'comfort blanket [that] justifies his deference to the family'.[62] More than this, given that Tucker's political affiliations are revealed when communist literature and pornography are simultaneously found in his suitcase, Barnes seems to be mocking revolutionary communism as a fantasy, just another working man's dirty little secret.[63]

The Ruling Class and 'Swinging London'

Rather, it is more likely that Barnes's play functioned less as a schematic delineation of the class system and more as a riposte to the notion of classlessness embedded in the media manufacture of Swinging London. As Jonathon Green argues in his history of the 1960s, *All Dressed Up*, the mid-1960s Carnaby Street and King's Road world of boutiques, 'dolly birds' in mini-skirts and psychedelia was 'an instant media myth'.[64] Much was made of the new classlessness of the London scene, but Green argues that it was highly self-regarding and elitist, and, apart from a handful of models, photographers and rock stars, class movement mostly worked in the other direction, with children of aristocratic families enjoying the decadent thrill of 'slumming it'.[65] Barnes's play on one level invites us to laugh at the aristocracy's inbred lunacy; on the other, it can be seen as reminding us, via the image in the penultimate scene of a House of Lords full of skeletons, and the final murder, that the morality of a fusty Victorian hypocrisy is still Britain's dominant cultural mode.

Hence, the play seems to be taking place in a world that is a curious mix of the mid-twentieth century (references to Bert [*sic*] Bacharach and W.C Fields) and the *fin-de-siècle* (a cape and deerstalker, covered piano legs and Elgar's 'Pomp and Circumstance').[66] As Michael Billington has remarked, the play's comic critique of 'ancestor-worshipping' is that the earl 'believes he is living in Victorian England: as a result he is regarded as sane and becomes a pillar of the House of Lords'.[67] It is also interesting that ultimate, deranged wickedness should be represented by Jack the Ripper, a murderer who may – according to some theories – have been linked to the aristocracy, rather than any of the serial killers or genocidal dictators of the twentieth century. Presumably, Jack the Ripper was felt by the late 1960s to have been sufficiently historically distant to be amusing, yet sufficiently well recognized to be theatrical shorthand for 'evil'.

So, despite differences in style and content, and *Early Morning*'s more thoroughgoing references to the dehumanizing effects of capitalism itself (as opposed to its particular expression within Britain in the 1960s), both plays are open to the reading that the 'angry, gleeful ghosts' of the Victorian period should be permitted to haunt us no longer, and yet are reliant on our recognizing their figures and narratives in order to make the plays' subversive qualities stick, and in order to create reference points for other, transcendent qualities.[68]

Oliver! and the world being lost

A very different view of the Victorians can be seen in the film of the musical *Oliver!* Jeffrey Richards, echoing to some extent the point of view of Miles Taylor quoted above, has argued that 'The 1960s, affluent, liberated, "swinging", saw the Victorian era as utterly remote, a picturesque Christmas card/chocolate box/olde-worlde fantasy land full of kitsch bric-a-brac.'[69] While it is true, as he goes on to state, that the musical *Oliver!* hit upon a winning formula that was subsequently followed by the musicals *Pickwick* (1963), *Two Cities* (1969), *Hard Times* (1973, set in a circus ring) and *Great Expectations* (1975), I shall argue here that the film's images and settings were not 'utterly remote', nor a 'fantasy land', but, in part, poignant reminders of the working-class community life that was under threat from modernity.[70] Raphael Samuel perceptively remarks that *Oliver!* 'belongs to a period in which attitudes to the Victorian were becoming much more ambiguous', observes that Bart had already written the stage show *Fings Ain't What They Used to Be*, 'a requiem for a world that was being lost', and goes on to argue that in *Oliver!* he 'treats street life itself as colourful and interesting rather than squalid'.[71] However, even this attitude is ambivalent in the film, as I shall argue.

To illustrate this ambivalence, we might usefully look at one of the two biggest set-piece numbers in the film, 'Consider Yourself'. The song is triggered by Oliver's meeting with Dodger, whose invitation is taken up by the whole of London's labouring life: a pavement artist, a group of police officers prancing in formation, women with baskets of vegetables, butchers throwing each other parcels of meat and chopping it with a cleaver, street children parading by on donkeys playing reeds, whistling newspaper boys, mountebanks and circus tumblers. At one point the song's jollity appears to be under threat by the sudden appearance of three screaming child chimney sweeps, but it turns out that they are only screaming because their bottoms are being singed (and are quickly relieved by sitting in a trough), not because they are bemoaning the misery of child labour. In the song, Oliver is invited into a community of mostly working-class tradespeople by Dodger, who steals from them, and thus can hardly be considered 'your mate' or 'one of the family'. He is shown stealing bread, untying a washerwoman's apron and taking fruit from a passing barrel.

Dodger makes spurious claims to like and accept Oliver 'after some consideration' (i.e., having seen how 'green' he is), and invites him to join a community to which he himself doubtfully belongs. There is a bait-and-switch strategy at work, for Dodger will, of course, introduce him to a much lower stratum of society (indicated by Dodger leading Oliver off down a sinister-looking passageway as the song ends). The song is a lie that is taken up by the workers as a truth. On a realistic level it is, of course, ridiculous to portray working-class Londoners of the 1830s as full of enough energy to perform high-kicks when going about their appallingly paid, back-breaking work, and there is something faintly disturbing about this massed response to Dodger's invitation, sung by the chorus not to Oliver (who it seems has not spoken to anyone else since arriving in London), but with their eyes facing forwards, like ranks of automatons. One might even, influenced by the analysis of Victorian society in *Early Morning*, see the performance as a metaphor for the way capitalism treats its workers as if they are themselves machines.[72]

However, on the level of sentiment, the sequence functions as a tribute to 'a world that was being lost'. It can be seen, through the energetic formation dancing, as a celebration of the sheer energy and industry of the Victorian age, where every worker has their rank and specialized task, just as they have their own street cries (taken up in 'Who Will Buy?') and recognizable clothing, just as in George Cruikshank's famous Victorian illustration 'The British Bee Hive', showing each level of society.[73] It might, moreover, and to take up Samuel's point, be read, like *Fings Ain't What They Used to Be*, as a 'requiem' for the working-class life of the mid-twentieth century, a nostalgic celebration of knowable communities where even the neighbourhood thieves were tolerated and incorporated.

Why should working-class communities have felt under threat, or as if their world had already been 'lost', in the 1960s in particular? Why might such a vision of working life have carried such resonance with theatre and cinema audiences? During this decade, the slum-clearance programmes were put into effect, sweeping away many rundown and often bomb-damaged Victorian neighbourhoods and replacing them with new towns and estates on the outskirts, which were viewed with ambivalence by the people they were intended to benefit.[74] According to Hewison, new Local Authority powers of 'slum clearance' wiped out 80,000 houses a year from the 1950s on, and by 1965 there were some 27,000 flats in new buildings over ten storeys high.[75] In the language of the architects and town-planners, 'Victorian' was deployed to describe anything old, dilapidated and unsafe. As Dominic Sandbrook's account of changes to housing in the 1960s shows, Geoffrey Moorhouse's influential and polemical *The Other England*, published in 1964, had referred to people in Openshaw, Lancashire, living in 'Victorian cave-dwellings' and to 'the decrepit building of the Industrial Revolution' in the Midlands, while Coates and Silburn's academic study *Poverty: The Forgotten Englishmen* focused on 'a typical late Victorian, working-class, city-centre neighbourhood in acute decline in Nottingham'.[76] By contrast, it was asserted that 'smart typists and skilled young workers will not put up with Victorian by-law streets any longer', and Moorhouse supported the plan to demolish the Victorian slums on the fringes of Birmingham in order to make it a future-facing city.[77]

The aesthetic, health and cultural consequences of the 'modern brutalist' style of building shops, offices and homes are now well known, but in 1968 attitudes, it is fair to say, reaching a turning point. The explosion at the Ronan Point development in Newham, East London, in May of that year, in which 33 people died, highlighted the shoddy and unsafe building practices that could occur during construction of the new-style tower blocks, yet local residents were compelled to continue moving into the buildings.[78] The Thamesmead housing development, situated east of Woolwich, was extremely unpopular: the first family took up residence in June 1968, but no one else could be persuaded to join them until 1969.[79] In the North-East of England, meanwhile, the leader of Newcastle Council, T. Dan Smith, in collusion with corrupt architect John Poulson, forced thousands of families into substandard accommodation in order to enrich themselves (a story later fictionalized as one of the major plot strands in Peter Flannery's 1982 play *Our Friends in the North*).[80]

As Raphael Samuel argues, the Ronan Point disaster was followed by 'a much more widespread disenchantment with the modernism which the motorway boxes of the civil engineers, the sodium lights of the highway departments, as well as the "deck-access" walkways and concrete canyons of the New Brutalist architecture all represented'.[81] Paul Addison cites the 1963 Ministry of Transport report *Traffic in Towns*, which became 'a manual for urban planners' as 'eighteenth and nineteenth century streets and squares [tended to be sacrificed] in the interests of expressways, subways, and multi-storey car parks'.[82] Robert Hewison discusses the psychological effects of such displacement, and quotes Elspeth King, then curator of the People's Palace Museum in Glasgow, who describes the process as 'taking a rubber to the map and just rubbing places out and rebuilding them'.[83] Hewison extends this notion of the sense of loss, caused by modernization, to the rural landscape too, pointing out that Britain lost one half of its pre-1600 woods between 1947 and 1980, along with thousands of miles of hedgerows, and large farms took over: 'architectural and scenic differences were ironed out under the weight of mediocrity and uniformity'.[84] Meanwhile, the Beeching Report of 1963 had led to 3000 miles of abandoned railway lines and 20,000 acres of derelict railway land (by 1982); Hewison suggests that modernization itself seems to produce dereliction.[85]

Reactions against this wave of modernist building were as old as Ian Nairn's *Outrage*, a special issue of the *Architectural Review* published in 1955 as a polemic against environmental degradation and 'subtopia'. Nairn's 1966 *Observer* article 'Stop the Architects Now' provided an influential voice for the movement, alongside those of the poet John Betjeman and the critic F.R. Leavis (who wanted to prevent the demolition of the Victorian East End and 'Dickens's London').[86] Sandbrook notes that by the late 1960s 'Rather than rushing to clear their Victorian slums, local authorities were becoming interested in preserving and renovating them.'[87] Samuel cites the Civic Amenities Act of 1967 as important, since it gave planning officers the power to designate 'conservation' areas, 'traditionalizing rather than modernizing the townscape'.[88] For the many residents of old working-class neighbourhoods that had been demolished, however, this turn had come too late. The watching of *Oliver!* may not have brought those communities back, but it gave a (no doubt idealized) inkling of how the Victorian communities that were originally built around might have operated: a public, street-and-square-based life made manifest for the panoramic cinema screen, and contrasting strongly with the balconies, stairwells and lifts, the closed, semi-private spaces of the tower block. To borrow a phrase from Raymond Williams, whose interpretation of Dickens will be investigated later, *Oliver!* conveys, in some form at least, the idea of a 'knowable community'; the city, as he says is true of Dickens's writing, 'is shown as at once a social fact and a human landscape'.[89]

The middle-class reaction against modernity was different but no less important. It was in the late 1950s and 1960s that the middle classes first began to preserve original features, such as fireplaces, coving, tiling and floors, in Victorian houses, rather than modernizing them with gas fires and panelling as the immediate post-war generation had done.[90] Residential areas that had been rundown and used for lodging-houses were bought up and improved by middle-class 'knockers-through', subjecting neighbourhoods to 'gentrification'.[91] As Gardiner points out, it was only in the 1970s that the old definition of antique (i.e., anything pre-1840) gave way to including things over 100 years old.[92]

The reaction against modernity in 1960s fashion

This growing bourgeois fondness for the individualities of Victorian housing coincided with the countercultural trend, in the late 1960s, for dressing in Victorian-style pea-coats, military jackets, top hats, ruffled shirts, boating blazers, capes and velvet suits. Two of the most mythologized fashion boutiques in accounts of the 1960s are Granny Takes a Trip, on the King's Road, and I Was Lord Kitchener's Valet, on the Portobello Road, both names drawing attention to the idea of young people dressing up in the clothes of their grandparents' generation, eclectically mixing styles to give them a 'psychedelic' makeover. Samuel mentions 'the wistful turn in late 1960s counter-culture' and 'a whole series of short-lived period revivals which followed the Art Nouveau craze of the late 1960s'.[93] The Victorian and Edwardian seemed to recur in 1960s fashion at least as much as other styles, however. Sandbrook describes I Was Lord Kitchener's Valet as overflowing with 'Union Jacks and imperial memorabilia'.[94] The longer hairstyles, sideburns and moustaches that were to dominate male fashion until the early 1980s constituted the most hirsute look for men fashionable since the turn of the twentieth century. The new trouser style was the flare, based on nineteenth-century naval 'bell-bottoms'.[95] The popular television character Adam Adamant sported a 'Victorian look', and of the three fashionable 'swinging London' clubs, two had a Victorian theme (the 'Victorian whimsy' of Pickwick's and Scottish Baronial style of the Scotch at St James).[96] In women's fashions, Biba was developing a decadent, vampiric look evocative of the 1890s, and Laura Ashley was selling increasing numbers of dresses whose style was 'immersed in Victorian revivalism and the spirit of William Morris'.[97] Samuel does note that

'There was a very strong camp element in the late 1960s vogue for dressing up in period clothes, one which gave free play to fantasy and fetishism, while at the same time caricaturing or sending up class and gender stereotypes', while Jonathon Green argues that 'Fashion, once a badge of maturity, had reversed direction. Led by [Mary] Quant it feted immaturity, endless youth. As the decade proceeded this moved into pure dressing up – boys as toy soldiers, girls as fairy princesses: the upper-class nursery laid out for all to enjoy.'[98] In explaining this fashion for dressing-up, John Gardiner asserts that there was a demographic shift at work in the 1960s' fondness for Victoriana, and that it began after the dying out of the last Victorians by upbringing, such as Churchill in 1965, Clement Atlee in 1967 and Bertrand Russell in 1970.[99] He also sees, more practically, the dying of the last generation of Victorians in the 1950s and 1960s as allowing an influx of clothes, jewellery and furniture onto Portobello Road, available cheaply.[100]

In a similar way to housing and clothing, English pop music of the late 1960s might be said to have been reaching towards and re-inhabiting styles that had only recently died out. Perhaps it is something more than a coincidence that a style evocative of Victorian or Edwardian music hall can be detected in the use of call-and-response, funny voices or emphatic cockney delivery, parochial settings or the focus on eccentric character portraits in such songs as the Kinks' 'Dedicated Follower of Fashion' (1966) (a distant cousin of music hall standards 'Gilbert the Filbert' and 'Burlington Bertie from Bow'), and also the Small Faces' 'Rene' and 'Lazy Sunday Afternoon' (1968), The Scaffold's 'Lily the Pink' (1968) and, probably the inspiration for much of the above, the psychedelic eclecticism of The Beatles' *Sergeant Pepper's Lonely Hearts Club Band*. That album's title track has been described by Ian MacDonald as 'a shrewd fusion of Edwardian variety orchestra and contemporary "heavy rock"'.[101] During the 1960s, pop music had begun to attract young people to concerts, undermining the traditional family appeal of the variety bill; it is interesting that rock musicians towards the end of the decade should begin to be nostalgic about one of the entertainment forms they themselves had displaced.[102]

Declinism and British identity

However, what may have begun in the 1960s as camp and dressing-up by a small, bohemian section of London had, by the 1970s, become adopted by the mainstream and lost its ironic connotations. As Hewison's *The Heritage Industry* and a 2007 BBC4 documentary entitled *The 1970s' Edwardian Resurrection* both argue, during the 1970s the flirtation with pre-1914 objects, stories and styles became a full-scale nostalgia, or 'heritage' boom. This was the era when a whole industry was built around reproduction stripped-pine 'country kitchens' that resembled the sculleries of 1970s period dramas like *Upstairs, Downstairs* (see p. 41). The documentary interviews Winston Fletcher of the advertising firm Fletcher Shelton Delaney, who says of the commercials for bread and herbal shampoos that played with imagery of cobblestones, traditional bakers and workers in the fields, 'By the 1970s, particularly because of the economic difficulties, a lot of people were beginning to feel that the gilt had come off the gingerbread, and that the consumer society wasn't quite what it was cracked up to be', and that these advertisements harked back to a supposedly more pure period.[103]

This sense of crisis and national decline, although popularly associated with the 1970s (Michael Billington claims that 'Britain underwent something very close to a national nervous breakdown in the early Seventies'), was palpable from the late 1960s on, although, as both Addison and Sandbrook make clear, it is a long-standing feature of British thought.[104] The press baron Cecil King was formulating his emergency government campaign in 1968, and Lord Mountbatten came close to agreeing to be the figurehead for King's planned coup.[105] The Conservative grandee Quintin Hogg made his famous comment that 'we are a people that has lost its way' and that Britain was 'in the act of destroying itself, and will surely do so if we go on as at present'.[106] The Wilson government launched its slightly desperate-sounding 'I'm Backing Britain' campaign for people to buy more domestically produced goods in an attempt to ameliorate the balance of payments crisis.[107] Perhaps most divisively, in April 1968, Enoch Powell made the speech that has since become known as 'Rivers of Blood', where he likened the rate of immigration to 'a nation busily engaged in heaping up its own funeral pyre'.[108] It is sometimes forgotten how popular this speech made him with some sections of the populace: the London dockers marched in his support as the Race Relations Bill was going through parliament, while the Conservatives had a strategy in place for preventing Powell, because of his popularity with voters, from becoming party leader if Edward Heath lost the general election in 1970.[109] The ways in which race and immigration were used as symbols of national decline, and how plays about the Victorians as empire-builders offered alternative scenarios to this, forms the focus of Chapter 2.

We can see this sense of confusion about British identity, and the ways in which it was changing, reflected in television drama of the 1970s.

Donald Wilson's production of *The Forsyte Saga*, screened in 26 episodes from 1967 and covering the period 1879–1926, was immensely popular, and it paved the way for other family sagas during the 1970s, both original and adapted from novels, such as *The Pallisers* (1974), adapted from Anthony Trollope's series of novels, *Upstairs, Downstairs* (1971–5) and *The Onedin Line* (1971–80).

What can be seen in *The Forsyte Saga, Upstairs, Downstairs* and the BBC's *The Duchess of Duke Street* (1976–7) is an attempt to retell the story of the transition into modernity, from the nineteenth to the twentieth centuries, and to trace the emergence of modernity: the *Forsyte Saga* takes the longest stretch of history, while the first series of *Upstairs, Downstairs* was set in 1903 and continued until the 1930s; *The Duchess of Duke Street* began in 1900, the last full year of Victoria's reign.[110] There is a strong focus on working life, particularly in the latter two, and the experience of the domestic servants: a sense of the nation engaged in an act of remembrance for, and a fascination with, how it used to live. *The Duchess of Duke Street* can be seen, like the 1978 LWT series *Lillie*, telling the story of Lillie Langtry, as having affinities with the second-wave feminism that was coming to cultural prominence in the 1970s. In both, ambitious women have to negotiate and rise in a male-dominated world. Louisa Leighton, the protagonist in *The Duchess of Duke Street*, argues with her mother about 'getting on in the world', her having rejected an unsuitable man, and her mother's refusal to allow her to stay on at school and become a teacher.[111] She is given the job as assistant to *Chef de Cuisine*, Monsieur Alex, only because there were no male applicants, and must prove herself equal to the attentions of the wealthy Mr Charlie as well as the petty jealousies of female members of the household staff (as with *Upstairs, Downstairs*, there is a fascination, in the first episode, with the processes of cooking a feast for the Prince of Wales, and the view from the kitchens, rather than the dinner party conversation of the nobility).

Anne Onedin, the heroine of the BBC's long-running original drama *The Onedin Line* (created by Cyril Abraham and set in the Liverpool of 1860), can equally be seen as a clever, businesslike woman who marries James Onedin in order to keep the ship, the *Charlotte Rhodes*, in the family, and travels with him on trading voyages. In the second episode she has to navigate the ship home when James falls ill, as well as deal with the superstitions of the obstinate Captain Baines.

The Onedin Line can also be said to belong to another category of Victorian television of the 1970s – the story of the ambitious individual who defies the prejudices of the time and helps make Britain great.

There was Yorkshire Television's *Dickens of London* in 1976, and another flamboyantly dressed novelist in ATV's *Disraeli: Portrait of a Romantic* in 1978, the story of the 'one-nation conservative' prime minister who says, 'I refuse to let myself be beaten' and who promises 'to work for the good of the nation as a whole'.[112] James Onedin, similarly, defies the economic pessimism of his brother Robert, who says, 'You speak so grandly of the world as your oyster, but that shell has long been prised open.'[113]

This craving for the minutiae of Victorian and turn-of-the-century living was not manifested as strongly in theatre, and it is arguable that television as a medium is more suited to this kind of drama. It can make more use of sets, location filming and camerawork (which is able to depict items and processes in close-up). The 'serial drama' format, as open-ended in some ways as a soap opera, also has the space and time to give a sense of the daily rhythms of work. As the next chapter investigates in more detail, new writing on the Victorians for the theatre during the 1970s tended to focus on the British Empire, as a way of coming to terms with its comparatively recent break-up, and also with the implications of the 1960s' sexual liberalization and controversies over race and immigration. Vigorous political use was made of the Victorians during the 1970s by agit-prop theatre companies, too, as explored further in Chapter 4. However, there are few examples of plays that explore the social minutiae of a Britain that has been lost until close to the end of the 1970s.

The theatre of everyday life

Noel Greig's *The Dear Love of Comrades*, first performed at the Oval House in March 1979, revisits the life of utopian socialist Edward Carpenter, who campaigned for social equality and tolerance of homosexual activity with equal vigour. Set between 1891 and 1898, the play shows Carpenter as a figure whose life and view look forward to the twentieth century with an optimism that a late 1970s audience may have felt was misplaced. In the discussions in the early part of the play, and particularly in the picnic scene, a range of contemporary progressive opinion is explored, all of which will have their impact on the twentieth century: anarchism, the decline of the Christian faith, pacifism and animal rights.[114] As discussed in the Introduction, a pattern of emergence is being presented here, with men like Carpenter seen as possessing the kernel of social thought that will become part of the twentieth-century landscape. Later, Carpenter's freewheeling existence is contrasted with the outlook of the well-meaning but conventional Independent Labour Party candidate Frank Simpson.[115] Raphael Samuel argues that 'The historicist turn in British culture coincided with the decline of Labour as a mass-membership party, with the demise – in Britain as in other countries – of socialism as a worker's faith.' Audiences at the time will surely have found it tempting to compare the Labour Party in its formative phase with the then Labour government under James Callaghan, and quite possibly mourn the loss of the early, transformative socialist vision.[116] They may also, presumably, have drawn connections between Carpenter's 'free love' lifestyle and some of the difficulties engendered by the new sexual freedoms since the 1960s.[117]

John Downie's *Mary Ann: An Elegy*, first staged at the Edinburgh Festival in 1979, tells the story of Mary-Ann Cotton, a young widow in County Durham in 1873, who was hanged for poisoning her son and several of her lodgers. Stylistically, the play is somewhere between a social-realist drama (it is preoccupied with socialism and trade unionism, and makes room for long disquisitions on the role of the hangman), a hallucinatory Bond-style play (in which two sides of Mary-Ann argue and fight and confront different villagers at different times) and a Peter Barnes or Snoo Wilson-style series of pointed pastiches (the death of Joe Nattrass is enacted as melodrama, and there is a hallucinatory courtroom scene that borrows from music hall and circus styles, with a chorus, rhymed speech, song, slapstick and ventriloquism).[118] Nevertheless, like television drama of the period, it seeks to uncover and confront the hidden history of women who had to endure secret pregnancy and abortion, sexual double standards and even incest.[119]

Most significantly, in 1978 the Cottesloe at the National Theatre staged Keith Dewhurst's *Lark Rise* and its sequel, *Candleford* – tales of rural Oxfordshire in the 1880s – and presented them together as *Lark Rise to Candleford* in 1979. Although there is little attempt to situate the characters in terms of contemporary politics (apart from a short discussion of Gladstone), it is unfair to dismiss the plays as appealing primarily to 'sentiment and nostalgia'.[120] Seen in the light of the dramas discussed in this chapter, Dewhurst's intention to highlight the connections between the Victorians and ourselves, our 'common humanity' as Dewhurst calls it in his introduction, is part of an important cultural coming-to-terms with modernity, and is similar to the television dramas discussed earlier in several key ways.[121] First, the plays dealt with the everyday manual labour and lives of the working class, not the dashing metropolitan lives of the Victorian elite. Secondly, in using Emma and Albert Timms's daughter Laura, aged ten at the start of the first play, as occasional narrator, the plays offer a female perspective on a village life that seemed, on the surface at least, dominated by patriarchal privilege (the squire, Sir Timothy and the hunt) and male brawn (the harvesters, the blacksmiths at the forge and, later, Laura's domineering husband who belittles her writing ambitions).[122] Thirdly, as with the long-running original television dramas mentioned above, Dewhurst does not have to follow a rigidly paced single plot but can be anecdotal, and give a succession of impressions rather than a single clear line of action. As in serial drama, characters are introduced as part of the social mix but not necessarily fully utilized; one of the main threads in *Candleford*, Mrs Macey and her husband who is secretly in prison, is never concluded: she simply leaves to be with him.[123] As in *The Duchess of Duke Street*, small social distinctions take on great importance: field workers' wives regard a stonemason's wife as 'a bit la-di-da', and one cousin addresses another by her full name and title because she owns a post office.[124]

However, one of the factors that seems to have made *Lark Rise to Candleford* a success in the 1970s was its staging as a promenade performance, where the audience was encouraged to walk among the actors. By having the audience standing among the labourers, seeing their physical exhaustion, or by showing the old man, Sharman, being taken forcibly away from among them to the workhouse, Dewhurst and the director, Bill Bryden, could be said to be evoking empathy for the narrow, rural world-view of a century earlier, in which the sea and Oxford are equally, unimaginably far, without encouraging sentimental nostalgia.[125] It might be said to have something in common with the artist Cornelia Parker's show *Never Endings*, discussed in Chapter 6: the urge to connect with, to immerse oneself in, the intangible ephemera of the everyday rhythms of those who are long-dead but who seem to have a form and fixity (as historical figures, or as workers secure in their place and function) that we lack.

Samuel has drawn connections between the use of 'free-floating space' in *Lark Rise to Candleford* and the 1960s cult of immediacy, a countercultural rejection of the proscenium stage. He also notes that the Theatre in Education movement, which grew in the 1970s, popularized the idea of re-enactment as a trigger for historical empathy, with 'grandmother's wash day' or the 'Victorian Day' becoming the primary school fixture it is today.[126] But I have aimed to demonstrate in this chapter that, for adults during the 1960s and 1970s, there seems to have been a palpable sense of the loss brought about by modernity, in the dislocations of post-war rehousing and town planning, in the loss of optimism about the future of society and Britain's place in the world, and even in the privatization and mediation of the experience of listening to music (the transistor radio instead of the parlour piano or variety show, what MacDonald has called the process of 'desocialisation by technology').[127] This sense of loss made British culture more sincerely interested in the Victorians and how they coped with their own transitions to modernity, and unable to laugh them off as irrelevances, or castigate them for their ongoing influence, as Bond and Barnes seem to suggest. Cora Kaplan states in *Victoriana* that 'The Victorian as at once ghostly and tangible, an origin and an anachronism, had a strong affective presence in modern Britain in the supposedly libertarian 1960s and 1970s, when the nation was thought to be on its way to becoming a classless and multicultural society', and this chapter has attempted to begin to flesh out how such a contradiction could persist, and how this might apply to British theatre.[128] The further fears engendered by this nascent multicultural society, and the way in which race was viewed as a result of the 1960s supposed sexual revolution, are the themes that will be applied to this period's 'Empire plays' in the next chapter.

2
Staging the Empire

In this chapter, I intend to focus on plays about the British Empire in the Victorian period, a popular subject and setting for a series of high-profile works from the late 1960s to the early 1980s. In particular, I wish to examine how these plays represented sexuality and race, and how this connected with wider public concerns about immigration, national decline and the 'permissive society' during the 1970s. I begin by exploring the way in which these empire plays – principally Charles Wood's *H*, Tony Harrison's *Phaedra Britannica*, Simon Gray's *The Rear Column*, David Pownall's *Livingstone and Sechele* and Caryl Churchill's *Cloud Nine* – can be read in terms of the sexual liberation movements in western Europe from the late 1960s onwards, and the New Left's incorporation of Freud and psychosexual alienation into its Marxist analysis in particular. This leads me to return to Foucault's repressive hypothesis, and to consider this in the light of these post-1968 plays' urge to 'speak the truth about sex'. This urge, I argue, is a doomed one, not only since in order to 'liberate' the Victorians' sexuality on stage one must perform an act of historical ventriloquism, but also because, at 40 years' distance, it becomes clearer that what post-1968 liberal playwrights considered 'sex' was actually a historically bound 'sexuality', predicated on the male gaze and a degree of sexual violence. I use the 1975 musical spectacular *Ipi Tombi* as a point of comparison for the sexualized depiction of colonized peoples.

Broadening the scope of the chapter somewhat, I use Stuart Hall et al.'s 1978 book, *Policing the Crisis*, and in particular its analysis of the conservative reaction to 1960s social liberalism and immigration, to add a further dimension to the context in which empire plays were received. Finally, I suggest that the plays can be read as reversing racist stereotypes of black and Asian people as muggers or native 'savages', implying

that it is the Victorian empire-builders who have been the true historical 'savages'. This liberal cosmopolitan outlook, characterized by Hall,
which questioned British claims to moral superiority and enjoyed the
benefits of the 'permissive society' during the 1970s, was, I will conclude, to be the target of Hall's other group, the resentful, conservative
lower-middle class, in the coming decade, with its twin figureheads of
Mary Whitehouse and Margaret Thatcher.

Empire plays as a 1970s phenomenon

The plays that form this chapter's source material are those that present,
in an imagined form or in one based on historically documented events,
British imperial rule during the Victorian period (or whose events and
characters strongly suggest the Victorian period, as with the Com-
modore and Georgiana in Edward Bond's *Narrow Road to the Deep North*).
Narrow Road could be counted as the earliest of these, first staged at
the Belgrade Theatre Coventry in 1968, and produced at the Royal
Court Theatre in February 1969 as part of a 'triumphant season' of
Bond plays also including *Saved* and *Early Morning*, to celebrate the
defeat of the censor.[1] Charles Wood's play '*H*', set in 1850s imperial
India, had premiered earlier that same month in 1969. In the 1970s,
Tony Harrison's *Phaedra Britannica* appeared at the National Theatre in
September 1975, Simon Gray's *The Rear Column* at the Globe Theatre,
London, in February 1978, David Pownall's *Livingstone and Sechele* and
Caryl Churchill's *Cloud Nine* in 1979, John Spurling's *The British Empire
Part One* at the Birmingham Rep in 1980, and Peter Nichols' *Poppy*, for
the Royal Shakespeare Company (RSC), premiered at the Barbican in
September 1982. To this list might be added Briony Lavery's *Zulu* (1981)
and *The Black Hole of Calcutta* (1982), written for the National Theatre
of Brent and dealing with the 1857 Sepoy Rebellion.[2]

While the above list may not seem a prodigious number of plays
to have been produced over the period of more than a decade from
1968, it is the prominence of the venues that is worth noting first of
all: these are plays that were performed in major subsidized theatres
and those with reputations for new writing, such as the National
Theatre, the RSC, the Royal Court and the Lyric Theatre, Hammersmith.
Gray's play was given a West End opening and directed by Harold
Pinter. Therefore, British imperial behaviour during the Victorian
period was a topic during the 1970s that appealed to writers, directors and/or literary managers, and was felt to be important enough
to justify the use of their resources. I have used a cut-off point of

1982 in this classification, since empire plays of this nature had begun to peter out by that point. Hence, the latest play that this chapter analyses in detail dates from 1979, when the economic and ideological ground in Britain began to shift significantly, as Chapter 3 will discuss.

The fashion for empire plays between the late 1960s and the mid-to-late 1970s was to some extent made possible by the 1968 Theatres Act, since the Lord Chamberlain's Office, in addition to banning representations of God and of past and present monarchs in work that was not sufficiently 'serious', had also been known to censor representations of public figures (as with Churchill) and actual persons, living or dead (as when, for instance, a play about the trial of Oscar Wilde was refused a licence in 1946).[3] The tone of these imperial plays can also be seen in the context of theatre from 1968 on pushing the boundaries of taste that had previously been enforced by a member of the Queen's household. Bill Gaskill has commented that the end of censorship 'initially meant bums and tits', presumably having in mind the opening of *Hair* on the night (28 September 1968) when the Theatres Act became law.[4] As Nicholas de Jongh has noted, the Theatres Act paved the way for risqué revues in the early 1970s, such as *Oh! Calcutta* and *The Dirtiest Show in Town*.[5] However, a further reason for focusing on the period up to the end of the 1970s is that the case of Howard Brenton's *The Romans in Britain*, first performed at the National Theatre in 1980 and also a play about British imperialism, indicated that there were still, potentially, limits on this new freedom of expression in the theatre despite the end of pre-censorship. The play's director, Michael Bogdanov, had a private prosecution brought against him by Mary Whitehouse of the National Viewers and Listeners' Association; the prosecution hinged on the question of whether the stage simulation of buggery constituted procuring an act of gross indecency.[6]

Changing representations of empire in cinema

The debunking of British imperialism in plays from 1968 on also took its cue from cinema, where Tony Richardson's *The Charge of the Light Brigade*, scripted by '*H*'*s*' author Charles Wood, marked a pronounced departure from the conventional filmic depiction of the British at war. As Raphael Samuel makes clear, it was the empire films of the 1930s that 'established an iconography on which a generation of film-makers was to draw'.[7] Even in 1964's *Zulu*, although a degree of class antagonism is dramatized in the conflict between Bromhead (Michael Caine) and Chard (Stanley Baker) over who is to command the defence of

Rorke's Drift, the final moments are uncomplicatedly patriotic, listing all eleven soldiers who were awarded the Victoria Cross for the action, as a military choir insists that 'Welshmen will not yield'. By contrast, in *The Charge of the Light Brigade*, the personality clashes between Captain Nolan and Lords Lucan, Cardigan and Raglan are central to the disaster depicted in the film. The powerful sense of the wrong people – amateurish, out-of-touch aristocrats rather than thrusting meritocrats – being in charge is highly evocative of the rebellious mood of the late 1960s, and is encapsulated by John Gielgud (as Lord Raglan) and his celebrated line: 'It will be a sad day when England has her armies officered by men who know too well what they are doing. It smacks of murder.' Like Lindsay Anderson's violent public school fantasy *If . . .* , also released in 1968, *The Charge of the Light Brigade* signals an impatience with deference and tradition.

By 1975 and John Huston's *The Man Who Would Be King*, critiquing Victorian imperial assumptions of superiority seems to have become a familiar position, although the film's status as an adaptation of a short story by Kipling means that this critique comes originally from the Victorians themselves. The central characters, played by Michael Caine and Sean Connery, are a pair of roguish ex-soldiers who hit on a scheme to seize control of and loot the fictional country of Kafiristan. When they arrive there, Danny (Connery) is taken for a god and given the treasures of Alexander the Great. As we will find to be a recurring motif in the 1970s empire plays, it is sex – and sex's power to trump even money – that proves to be the conspirators' undoing in *The Man Who Would Be King*. Danny wishes to stay in Kafiristan and take a wife rather than steal the treasure, but at the wedding ceremony his chosen mate bites him and the priests see that he is bleeding, and hence a mortal. Needless to say, the two are set upon and bloody revenge is exacted. From this very small sample, then, it might be said that the focal figures in empire films shifted in these years from the commanding officers (*Zulu*) through the rebel captain (*Charge of the Light Brigade*) to two imperial freebooters, uttering their characteristic oath, 'God's holy trousers' (*The Man Who Would Be King*).

Foucault, the New Left and sexual liberation

This chapter will now begin to discuss some of the social and intellectual currents behind the sexual liberalization of the 1960s and 1970s, for which the Theatres Act was both a symptom and a catalyst. Michel Foucault's essay 'We "Other" Victorians', which forms the first part of

The History of Sexuality: 1, begins with the ringing sentences, 'For a long time, the story goes, we supported a Victorian regime, and we continue to be dominated by it even today. Thus the image of the imperial prude is emblazoned on our restrained, mute and hypocritical sexuality.'[8] The use of the qualifying aside, 'the story goes', is, of course, crucial to Foucault's analysis – his argument that our past repression and present or future liberation is a story we tell to convince ourselves of our modernity. It is also interesting that Foucault makes use of the idea of an empire of prudery, presumably as a metaphor for the way in which this system of power/knowledge spreads into every corner of our lives. Foucault goes on to explain that the reiteration of this 'story' provides 'something that one might call the speaker's benefit. If sex is repressed, that is, condemned to prohibition, nonexistence, and silence, then the mere fact that one is speaking about it has the appearance of a deliberate transgression.'[9] It is the transgressiveness of making sex appear to speak on stage, in the plays about empire that this chapter covers, that I wish to focus on. Foucault goes on, 'What sustains our eagerness to speak of sex in terms of repression is doubtless this opportunity to speak out against the powers that be, to utter truths and promise bliss, to link together enlightenment, liberation, and manifold pleasures.'[10] I would like to take a few sentences to consider Foucault's terms, 'the powers that be' and 'enlightenment, liberation, and manifold pleasures', and how they might apply to British and continental European culture in the 1960s and 1970s.

The liberalizing of societal attitudes to sex in Britain from the late 1960s can perhaps be seen to have three strands. First, there was the liberalizing that came from within the Establishment, in particular Roy Jenkins's period as a liberal, reforming Home Secretary in the late 1960s, when abortion was legalized, the laws on homosexuality were liberalized, divorce was eased and, of course, the pre-censorship of theatre ended.[11] The second strand was pressure from the counterculture in the name of freedom of behaviour and expression. This is exemplified by the enthusiasm of radical bookshops, like Indica and The Paperback Book Shop, for disseminating pornography, and also by *Oz* magazine, most notoriously with its 'School Kids Issue'.[12] The third strand includes more cogently political schemes of thought from the New Left, where the throwing-off of sexual repression is held to be a revolutionary act.

The schemes of thought in this third strand might be seen, broadly and to some extent, as the incorporation of ideas about sexual repression, derived from Freud, into a Marxist analysis of western capitalism. For Herbert Marcuse in the late 1960s, for instance, society after the qualitative change of revolution (as opposed to the quantitative change provided by the affluent society) would reflect a 'new sensibility' that 'expresses the ascent of the life instincts over aggressiveness and guilt', since they would be striving for a 'free society' but also a 'free human existence'.[13] Marcuse had a vision of 'Society as a work of art...the most radical possibility of liberation today.'[14] Similarly, Erich Fromm, a Marxist of the Frankfurt School who, like Marcuse, was energized by the social protests of the 1960s, wrote a great deal about the way in which we have substituted genuine existence and experience – 'being' – for 'having', that is, artifice, the consumption of second-hand experience and capitalism's empty promises.[15] He argued that modern society had lost the differentiation between erotic love and mother love, and lacked even the words to talk about sex apart from obscene ones; the revolutionary change from having to being would therefore create a sexual openness and restore the person to his totality, 'or, as I would rather say, to his reality...my heart and my feelings can be just as rational as my thought...Most of us are somewhat embarrassed about having feelings at all.'[16] Finally, situationism could be said to be a movement with some similarities to New Left thought (although it has its roots, as Stephen Barber demonstrates, in Dada, surrealism and the Lettrist artistic movements of interwar and post-war Paris).[17] The situationists rose to prominence during the student protests that were part of the Paris disturbances of May and June 1968.[18] In 1967, one self-styled situationist leader, Guy Debord, published *The Society of the Spectacle*, and his description in this book of 'the spectacle' and its 'ceaseless manufacture of pseudo-needs' is not far removed from contemporary Marxism's emphasis on the alienated consumer.[19] Debord describes the revolutionary consciousness required to overthrow the spectacle as 'Consciousness of desire and the desire for consciousness', and he claims that when the spectacle is dissolved, 'the authentic *journey* will be restored to us, along with authentic life understood as a journey containing its whole meaning within itself'.[20]

To return to Foucault, then, the promise of bliss, of liberation, of the revelation of the truth about ourselves by sexual openness, was very much an attitude that had had discernible effects in post-1968 western Europe at the time when Foucault began the publication of his *History of Sexuality* project (in 1976) and, as mentioned above, the 'powers that be' had been sympathetic to some extent. By situating these empire plays in the context of the liberalizing effects of the 'permissive society' (as it was pejoratively called in Britain), I hope to shed new light on the plays featured in this chapter.[21] Playwrights of the time can be seen as choosing to set dramas in the Victorian age because it represents the height of society's repression of sex, and also the point at which capitalism is most visibly brutal and bloody, keeping the masses hungry while a few factory owners grow immensely rich. There is, of course, a logical flaw with this set of assumptions: why, if capitalism was at its most brutal in the nineteenth century, should revolution be more imminent now than then? However, I do not wish to argue that these playwrights (Bond is perhaps the exception[22]) themselves advocated revolution, merely that their use of sexual behaviour as a metonym to highlight the futility and corruption inherent in the British imperial mission, and to force a more critical reading of the English sense of moral superiority, was a stream of thought that these plays shared with contemporary Marxism and that may have been read as such at the time.

In passing, it is worth noting that Marx himself saw British imperialism as largely an expression of the needs of capital – for slave labour and cheap raw materials, and finally as an outlet for Britain's resultant surplus production; to Marxists in the 1960s and 1970s, the plays might be seen as depicting imperialism in order to depict the crisis in capitalism writ large.[23] Furthermore, these plays seem to be using the Victorian-imperial setting in order to argue that on one level, what drives imperial conquest is a displaced sexual drive that cannot find expression in British society at home. As Marx pointed out, in a passage that uses metaphors of undressing to bring the point home, 'The profound hypocrisy and inherent barbarism of bourgeois civilization lies unveiled before our eyes, turning from its home, where it assumes respectable forms, to the colonies, where it goes naked.'[24]

Sex and empire in the theatre

Before considering some of the problems of using the Victorians to critique imperialism as a repressed sexual desire (possibly fostered by the contradictions of capitalism), it is worth looking at how far these plays do foreground sex. Charles Wood's '*H*', performed by the National Theatre at the Old Vic in 1969, is, alongside Bond's *Narrow Road to the Deep North*, the earliest of these theatrical debunkings of the Victorian ideals of empire, and it uses themes of performance, class and sexual violence in order to do this. It is one of the very few Victorian plays of the period that focuses on a famous historical event, the Sepoy Rebellion (or, to give it its better-known but pejorative name, the 'Indian Mutiny') of 1857. Wood makes it clear that he wants to break the fourth wall down by making the action push at and tear through the safety curtain. Throughout the many disjointed scenes, the idea that the imperial mission is a performance or script is brought home to us by General Havelock addressing the men in what appears to be his own voice, which is then revealed to be a recording that he is miming to (a trick later performed by Surgeon Sooter), or by the bombardier and the sepoys making the 'Whee. Bang!' noises of the British being shelled as they watch a *tableau vivant* of wounded sepoys.[25]

There are many sudden reversals of sentiment, too, as if to prevent any character from seeming to be heroic. Although Jemadar, a rebel leader, is condemned to die, the British officer Neill kisses him and voices a paean to the lost days of mutual endeavour and understanding – and then throws a pigskin at him.[26] On the eve of Jemadar's execution, just as we might be expected to see the rebel leader as heroic, Jones-Parry condemns Indian traditions, such as marrying children: 'and do not deny it,/I have seen them die with their/bowels ruptured by your cocks'.[27] This stark language forces us again to consider the British imperialists' moral arguments, an impression that is then immediately undermined by Jones-Parry's name-calling, 'cherry merry bamboo'.[28] At the execution itself, Jemadar says that the English 'are as the wind' and 'as the grain of sand', to which Jones-Parry responds with a patriotic speech of defiance that one would expect to save the day and restore the British character's sense of superiority (and, perhaps, the audience's sense of feeling superior to their jingoism), but, in fact, the speech 'embarrasses everybody'.[29]

There is one scene where, after the capture of Cawnpore, the soldiers are allowed a day's looting in the city, and the rebels' attack on the women and children's quarters is shown being transformed from historical event to spectacle, an 'outrage' with the pronounced sexual dimension of the rape of white women, for the newspapers back home. A soldier cuts a dead girl's hair off so that each man can send a portion home to add urgency to their call for vengeance; the soldiers scratch emotive slogans on the wall after the event, like 'Revenge, I am slain'; the literate ones take requests from the illiterate. Harry, General Havelock's son, seems to have no sentiment whatsoever about it; the weeping soldiers sicken him.[30]

The sexual drive behind imperialism is symbolized in '*H*' by the monkey god Humayon, who performs an 'obscene and insulting dance' during the fighting, squirting at Captain Jones-Parry with his oversized phallus.[31] In a later reappearance, as the monkey god beckons on the sepoys, Jones-Parry manages to shoot him.[32] But is Humayon real, a kind of sepoy ensign or mascot, or a figment of Jones-Parry's imagination,

the bestial, ungovernable India of his fears? It hardly seems coincidence that the squirting phallus appeared in the scene following the one
where Jones-Parry's wife is assaulted by the bombadier. As the bombadier
insists, as he awaits the firing squad near the end of the play,

> It is not the English holds India,
> It is the Irish and the Jocks,
> And they does it through their,
> Pricks.[33]

Although voiced by a coarse, sadistic, discredited soldier, this speech
seems to support Marx's interpretation of barbarism going naked in
the colonies. The imperial mission to spread 'bourgeois civilization' is
revealed as hypocritical through its methods of domination.

A similar unmasking of the sexual forces behind conquest and colo-
nization takes place in *Phaedra Britannica*, Tony Harrison's 1975 adaptation of the Phaedra myth, set during the British Raj, and produced by
the National Theatre at the Old Vic. The governor, wrongly suspecting
his son Thomas of seducing his stepmother, banishes him, but on his
way out of the city the Hindu god Siva rises up in front of Thomas,
causing the horses to bolt and killing him. Harrison's introduction to
the play discourages us from reading this as a simple act of the gods. He
emphasizes how often in the play India is apostrophized as a capricious
and corrupting force, and there are abundant examples: 'Oh India got
into us somehow!'; 'how much more/Persecution has India in store?'[34]
In fact, it is the imperialists, not any 'spirit of India', who are responsible
for corruption and degeneration. The governor, the most sexually vora-
cious character, announces his reform after a close brush with death,
but then, unable to accept the possibility of his wife's hidden lust for his
son, he punishes the son instead. These self-deceptions can be read as
what Freud would call transference: the 'repressed impulses of love, hate
and fear' being redirected to a different object.[35] The governor transfers
his own lusts onto mysterious India, and transfers his fear and hatred of
his wife's taboo sexual drives onto his son. So much repression is taking place in order to propel Thomas, the only member of the family
free from hypocrisy, out of the city, that a beast emerges in the precise,
uncanny form into which those unconscious desires had been displaced:
a god of ancient, savage, mystical India.

A rather more gentle critique of imperialism is offered in David
Pownall's *Livingstone and Sechele*, which premiered at the Traverse
Theatre, Edinburgh, in 1979 before being revived at the Lyric's studio

in Hammersmith. Pownall's drama is based on historically documented characters: the Scottish Presbyterian missionary David Livingstone, his wife Mary, and Sechele, chief of the Crocodile People, and his favourite wife, Moko. Having lived among the Crocodile People for four years, Livingstone still has not managed to successfully convert Sechele to Christianity, and the rest of the tribe are indifferent or actively hostile to the doctrine. For Sechele, despite his admiration for Livingstone and knowing much of the Bible by heart, the sticking-point that makes him backslide shortly after each announcement of conversion is his passionate love for his fourth wife, Moko, whom he would have to give up as a Christian, entering instead into a monogamous relationship with his first wife. The way in which the play ends with Sechele promising once more 'I will never let you down again' and the singing of the alphabet song to the tune of 'Auld Lang Syne', as at the play's opening, highlights this sense of indecision and events repeating themselves.[36] The play has its dark elements, critical of colonialism. Mary insists that Moko must abandon the child with which she is pregnant, because it was conceived after Sechele was baptized, and is thus illegitimate. Then, at the end of Act 2, Mary herself is in the final stages of pregnancy, and Sechele is ordered to collect all the people's water, in this drought-plagued village, in a big jug with Admiral Nelson on it. Although *Livingstone and Sechele* was marketed (at least judging by the Hampstead programme) as a knockabout comedy,[37] the situations outlined above seem to be pointing to the futility of overcoming desire with imported doctrine, and again, with the jug, to be suggesting an image of sucking the people dry.

Caryl Churchill's *Cloud Nine*, devised with Joint Stock Theatre Company and first performed at the Royal Court in 1979, also points to the monster at the heart of the civilizing mission, in the form of Harry Bagley, trapped between his affair with imperial administrator Clive's wife Betty, his sexual liaison with the servant Joshua and his abuse of Clive and Betty's son Edward. However, moral judgement is made much more difficult for the audience by the fact that in the first act of the play, the Victorian age is represented through farce, with cross-gender casting making the scene even more dramatically heightened (where the second act, set in the late twentieth century is shown more naturalistically). As in farce, in the Victorian sequence, everyone is perpetually on the verge of being caught in the act. Churchill's play seems to echo Freud's pessimism that desire is, in Cohen's words, 'an aimless and fickle *drive*', 'modelled on confusion... excessive and uncontainable'.[38] At the end of the first act, it appears that the colonists are about to pay the price for their sexual and economic exploitation of the Africans and their hypocritical attempt to impose Christian values, when the servant Joshua raises his gun to shoot Clive.[39]

Simon Gray's *The Rear Column*, meanwhile, is a naturalistic drama set in Africa, having much in common with a psychological thriller like Conrad's *Heart of Darkness*, and a similar sense of moral unease with colonialism. Bartellot is placed in command of the Rear Column by Henry Morton Stanley, Victorian adventurer, empire-builder and profiteer, who has marched on with the rest of the troops to Emin Pasha. His instructions are to await the arrival of the mysterious Arab warlord, Tippu-Tib, but, as the weeks turn to months, supplies run low and Bartellot's leadership is challenged by his impatient fellow officers. It is these shifting allegiances, and Bartellot's descent into madness, that are the main focus of the play, as the gentlemanly values of duty and honour give way to capitalism's ruthless dynamic. Bartellot and his gentleman-naturalist ally Jameson become trapped by these old-fashioned values, being unwilling to disobey orders or desert, and eventually being tricked, by their gentlemanly generosity, into a blackmailing opportunity by Tippu-Tib.

Both *H* and *The Rear Column* feature moments where imperial soldiers, in the midst of asserting their higher, rational qualities, suddenly and impulsively perform actions associated with beasts (vampires, even): Bartellot in *The Rear Column* confesses to having held one of his African porters at gunpoint as he bit into his wife's neck, and Surgeon Sooter bites off Jones-Parry's finger when he is reluctant to have it amputated.[40] These incidents might call to mind some of Marx's favourite metaphors for capital as the consumer of human life: it is a Shylock, demanding its pound of flesh, a lynx, a werewolf and finally a consumer of 'muscles, nerves, bones and brains'.[41] They might also be placed alongside the figure of Sweeney Todd in Stephen Sondheim and Hugh Wheeler's 1979 musical, set in mid-Victorian Britain, where Todd decides to follow the logic of capitalism and allow man to literally devour man in the form of meat pies: 'It's man devouring man, my dear/And who are we/To deny it in here?'[42] What these characters and actions have in common is that they represent something bestial, even cannibalistic, at the heart of 'civilized' man, whether he is concealed in the metropolitan environs of London or supposedly 'civilizing' indigenous peoples himself.

From sex to sexuality

As has previously been argued, the recurrent linking of sex and empire does not demonstrate that these plays were Marxist in intent or function (anyway, any revolutionary message that the plays might contain is hemmed in by the historical setting: they represent a historical failure without agitating for any post-revolutionary utopia). Rather, the 'repressive hypothesis' that gained in popularity from the late 1960s was a theatrically arresting and fashionable way to critique imperialism and Victorian-derived ideas of Britishness; furthermore, the easing of theatre censorship made possible more sexually provocative drama that pushed the boundaries of taste. In this sense, the plays might be viewed as a form of confession, in the terms in which Foucault discusses it in *The History of Sexuality: 1*. 'We have since become a singularly confessing society,' he asserts. 'The confession has spread its effects far and wide... One confesses – or is forced to confess.'[43] The confession is seen as crucial because, 'Spoken in time, to the proper party, and by the person who was both the bearer of it and the one responsible for it, the truth healed.'[44] Certainly, in surveying the plethora of television chat shows, magazines and other confessional formats available in 2011, it seems clear that Britain has become a more openly and publicly 'confessional' society since the late 1960s. However, there are obvious problems in comparing these empire plays to confession, for they may be culturally 'spoken in time' (i.e., disseminated at a time when British culture was dismantling its empire and perhaps more receptive to such revisionism), but it is doubtful whether these imperial confessions were spoken to 'the proper party' (would that be Britons, 100 years later, or the descendants of the colonized peoples, or both?), and they were certainly not delivered by those who bore responsibility for the British Empire. It can be argued that there is an act of historical ventriloquism taking place, in which the playgoers' ancestors are made to confess in order to liberate, in order that 'the truth' might heal – but at little personal moral cost to the audience member, unless they happened, for instance, to be a descendant of General Havelock or Henry Morton Stanley.

Moreover, Foucault's ideas about sex suggest some further thoughts on the difficulties and contradictions of these plays' indictment of sexual repression while they also depict certain types of sexual behaviour. I would like to draw the distinction, as Foucault does in my reading of *The History of Sexuality*, between three categories: 'sexuality', 'sex' and 'bodies and pleasures'. Sexuality, as the title of his books indicates, was for Foucault a culturally and historically contingent set of ideas rather than a 'natural' or 'common-sense' range of behaviours or practices. He usefully defines sexuality in *The History of Sexuality: 2* as being constituted in three ways: first, in terms of knowledge about sexual behaviour; secondly, in terms of the systems of power that regulate sexual acts; and thirdly in terms of 'the forms within which individuals are able, are obliged, to recognise themselves as subjects of this sexuality'.[45] Towards the end of the first volume of *The History of Sexuality*, Foucault begins to draw a clearer distinction between this historically variable 'sexuality' and the notion of 'sex', the latter terms being no more historically and culturally transcendent than the former: 'it is precisely this idea of sex *in itself* that we cannot accept without examination. Is "sex" really the anchorage point that supports the manifestations of sexuality, or is it not rather a complex idea that was formed inside the deployment of sexuality?'[46] In other words, 'sex' is an idea of purity and transcendence constructed within the constructed idea of sexuality itself; and he continues, in the modern period 'one sees the elaboration of this idea that there exists something other than bodies, organs, somatic localizations, functions, anatomo-physiological systems, sensations, and pleasures; something else and something more, with intrinsic properties and laws of its own: "sex"'.[47] 'Sex' is 'sexuality's' notion of an unchanging truth at the heart of itself, when, in fact, Foucault argues that 'sexuality is a very real historical formation; it is what gave rise to the notion of sex.'[48]

The notion of 'sex' gained currency because, Foucault explains, it 'allowed us to group together, in an artificial unity... and it enabled one to make use of this fictitious unity as a causal principle, an omnipresent meaning, a secret to be discovered everywhere'.[49] We were thus encouraged to 'believe in the sovereignty of its law', when in fact 'we were moved by the power mechanisms of sexuality'.[50] As a way of escaping these preformed ideas, one ought instead to focus on bodies and pleasures: 'The rallying point for the counterattack against the deployment of sexuality ought not to be sex-desire, but bodies and pleasures.'[51] Presumably the point here is that biological sexual responses can to some extent be measured and are stable within the species *Homo sapiens*; and therefore to identify a pleasure and a body that experiences it is to specify a 'sexual' act, but without the cultural baggage that deployment of the word 'sexual' would inevitably bring into play.

I think Foucault's distinctions are very useful in helping to theorize what seems strange and 'other' about these empire plays, 30 to 40 years on, and perhaps in helping to explain why very few of them have been revived with any frequency. Plays about the Victorians after 1968 sought to liberate Britain's past from stuffiness, repression and hypocrisy; their intention seems to have been to present a humanist perspective where the Victorians experienced 'sex' just like us, but simply could not admit it, as we healthy moderns do. However, what the plays actually reveal to a present-day perspective is that the representation of 'sex' is actually a historically bound 'sexuality' that was very much of its time.

Rape, paedophilia and nudity

We can see this, first, in the plays' treatment of rape. In Charles Wood's *H*, there is an unsympathetic portrayal of Mrs Jones-Parry, who is captured and raped by the Anglo-Irish bombardier who is fighting on the Indian side in the 1857 rebellion. On her return to the British camp, months later, she displays no compassion for the lower ranks and still expects privileges;[52] the play could be seen as arguing that the rape is just deserts for her class-bred petty snobbery, or that wives of the officer-class have no capacity for empathy and therefore their suffering is lesser or of a different quality as a sexual assault. In Bond's *Narrow Road to the Deep North*, the evangelist Georgiana, driven mad by the Sunday-school massacre, fears that she will be raped when she sees Kiro, crying, 'Ah! He's going to rape me! I'm going to be raped!...He'll split me up and open me out!' As Kiro takes out his sword to commit suicide, Georgiana responds, 'He's going to murder me! Murdered before I'm raped! I shan't know what it's like!' which suggests that she secretly wishes to experience rape and is rather disappointed that she might die first.[53] Among other post-1968 Victorian plays, we might also include in this classification the rape of Florence Nightingale by Queen Victoria in *Early Morning*,[54] and the farcical treatment of abduction and sexual assault in the first act of Snoo Wilson's play *Vampire*, produced at the Royal Court in 1973.[55]

Secondly, the inclusion of a quite sympathetic paedophile figure in *Cloud Nine*, and the way in which his abuse of Edward is never openly addressed and condemned, also suggests that these plays hail from a time with different notions of 'sexuality'. As Max Stafford-Clark commented in 1999, the play's second act, set in 1979, now itself seems 'quaint and historical' where at the time it seemed 'absolutely contemporary' (the recent revival at the Almeida Theatre in November 2007 accordingly dressed the cast in the second act in 1979 'period costume').[56] Nevertheless, the contents of Churchill's play have become so familiar from inclusion in textbooks for A-Level theatre studies and undergraduate courses that its deeply disturbing implications in performance can sometimes be overlooked.[57] In Act 1 Scene 2, we learn from Edward's conversation with his 'uncle' Harry that they have had a sexual relationship for some time; the fact that it is partly an act of hero-worship on Edward's part and viewed as a romance ('I wish the others would all be killed. Take it out now and let me see it.') emphasizes that the boy does not see himself as a victim of abuse.[58] Of course, the role of Edward, as in the original casting, seems always to be played by a woman

(Julie Covington in the original; Nicola Walker in the Almeida revival). This might serve to emphasize that we are being asked to imagine a situation, rather than being shown it (in a worst-case scenario, Mary Whitehouse presumably could not have launched a private prosecution against the play because all that is actually being 'shown' is a romance between a man and a woman); it also fits in with the play's undermining of rigid gender roles and sexual orientations. Nevertheless, the exchange appears within the context of what can be read as a cross-dressing farce. If it were a new play opening tomorrow, *Cloud Nine* might well be facing calls – as a result of its suggestions of paedophilia – to be altered so that Bagley is seen to be less appealing, more of a typical offender figure, with Edward a more clearly traumatized victim. Alternatively, the play might face criticism from gay rights campaigners, since Harry's suggestion to Joshua, 'Shall we go in a barn and fuck?', could be taken as unhelpfully associating homosexual behaviour with paedophilia.[59]

What appears to have happened to rape and paedophilia in the years since the 1970s is that, perhaps as a result of feminism in the 1970s and 1980s in the former case and tabloid campaigns since the 1990s in the latter, these actions have come to be seen as outside the spectrum of sexuality, and linked to violence, coercion and abuse (of strength, of power) instead. In the period 1969–79, rape and underage sexual activity seem to have been topics that could be joked about in the name of permissiveness (or liberation).

The third area where the portrayal of sexuality in these empire plays seems to come from another age is in their use of nudity, a feature that is not obvious from reading the scripts but that, I argue, can considerably influence the effect of the work in the theatre. In Pownall's *Livingstone and Sechele*, the formidable stage presence of the character Moko is perhaps weakened by the fact that the actress, on the evidence of a production photograph of Anni Domingo from the Lyric production, was topless (it illustrated a review by Christopher Hudson in the *Evening Standard* entitled 'Body and Souls'). In a similarly prurient vein, an (unattributed) review of Simon Gray's *The Rear Column* in the *Sunday Times* a year earlier remarked on a topless extra, 'but I suppose she has to be there, else how, in an otherwise all-male play, could we be shown a pair of nice brown titties?'[60] It is difficult to know how to interpret the tone of this last comment; certainly there is a cynicism about the idea of nudity being something that helps to sell a play with an imperial theme, but is the reviewer revealing a personal predilection for 'nice brown titties' or is he commenting sardonically on having objectivized images of colonized people foisted upon him against his will?

We might gain something of an insight into the reviewer's attitude if we consider it in the light of the storm over *Ipi Tombi*, a musical spectacular that ran at Her Majesty's Theatre from November 1975. The production was billed as a celebration of the Zulu people and an exuberant portrait of modern South Africa, packed with song and dance. However, the reviews of the time were in little doubt that this counted as 'a brown tits-and-ass show' where 'the girls wear brown, flesh-tinted knickers, presumably so that the Upper Circle may think they are bare' and 'the well-developed ladies [wear] generally a modest little woll [sic] chest from which escape in whirling motion the handsome bare breasts'.[61] Again, we might detect a certain confusion between these reviewers' distaste for selling 'tits-and-ass' and their precise location for their readers of where, and to what extent, it can be found. The musical's title, the producer Bertha Egnos explains, means 'Where are the girls?' in Xhosa, as if in coded reference to the voyeuristic expectations of the audience.[62]

Eleven members of the cast of *Ipi Tombi* were also involved in a dispute with the show's London management, Ray Cooney Ltd, over rates of pay, and later formed their own breakaway theatre company, refusing to return to South Africa because they feared they would be arrested when it became known that they had been involved in industrial disputes.[63] Press cuttings regarding this episode nestle alongside reviews of the show in the V&A Theatre Collection file on *Ipi Tombi*, and serve as a reminder that the show became a part of the history of apartheid and the European colonial legacy that its depiction of cheerful tribespeople was seeking to occlude. Equally, the empire plays under discussion here did not operate in a vacuum; their occasional use of naked African characters can be seen, from a twenty-first-century perspective, as an uncomfortable reminder of the objectification of 'native' women, or at least their tendency to be objectified by reviewers as 'nice brown titties', even in plays that, textually, seem to be lamenting the iniquities of the British imperial mission.

The emergence of black British theatre

A further contextual dimension to these empire plays is that they were being staged at a time when black and Asian playwrights' work was beginning to be staged in Britain. As Dominic Hingorani notes, 'Naseem Khan's ground breaking report "The Arts Britain Ignores" in 1976 officially recognized that "ethnic arts" should not be regarded as an "exotic" extra operating outside of British theatre but should be understood, funded and fostered as though they were a *part* of British theatre.'[64] The following year, Tara Arts was founded by the young student Jatinder Verma; Hingorani classifies its first phase as being from 1977 to 1984, where the company 'concerned itself with a range of subjects, including the postcolonial reworking of historical events on the Indian subcontinent in *Inkalaab 1919* (1980)'.[65] Michael Macmillan names some of the black theatre companies that also emerged in the 1970s, including the Dark and Light Theatre Company (later called the Black Theatre of Brixton) founded by Frank Cousins, and Temba Theatre Company, founded by Alton Kumalo (these two, Roland Rees points out, together 'produced more black plays in two years than the whole of English theatre had in the previous twenty-five'), and mentions the opening of the Keskidee Centre, one of London's first black arts centres.[66] Caryl Phillips notes that playwrights Mustafa Matura, Michael Abbensetts, Leigh Jackson and Alfred Fagon began to have their work performed in more prominent venues as the 1970s progressed.[67]

Immigration and national bogeys

Whether the subject matter of these black and Asian playwrights and companies was historical or contemporary, it must have been increasingly clear as the 1970s progressed that the British version of the colonial and post-colonial experience was not the only one being heard. While it might be possible to read the empire plays in this chapter as self-pitying meditations on national decline and the loss of empire, in this final section of the chapter I argue that they can be more usefully interpreted as liberal responses to public concern over immigration, calling into question the 'national bogey' figure of the black criminal by drawing attention to Britain's own Victorian crimes abroad.

The social study, *Policing the Crisis: Mugging, the State, and Law and Order*, by Stuart Hall, Chas Critcher, Tony Jefferson, John Clarke and Brian Roberts, is a fascinating text to read alongside these plays because it deals explicitly with the very contemporary issues – race and national decline – embedded in the subtext of the empire plays. The book is a response to the media storm over 'mugging' in the early 1970s, and the way in which young black men in particular were targeted and stereotyped as potential muggers. It begins by comparing public fear about street crime with the panic over garrotting in Victorian England: 'Credulity became a social obligation . . . the garrotters, lurking in the shadow of the wall, quickening step behind one on the lonely footpath, became something like a national bogey.'[68] Hall et al. use the idea of 'moral panics' first proposed by Stan Cohen to describe reactions to the battles between mods and rockers in the 1960s. He defines a moral panic as when 'A condition, episode or group of persons emerges to become defined as a threat to societal values and interests; its nature is presented in a stylized and stereo-typical fashion by the mass media; the moral barricades are manned by editors, bishops, politicians and other right-thinking people....'[69] The authors link the moral panic over mugging in the 1970s to anxieties over social permissiveness during Roy Jenkins's period as Home Secretary: there was the fear that 'the erosion of moral constraints, even if not directly challenging the law, would in the end precipitate a weakening in the authority of the law itself'.[70] This anxiety is displaced, the book argues, onto various scape-goats, of whom immigrants are among the most highly visible and vulnerable.[71]

Dominic Sandbrook's recent reading of the debates about immigra-tion and 'the permissive society' is remarkably similar to the conclusions that Hall et al. drew at the time. He argues that 'Racism did not exist in a vacuum: it was based on old ideas of British imperial predomi-nance, and by the late sixties it had become interwoven with broader anxieties about cultural change and national decline', while earlier he had stated, 'The answer is that sex worked as shorthand for other, more general anxieties about morality, modernity, social change and national decline.'[72] In 1976, Britain was forced to appeal to the Inter-national Monetary Fund to stem its balance of payments deficit, and the American-produced document on Britain's financial situation at the time, *The Hudson Report*, contained the significant wording:

> Britain in the 1970s is largely a creation of the mid-Victorian period...Many of the country's problems are Victorian problems or stem from attempts to operate Victorian solutions in a society that exists in a late twentieth-century world. In a nutshell, Victorian Britain attempted to come to terms with a crude industrialism; the Britain of the 1970s has refused to look beyond it.[73]

These additional views might be taken to indicate that the 'national decline' discourse was not one that Hall et al. simply set up as a straw man to bolster their own arguments.

Policing the Crisis formulates a view of English conservatism based on notions of 'respectability', 'work', 'social discipline', 'the family', 'the city' and 'the law'.[74] This 'traditionalist "English ideology"' also includes the "quiet, unspoken" assumption of the inbuilt superiority of

the English to former ' "natives" – colonised or enslaved peoples, especially if they are black'.[75] Middle-aged and older people were especially
likely to be prone to social anxiety regarding the breakdown of these
values, a 'sense of loss' that 'In ways which are hard to locate precisely... also had something to do with the experience of the war and
the decline and loss of Empire – both of which had contributed, in their
different ways, to the ideological 'unity' of the nation'.[76] This is why, to
such sections of the population, the folk devil is such a potent spectre
to raise:

> In one sense, the Folk Devil comes up at us unexpectedly, out of the
> darkness, out of nowhere. In another sense, he is all too familiar; we
> know him already, before he appears. He is the reverse image, the
> alternative to all we know: *the negation*. He is the fear of failure that is
> secreted at the heart of success, the danger that lurks inside security,
> the profligate figure by whom Virtue is constantly tempted...[77]

Consciously or otherwise, the empire plays can be read as putting forth
the idea of an alternative (or pre-emptive) folk devil, the British imperialist. In the form of Bartellot in *The Rear Column*, Surgeon Sooter in *H* or
Harry Bagley in *Cloud Nine*, he both 'comes out of the darkness' of the
corners of empire, and yet 'we know him already, before he appears'
as the *Boys' Own* hero derived from the works of Kipling and Rider
Haggard. Even without explicit references to cannibalism, each of the
empire plays discussed in this chapter does indeed use individual characters (Georgiana, Jones-Parry, the governor) to explore the failure at
the heart of imperial success, the danger inside the supposed security of
the empire as a big, happy family, the virtue that (seemingly inevitably)
gives way to profligacy.

Reactions to a changing Britain

All this may seem quite obvious in the twenty-first century; it has
become something of an orthodoxy to decry the effects, if not necessarily all the aims, of the British Empire. However, in the 1960s and 1970s,
with decolonization still taking place and the empire a recent memory,[78]
such views might still be regarded as unpatriotic by Hall et al.'s 'traditionalist English', who celebrated the Queen's Silver Jubilee in such
numbers in 1977 (as Jon Savage points out, it seems likely that steps were
taken to ensure that the Sex Pistols' Jubilee protest 'God Save the Queen'

never reached number one in the summer of that year, and that the association with anti-royal attitudes led to punks being assaulted and becoming another version of Cohen's folk devil).[79] Hall et al. identify two sharply differentiated responses to such processes as social liberalization and immigration. On the one hand is the cosmopolitan 'fraction' of the middle class, whose opinions could be seen in the 'abstract analysis' of the 'quality' Sunday newspapers.[80] It is this 'fraction' that I believe the empire plays of the 1960s and 1970s spoke to: audiences with liberal leanings who took a relaxed view of 'permissiveness' and were suspicious of the anti-immigration, populist conservatism that came to be known as Powellism.[81]

On the other hand, Hall et al. identified a resentful lower-middle class, prone to looking for scapegoats:

> As the tide of permissiveness and moral 'filth' has accumulated, and the middle and upper classes have lowered the barriers of moral vigilance and started to 'swing' a little with the permissive trends, this lower-middle-class voice has become more strident, more entrenched, more outraged, more wracked with social and moral envy...This is the spear-head of the moral back-lash, the watchdogs of public morality, the articulators of moral indignation, the moral entrepreneurs, the crusaders. One of its principal characteristics is its tendency...to give voice on behalf of everybody.[82]

It is from this group, and in order to represent it, that Mary Whitehouse sprang, with her National Viewers and Listeners' Association's talk of permissiveness and national moral decline. As Sandbrook remarks, 'More than any other individual, Mary Whitehouse popularised the issues of permissiveness and moral corruption, and she was undoubtedly one of the best-known and most controversial women of the sixties and seventies.'[83] Sandbrook goes on to compare Whitehouse with Margaret Thatcher, and it is this connection with which I wish to finish. Thatcher, too, can be seen as a product of the resentful lower-middle class; she too cited Powell as a major influence, and regarded the 1960s as a 'decade of excess, self-indulgence and moral decline'.[84] The election of Thatcher's Conservative Party to government in May 1979 helped bring about a national change of mood. As playwrights began to focus more on poverty and iniquity at home (often, as the chapters on Dickens and biodrama will explain, using the Victorians to do so), plays about the empire became less frequent. Michael Billington has asserted that during the 1980s, 'the Arts Council itself transformed from an independent funding body into a pliable instrument of government', and, if his case is accepted, then it follows that major subsidized bodies, such as the RSC and the National, would be nervous about putting on too many anti-patriotic plays.[85] Meanwhile, before the end of her first term of office, Thatcher had, as we shall see, invested the Falklands conflict with language suggesting a return to imperial values and Britain's status as a world power.

3
Staging Dickens

When we describe things as 'Victorian' in a pejorative sense, we often supplement it with the adjective 'Dickensian'. James Thompson has argued that 'As the currency of the adjective "Dickensian" suggests, images derived from Dickens have done much to colour perceptions of the Victorian past', while John Gardiner writes that Dickens 'looms large ... in our retrospective sense of the Victorian age'.[1] Newspaper journalism habitually uses 'Dickensian' as shorthand for all that was grim and harsh about the Victorian era, as if Dickens himself is to blame for the poverty and institutional neglect that he wrote so passionately against.[2] Dickens has also become a major player in the heritage industry, where adaptations of his works are just part of a wider associated network: guided tours, themed villages, blue-plaque locations, sell-through DVDs and so on. He represented, Peter Ackroyd insists, something profoundly English to the English about themselves, and thus he can be seen as a critical lynchpin, linking national character, our Victorian past and our commercial present.[3] Dickens adaptations have certainly featured heavily in the overall representation of the Victorians in theatre. Even excluding biographical dramas, parodies and Lionel Bart's *Oliver!*, this chapter draws on some 80 adaptations of his works. On television, it is Dickens adaptations like *Bleak House* (2005), *Oliver Twist* (2007) and *Little Dorrit* (2008) that are marketed as flagship classic serials by the BBC.

In this chapter I aim to explore the ways in which theatrical adaptations of Dickens have responded to the challenge posed by television – for audiences, and for a Dickensian voice perceived as 'authentic' – over the last three decades. In doing this, I highlight the central importance of ideas of community that Dickens has come to represent for contemporary theatre audiences, consider the importance of the RSC's *Nicholas*

Nickleby in this context and trace this back to the social crisis of the Thatcher years, where communities were felt to be under threat from the rampant forces of capitalism. Using the work of Raymond Williams as a starting point, I hope to uncover some of the material conditions that have given shape to theatre and television adaptations in their typical forms.

The wider debate over 'Victorian values' also helped to define Margaret Thatcher's premiership and the social mood of the 1980s. In this chapter, I characterize this mood as being influenced by two contesting ways of thinking about Britain at the time: the 'Hard Times' mode, which drew on Dickens for much of its resonance, and the 'Self-Help' mode, which proposed a new vision of personal responsibility and individual achievement reflecting a contemporary interpretation of Samuel Smiles's 1859 tract, *Self-Help*. However, I begin by querying Williams's use of two terms in regard to Dickens's fiction – the 'structure of feeling' and the 'knowable community' – rejecting Williams's conception of how fiction works, while still acknowledging the usefulness of these two concepts in a restricted sense: historicizing Williams's own historicizing terms. In considering stage adaptations of Dickens's works since *Nicholas Nickleby*, I argue that two main styles have emerged – the 'world on a stage' and the 'studio psychodrama' – both of which draw on the aesthetics, if not the methods, of David Edgar and of the theatre company Shared Experience under Mike Alfreds. I examine both theatre and television's contesting claims to Dickensian 'authenticity' and, finally, consider reasons for Dickens's long-lasting appeal in Britain.

Raymond Williams and structures of feeling

To begin with, then, I want to argue for the importance of Raymond Williams to our current understanding of Dickens, and why his forms of analysis need alteration if they are to help to fashion insights into adaptation. What Williams has to say about Dickens is important because it featured in one of his most successful books, *The Country and the City*, at the height of his influence in the early 1970s, after his involvement with the May Day Manifesto, and when he was regarded, as David Hare remembers, as a hero of the New Left.[4] It gives us an idea of what an influential critic, schooled in Marxist thought, wished to see in Dickens, and which, I believe, has influenced David Edgar's approach to adapting *Nicholas Nickleby*, which in turn influenced how Dickens has been perceived and adapted since.

In particular, the concept of 'structures of feeling' is extremely useful in any analysis of how the Victorians have been perceived since 1968. Williams demonstrates how illuminating cultural-materialist investigations can be in essays such as 'Commitment and Alignment', 'Crisis in English Studies' and 'The Bloomsbury Fraction', where he takes apparently common-sense assumptions about what terms like 'commitment', 'English literature' and 'the Bloomsbury set' mean and traces their historical formulation, often in the process revealing that the terms' current sense is strongly ideologically marked. Such a method has many similarities with a Foucauldian analysis, which overturns notions of common sense, power and linguistic categories.

Nevertheless, I argue that Williams fails to follow through the implications of his method in his more large-scale works on literature. There are Marxist assumptions underlying much of his critical work that the reader is required to bring to the work in order to fill in the gaps and to complete the argument. In a critical review of *The Country and the City*, Christopher Ricks complained that 'These are arguments which have to be *made*. He never works for them.'[5] I think one perplexing instance of this is his phrase 'structure of feeling'. Williams has defined it in several different ways over his career, and I shall use two definitions here as examples. When all the elements of a novel have been analysed, he argues in *The English Novel from Dickens to Lawrence*, 'There remains some element for which there is no external counterpart. This element, I believe, is what I have named the *structure of feeling* of a period, and it is only realizable through experience of the work of art itself, as a whole.'[6] In the earlier *Preface to Film*, Williams similarly states: 'The structure of feeling...cannot be merely extracted and summarized; it is perhaps only in art...that it can be realized, and communicated, as a whole experience.'[7] In other words, the structure of feeling is there but cannot be named, cannot be gazed upon, rather like the situationists' belief in the reality behind the spectacle. Although I readily accept that feelings can be commonly observed to have structures, in the sense of predictable sequences and patterns, the heart of the problem, for me, lies in Williams's insistence that the novel's structure of feeling 'can only be communicated as a whole experience'. This points to Fred Inglis's acknowledgement that Williams believed art to be the direct communication of experience.[8] Therefore, Williams might claim, he did not need textual evidence of the presence of that structure of feeling – the evidence was, by definition, extra-textual – he had read the novel, and felt something, and anybody else reading the book would feel the same thing, since they were reading the same words. For more recent readers, on the other hand, Wittgenstein and also Foucault and Derrida have all demonstrated that what we read is interpenetrated at every level by our own psychological limitations, the system of meanings and discourses in which we operate, and the distortions and displacements of language.[9] A modern adaptor of, say, *Great Expectations*, therefore, is very unlikely to share Williams's particular twentieth-century, New Left, class-conscious exegesis of the story, let alone come to the same conclusions about how the novel's structure of feeling is completed, given the famously ambiguous language of the novel's final paragraph.

The knowable community

In discussing Dickens, Williams brings his notion of the 'structure of feeling' into contact with the idea of the 'knowable community'. What he saw in Dickens's great novels of the city was 'A way of seeing men and women that belongs to the street.... Unknown and unacknowledged relationships, profound and decisive connection.... Obscured, complicated, mystified by.... This new and complex social order.'[10] Dickens is attempting to show us, Williams feels, what really connects city-dwellers, as if he is peeling back the false-consciousness of capitalism to show human brotherhood. Indeed, this is what Dickens, Williams argues, has dedicated himself to: 'The creation of consciousness – of recognitions and relationships – can be seen as the purpose of Dickens' developed fiction.'[11] Dickens is dramatizing 'a very complex structure of feeling', a modern city where men can be seen 'making their own worlds, carrying them about through the noise and the crowding'.[12] Dickens uses his narratives, his characters and his rhetoric to fight the prevailing assumptions of capitalism, of urban alienation and individualism, and gives a human face to impersonal institutions so that the model of society is always human relationships.[13]

Williams seems to be trying to co-opt Dickens into his favoured group of novelists writing about 'knowable communities'. In *The English Novel*, he asserts that the nineteenth century 'is a period in which what it means to live in a community is more uncertain, more critical, more disturbing...than ever before in history' and, later, that 'Most novels are in some sense knowable communities. It is part of a traditional method...that the novelist offers to show people and their relationships in essentially knowable and communicable ways.'[14] Although Williams is discussing Hardy here, the implication seems to be that even those writers who seem to be discussing urban alienation are actually revealing, reifying, a 'knowable community'. Of course, other readings of what

Dickens was up to are available: as Amy Hayward has argued in *Consuming Pleasures*, serial novels like Dickens's were more or less obliged to include a broad and varied cast of characters in order to maintain interest and sales.[15] Not only that, but such serial commonplaces as twins and doubles, characters being brought back from the dead and extraordinary coincidences were, and continue to be, generically typical devices for serials.[16] It could be argued that the fact that Dickens's novels tend to end with the revelation and clarification of obscure connections is not 'profound and decisive', but as much a fantasy of completion as his fairytale pictures of domestic bliss that conclude works as disparate as *David Copperfield* and *Bleak House*. It could be argued that Dickens was not suggesting to his audience that individuals really are connected in any kind of 'community' in such a way, but that such unlikely connections are a metaphor for human (indeed, Christian) brotherhood. It could be argued, in short, that Dickens's novels were not, predominantly, works of social realism.

I allude to such arguments not because I wish to pursue them as definitively correct in the context of Dickens's fiction; I only wish to make the point that Williams chose the social-realist, 'community' interpretation rather than any other. His Marxist convictions and New Left historical moment perhaps made it inevitable that he would. Furthermore, the term 'knowable community' is as problematic as any in Williams's vocabulary. The qualifier 'knowable' itself suggests a social-realist bias, and indeed his discussion of the term is most pronounced in *The Country and the City* when he discusses George Eliot's attempts to represent the rural poor.[17] In what sense are Dickens's characters 'knowable'? They are recognizable and memorable, certainly; and psychologically complex, in the later fiction, absolutely; but 'knowable' in the sense of having a documentary verisimilitude? Again, we come back to Williams's investment in the view that Dickens, like Eliot, must be communicating his verifiable impressions and experience for our instruction, which heavily outweighs the consideration, say, that he was fashioning a fiction along certain generic lines for our entertainment.

The term 'community' is even more slippery. Williams observed in his *Keywords* entry that the word 'seems never to be used unfavourably, and never to be given any positive opposing or distinguishing term', and yet this does not stop him using it extensively.[18] Today the multivalence of the term is probably more obvious than in the 1970s, when it seems to have been a word much more favoured by the Left than the Right – community theatre, community centres, community action. The generalization of the word's meaning might be said to have been accelerated by Margaret Thatcher's introduction of 'care in the community' (a euphemism for the widespread closure of mental hospitals) and the 'Community Charge' (the wildly unpopular Poll Tax). Since then, the media has, for the most part uncritically, relayed and adopted the Blairite, enthusiastic branding of everything from an ethnicity to a sexuality, from a group of religious believers through a geographical area to an online discussion forum, as a 'community'.[19]

Notional communities

This sense of a 'community', as it relates to reading and adapting Dickens, is worth further consideration. D.G. Myers, in a critique of Judith Butler, elucidates the distinction between 'a *formal* community like a city, in which everyone obeys the same laws, and a *substantive* community like a baseball team, in which everyone pursues the same goals'.[20] In Williams's ideal working-class community, I imagine, the formal and substantive communities are the same: the people live and work together on mutually understood terms, and all share the same hopes of socialist revolution. What we find in reality – and indeed, in fictional communities like Dickens's Coketown in *Hard Times* – is that members of a formal community can have strikingly different goals and views on how that community actually does, and how it should, function. So, instead of 'knowable communities', a term that raises many questions about what a community is and on what terms one may 'know' it, I propose the phrase 'notional community': an imagined community that a group, person or institution strongly wishes us to believe in the existence of, where the formal and substantive definitions overlap more or less exactly.

However nebulously conceived, 'community' was also, I want to argue, an important concept for the theatre-makers of the 1970s and 1980s who adapted Dickens's work, and led to very different interpretations of the novels on stage compared with those on television – differences that cannot be entirely explained by the medium for which the adaptations were written. It is in this sceptical, restricted sense that I would like to rehabilitate the phrase 'structure of feeling'. I suggest that the means of production and transmission do account for most of what differentiate the two media's choice of approach to adaptation, but that there are other cultural influences embedded in the form of both that date back to earlier conditions of production originating from the cultural shift brought on by recession and Mrs Thatcher's first term in office.

'Hard Times' as a structure of feeling

As Catherine Itzin notes, the Conservative administration elected in 1979 immediately signalled that the arts were to expect less from government in the way of subsidy and support: VAT was increased, Arts Council funding was dropped and local authorities' budgets were reduced.[21] Many theatre-makers, having grown used to the expansion of Arts Council' subsidy in the early 1970s, were now highly exposed. However, Thatcher's monetarist policies had far more than a financial effect on the arts. Particularly in the light of her re-election in 1983 on a wave of patriotic enthusiasm, and the defeat of the Miner's Strike in 1984–5, it became clear to many in the arts that British society was undergoing a decisive shift away from the consensus politics of the post-war period and, indeed, the (sometimes rapid, as in 1972) alternating between Conservative and Labour governments that had characterized the 1970s. Michael Billington is quite correct to point out that 'there has been a good deal of retrospective rewriting of history' in the connection between Thatcherite values and *Nicholas Nickleby*, and that 'it would have been difficult to pin down the exact nature of Thatcherism' in June 1980 when the play made its debut.[22] However, the play was such an immense success that it had an extremely long run: the RSC was continuing to tour a production as late as 1986, with stops at Stratford-upon-Avon, Newcastle and then the US.[23] Given its circulation for much of the 1980s, then, it is not unreasonable to suggest that the play came to be seen as a symbol of the resistance against Thatcherism's values, that is, the structure of feeling that I call 'Hard Times'.

I characterize the 'Hard Times' structure of feeling as a liberal and left-wing response to Thatcherism, which held that Britain was going through a period of immense change, comparable in some ways to that of the nineteenth-century 'social upheavals' that created 'a world of unfathomable economic opportunity but also one assailed by bottom-less social doubt', as Edgar characterized it in the 1980s.[24] With the erosion of the welfare state and the decline of heavy industry (such as mining, shipbuilding and steel), some families and communities, it was felt, were being left in pre-Second World War conditions of poverty and inequality. Furthermore, the pursuit of the profit motive was felt to be seeping into every aspect of life, including education and the arts. Edgar's 1988 essay collection, *The Second Time as Farce*, has the subtitle *Reflections on the Drama of Mean Times*, a slight echo of 'Hard Times', and James Procter has referred to the early Thatcher years as 'iron times' when, as he notes, Britain's gross domestic product fell by 4.2 per cent, its industrial production by 10 per cent and its manufacturing by 17 per cent, while unemployment rose by a record 141 per cent.[25] Stuart Hall et al. characterized Thatcherism as creating 'new times' in the 1989 essay collection *New Times: The Changing Face of Politics in the 1990s*. The terms 'mean times', 'iron times' (with an echo of Thatcher as the 'Iron Lady') and 'new times' all suggest an apprehension that the Thatcher years have ushered in a backward-looking new age that does not amount to social progress.[26]

With perhaps questionable taste, the discourse was picked up by popular culture. There was a 1981 Human League song with the title 'Hard Times' (the B-side to the hit single 'Love Action'), and the term was then Americanized into the 'hard times look', which was to become 'the uniform of the 80s: seriously ripped Levi 501s, a white T-shirt, motorcycle boots and a black leather jacket', which was announced in an edition of *The Face* style magazine in 1982 bearing the cover line 'Hard Times'.[27] The look was popularized by the pop group Wham!, whose early singles, such as 'Wham! Rap' and 'Young Guns (Go For It)', were written from the perspective of young people on the dole. Robert Elms' lead article in *The Face*'s 'hard times' issue seems to have caused some annoyance, expressed in the letters page of the magazine, at his aestheticizing of poverty, especially his final line, 'With any luck there's even harder times ahead.'[28]

Nevertheless, long before this, the phrase 'hard times' had become inextricably linked with Dickens's 1854 novel of that name, and its portrayal of the fictional Coketown. Hence, it is significant that one of the Dickens adaptations that came in the wake of *Nickleby*, and has been among the most long-lived, is Stephen Jeffreys' *Hard Times*, having first been performed in 1982 and revived in 1984, 1987, 1990, 1991 and 2001. One of the play's opening comments, spoken to the audience, that 'There never was such hard times seen in England before', could be taken as a reference to the state of England in the 1980s.[29] Echoing Dickens's novel, the work contrasts the joyless, profit-minded philosophy of the schoolmaster, Gradgrind, with the Bakhtinian festive space created by Sleary's circus (and Sleary, the representative of the marginalized, is given the final speech).[30] However, as Jeffreys explains, the play changes some details of the plot so that the protagonist, Stephen Blackpool, dies as the result of his individualism – his refusal to join with the workers – rather than as the result of an 'obscure promise', suggesting again that the adaptation has a polemical purpose in promoting organized, unionized resistance against Thatcherism.[31]

'Self-Help' as a structure of feeling

In contrast to 'Hard Times', the Thatcherite 'Self-Help' structure of feeling is perhaps epitomized by then-Home Secretary Norman Tebbit's comment, in the wake of the Brixton and Handsworth riots of 1981: 'I grew up in the Thirties with our unemployed father. He did not riot, he got on his bike and looked for work.' The implication was that the modern unemployed had insufficient self-discipline and initiative, and expected to live on handouts.[32] Moreover, as Raphael Samuel notes, Thatcherism offered a kind of inverted Marxism, where labour was seen as a fetter on the forces of production; where 'business' was privileged over the professions and carers, who were seen as a species of social parasite.[33] I have called the discourse 'Self-Help' because, as Adrian Jarvis points out, Thatcherism made the Victorian author Samuel Smiles and his book *Self-Help* into an inspirational tract, even though, as Jarvis argues, Smiles would have frowned on such 'speculative jobbery' as the City trading that Thatcherism did so much to encourage.[34] Helping to cement this link between the new Conservatism and the Victorians, Thatcher stated that the values of the Victorians were 'the values when our country became great' in an interview with Brian Walden on *Weekend World* in 1983. The comment caught the media's imagination, even though it could be said to have simply made more explicit the admiration for the Victorians that had surfaced in her 'New Renaissance' and 'Dimensions of Conservatism' speeches of 1977.[35]

As Billington again points out, it was not until a 1987 interview that Thatcher made the widely noted comment that 'There is no such thing as society. There are individual men and women and there are families.'[36] Nevertheless, it had long been the tendency of Thatcherism to question what she regarded as a prevalent sense of social entitlement and to play up the role of the entrepreneur: 'These people are wonderful, we rely upon them to create the industries of tomorrow.'[37] As Shirley Robin Letwin articulates it in her book *The Anatomy of Thatcherism*, Thatcher favoured 'the *vigorous* virtues' of people who were 'upright, self-reliant, energetic, adventurous, independent-minded, loyal to friends, and robust against enemies', rather than those who relied on the help of others or the state.[38] The family, as the 1987 remark makes clear, is equally a cornerstone of Thatcherism. Letwin again: 'it is the means whereby the moral qualities, and in particular the vigorous virtues, of one generation are instilled in the next...the Thatcherite sees the family as a band of individuals brought together in their common task of transmission'.[39] In summary, then, where the discourse of

'Hard Times' presented Thatcherism as a dangerous shift, disempowering millions through loss of work and opportunity, and then lecturing the dispossessed for their supposed moral failings, the discourse of 'Self-Help' held that it was up to the individual to make their own way in the world, and that to look after one's own interests, and those of one's family, was at the heart of one's moral and social responsibility, burdening the state as little as possible.

Edgar's *Nicholas Nickleby*

Into this atmosphere came David Edgar's adaptation of *The Life and Adventures of Nicholas Nickleby*, one of the most memorable features of which was what Samuel has called the adaptation's 'virtual reinvention' of the character of Smike, played by David Threlfall in the original production as a physically and developmentally disabled young man whose stuttering speech, pale looks and harshly cropped hair are a physical embodiment of the institutional neglect of Dotheboys Hall and, by extension, of England's most vulnerable.[40] As Edgar himself notes, Threlfall 'developed the physical characteristics of a twenty-year-old who had suffered profound environmental and nutritional deprivation', taking the lovable but clownish Dickens character and making his dialogue 'at least equivalent to the medically observable behaviour of retarded or schizophrenic people'.[41]

The moment where Nicholas turns the tables on Wackford Squeers and beats him for beating Smike was, if the cheering on the Channel 4 televised version is to be believed, one of the highlights of the original production, and one that was echoed in the 2006 Jonathan Church revival.[42] The revelation that Smike is actually the neglected son of the money-lender, and man of business, Ralph Nickleby, contributes to Ralph's ruin and suicide, and of course Smike himself dies, having at least been accepted into the bosom of Nicholas and Kate's side of the family. Such a character, so memorably acted, was likely, in the early 1980s, to be seen as representative of the most vulnerable people in society and their neglect in the new 'Hard Times'.[43] In a similar way to Marlene's daughter Angie in Caryl Churchill's 1982 play *Top Girls*, Smike has been betrayed by his family – the institution that is supposed to protect him if society will not. Hence both plays can be read as critiques of the Thatcherite praise for the family and its seeming irrelevance when it comes into conflict with the profit motive. Nicholas, similarly, has to seek a sense of family in the Crummles' company and with the Cheerybles, since Ralph will not look after his late brother's family.[44]

The style of Edgar's *Nicholas Nickleby* can also be seen as developing from the theatre of the period, and, in this context, it is a distinct mixture of the conservative and the bold, reflecting the uncertain atmosphere of the theatre industry at the time. As Edgar described it in his article 'Adapting Nickleby', Trevor Nunn, the artistic director of the RSC, had asked him to consider writing an adaptation of Dickens in 1979, as the RSC had already decided it was going to present an adaptation for its Christmas 1980 season; the choice was simply between *Nickleby* and *Our Mutual Friend*.[45] The choice of *Nickleby*, one of the early, comic novels, full of picaresque incident and the subject of an Ealing comedy of 1947 and a Ned Sherrin musical in 1969, might have been seen as a cosy and heartwarming option for a Christmas show, a variation on *A Christmas Carol*. But Edgar and Nunn's way of working was built on the agit-prop techniques of the 1970s: seeing the 1830s setting as 'a mirror of our times', using a Brechtian distancing technique to separate actor from role, and inviting the actors to research and discuss the project collectively and working from workshops to scripts.[46] *Nickleby* was large-scale – Edgar describes discussing the text in a 45-person circle – yet built on the stripped-down aesthetic of Mike Alfreds's Shared Experience, whose four-part, ten-hour *Bleak House* (with a much smaller cast) had been one of the theatrical sensations of 1976 and was still running at the Theatre Upstairs in 1978.[47] Elsewhere, Edgar is critical of 'the ascetic minimalism of the late 1970s', which had 'outlived its usefulness', and so we might conjecture that he wished to leaven his message about social iniquity with the aid of some sumptuous, hand-made costumes and elegant props, while still gesturing towards 'ascetic minimalism' with the bare boards, ladders and wooden scaffolding (with furniture stored upstage as in a lumber-room) which were present, on the evidence of the Channel 4 televised version filmed at the Bristol Old Vic, for much of the performance time.[48]

In another important sense, too, Edgar altered the Shared Experience technique: the terms of engagement with the audience changed from a collective encounter with the text to an entertainment that reached back to music hall and melodrama for many of its effects. In the televised version, we can see actors walking through the auditorium to reach the stage at the beginning of each episode; cast members, dressed as maids, appear to be acting as ushers.[49] Later, the actors work to 'incite' the audience in the strike scene, chase through the auditorium in the Dotheboys episode, and play to the audience as if it was Crummles's own audience in the actor-manager's patriotic spectacular, which ends Part 1. Samuel, discussing the play admiringly in *Theatres of Memory*, explores some of the ways in which it holds and brings together its audience. Nickleby's interactions with other characters are presented as secret, emotionally charged meetings that he characterizes as 'romances'; thus, in the course of the play, Nicholas has four separate romances, not only with the actress, Miss Snevellicci, but with his sister Kate, Newman Noggs and even Smike.[50]

The adaptation gets away with such romantic sentimentality for a number of reasons. Partly it is because the play came in three parts, totalling more than ten hours of performance time; the audience has spent much longer in the company of these characters than one normally would in the theatre, and has followed them on a considerable journey. Secondly, as Edgar freely admits, the supposedly Brechtian device of having the whole company of 40 actors as storytellers creates a more intense emotional longing for Ralph Nickleby's vision of the world to be disproved.[51] In addition, the audience is continually made aware of the company's presence as actors in a collective, swapping roles, moving the scenery: a performance is being made for these people, rather than a group of actors on a fourth-wall set who might be seen as simply 'going through the motions'. This company is very evidently working, sweating, for your approval, for your change of heart. Another dimension, of course, after the initial success of the play is that audiences will have come to the theatre fully expecting a transformative experience in which sentiment and melodrama are rehabilitated for a modern audience. There is also a sense in which people attending the show are witnesses – to Dickens's genius, to the power of his storytelling, to (as Edgar hopes) his continuing relevance to modern society, and – perhaps most important in a decade of cuts and government suspicion of the arts – an affirmation of the power of theatre, to bring people together and even to transform them.[52] Many commentators, notably Michael Billington, see *Nickleby*'s success in the 1980s in the context of audiences that 'looked to theatre to provide consolation in a time of increasing despair', and remarks that such grand theatrical events offered audiences the 'spiritual affirmation' they craved in an increasingly materialistic society.[53]

It is necessary to expand a little on this point before considering the further influence of the Alfreds/Edgar style (however difficult it may be to establish views about this conclusively). In adapting Dickens for the stage, the RSC could be seen as staking a claim on Dickens as 'for' the theatre, 'for' a left-wing notional community, against the monetarist policies of Thatcherism: in effect, answering the charge that Conservative values were traditional, truly British and proudly Victorian, before the whole 'Victorian values' debate of 1983 began. If Dickens, that icon of Englishness, the almost universally popular man of the people and social critic, could be claimed for the side of theatre-makers, then it would be almost as great a coup as claiming Shakespeare as anti-Thatcher.[54]

Nickleby's influence on Dickens in the theatre

Furthermore, in *Nicholas Nickleby*, by staging the characters' journey and making the audience an integral part of it, Edgar is reinforcing the need for a sense of community, or social responsibility: the final scene has the whole company singing 'God Rest Ye Merry, Gentlemen' while one of the young escapees from Dotheboys Hall collapses downstage centre and is rescued by Nicholas. Edgar is calling on us, as members of the community in the theatre, to guarantee a common humanity in this period 'assailed by bottomless social doubt' – that is, implicitly, both the 1830s and the 1980s.[55] A 'community feel' has been important in staging adaptations of Dickens ever since. Indeed, it was a preoccupation of theatre in the early 1980s in general. As mentioned in Chapter 1, the National had had a long-running success with Keith Dewhurst's *Lark Rise to Candleford*, an adaptation of a memoir of a rural Oxfordshire childhood in the late nineteenth century. Another National, Bill Bryden-directed production, 1985's *The Mysteries* by Tony Harrison, again had the actors interacting with, merging with and emerging from the audience. And one of Edgar's next projects was *Entertaining Strangers*, a 'community play' for the people of Dorchester, which transferred to the National in 1986. Similarly, Jeffreys' *Hard Times* can be said to combine many of the techniques that made Edgar's adaptation successful, cut to size for a touring company or studio theatre: it is possible to perform it with a cast of four. The script instructs the actors to come onstage and chat to the audience before the performance, in a way that recalls Bryden and Edgar's work above, as well as 1970s community plays like Red Ladder's *Taking Our Time*, which was also set at the time of the Chartists and that toured pubs and working-men's clubs in Yorkshire (and is discussed further in the next chapter).[56] However, a step into abstraction has been taken since the Red Ladder production. Although the audience is being treated as part of a notional community and the actors are also presenting themselves as such, they are much more anonymous and unknown to each other than workers at the same mine or factory.

In stage adaptations of Dickens, the audience is being called upon to play the role of someone belonging to a community rather than being welcomed into a real one.

Alongside such popular theatre conventions as audience interaction, Dickens adaptations have tended to use grotesque, exaggerated characterization to cement this bond with the audience, in stark contrast, as we shall see, to acting Dickens on television. In the RSC's *Nicholas Nickleby*, Mrs Crummles's pomposity, Miss Snevellicci's narcissistic self-dramatizing, Squeers's malevolence and the *commedia dell'arte* lasciviousness of Grice were all communicated with simple, recognizable postures, facial expressions and gestures: what Brecht referred to as something 'quotable', a *gestus* that indicated the character's position and outlook on the world. In Squeers's case, it was the squint, the whip and the self-satisfied hooking of the thumb in the waistcoat pocket; in Grice's, it was the gleeful, boyish movements and the Albert Steptoe-like leering and rubbing of the hands as he anticipated his wedding to Kate. This is especially important when actors transform from narrator through crowd member to individualized character: we instantly know who is speaking. In a similar vein, Giles Havergal's 1996 *David Copperfield*, when produced at the West Yorkshire Playhouse in 2005, featured a Uriah Heep whose appeal to the audience seemed similar to that of a stand-up comic presenting an eccentric character with a catchphrase – naturally, Heep's 'ever so 'umble' – that guaranteed audience mirth. Several adaptations of *Great Expectations*, in particular the RSC 2005 version, use Joe Gargery's 'ever the best of friends' and 'what larks!' as catchphrases to signpost the character's reappearance, and in John Clifford's 1988 adaptation, Magwitch is defined by his frequent repetition of his resolution, 'but I ain't a-going to be low'.[57]

The 'world on a stage' and 'studio psychodrama' modes

Most Dickens stage adaptations in the wake of *Nickleby* appear to have borrowed from it in one of two distinctive ways, which I have classified as two broad types: the 'world on a stage' approach and the 'studio psychodrama' approach. In the first type, the company presents itself as a notional community and makes a direct connection with the audience, which through its laughter, pathos and complicity feels itself to be part of their world. This 'world on a stage' approach has been used by Giles Havergal's 2005 adaptation of *David Copperfield,* and, in a highly original way, by Neil Bartlett for his *Oliver Twist* at the Lyric, Hammersmith, in 2004.

Significantly, Bartlett had the freedom as artistic director of the theatre to do so, an Arts Council subsidy, and a London audience that would perhaps be more receptive to a radical overhaul of a familiar text. He represented the novel as a 'Penny Dreadful' machine, with shades of Madame Tussaud's Chamber of Horrors, where the cast sprang to life and sang Dickens's narrative in chopped-up, staccato choral form.[58] There was still a great deal of physical inventiveness and, as I have described, interaction with the audience (Dickens's words were set, to macabre effect, to several nineteenth-century music hall songs). But the tone of this production seemed unmistakably different from the usual reverence for Dickens. Despite Bartlett's conceit of using 'Dickens' original language and nothing but', his production sets out to defamiliarize Dickens's world, its morality and its characters.[59] The 'Penny Dreadful' machine is entertaining and uncanny by turns, but it does not care if we like or admire it or not; it is a self-contained world with its own twisted rules. In taking the text down from its pedestal, drawing to our attention Dickens's sometimes shocking switches in tone, and finding theatrical analogues for them, Bartlett offers a method that evokes the 'world on a stage' as *Nickleby* did, but to altogether more disturbing effect.

Another recent inheritor of this 'world on a stage' tradition is the RSC's 2005 co-production, with Cheek By Jowl, of *Great Expectations*. Nick Ormerod's design was ingenious in its stripped-down, consciously stagey elements – pantomime cows and a speeding gate to represent the journey across the marshes, a fireplace for internal scenes, and the huge gates of Satis House – which were whipped into place as the company kept up with their own fast-paced narrative and physically brought their scenes into being. It was also a 'world on a stage' production because the large cast stayed onstage throughout, functioning as extras, stage-hands and, most importantly, witnesses to Pip's behaviour. At every turn, Magwitch, or Miss Havisham, or Joe and Biddy were watching how he conducted himself.

The second pattern of classic-novel adaptation that has grown in popularity since *Nickleby*, the 'studio psychodrama', takes the stripped-down aesthetic of Alfreds's Shared Experience, and uses an intimate space and a small cast to evoke the interior world of the novel in question. In this 'studio psychodrama' style, society and community exist only as abstractions. The audience is given the impression that they are trapped inside the head of the protagonist, or else the protagonist is a ghost, doomed like the Ancient Mariner to stop us and repeat their story. Such adaptations are usually performed in black-box studio environments, with a minimum of décor but often a profusion of dry ice, giving the impression that we are in a dream-world or on some other plane. Lighting emphasizes long, deep shadows, and a gauze or projections of expressionistic film sequences may be used to enhance the hallucinatory feel. Costumes are often monochrome. Doubling-up of roles means that new characters often bear an uncanny resemblance to old ones, dead ones and opposite ones.

Such an approach is popular for the novels of the Brontë sisters, and, as Chapter 5 explores, Shared Experience's *Jane Eyre* of 1996 might be regarded as a deluxe version of this kind of adaptation (it had a much more elaborate set than most 'psychodramas' and played to larger venues). However, the 'psychodrama' approach is also a very popular way of adapting *Great Expectations*, perhaps again because of its first-person, confessional mode. John Clifford's is one such version; the Manchester Royal Exchange's *Great Expectations* of 1984 is another, which Michael Ratcliffe in the *Observer* said was 'so determined to avoid the epic diversity of the RSC's *Nicholas Nickleby* that we never quite lose a feeling of breathlessness as 500 pages are squashed into three hours'.[60] Such adaptations, as the success of Jeffreys' *Hard Times* indicates, naturally had the advantage of being both cheaper and more portable than large-cast shows, like Peter Coe's 1985 *Great Expectations* at the Bristol Old Vic, which combined the casts of two repertory companies.[61] One fairly recent example is Neil Bartlett's adaptation for Aberystwyth Arts Centre in March 2007, a 'studio psychodrama' par excellence, with its use of dry ice, monochrome costumes, projections, a gauze and the hallucinatory quality of Estella's provocative dance.[62]

As will be clear from the list of features, I interpret this style of presentation as, in effect, Freudian rather than Marxist (as, in Edgar's hands, the 'world on a stage' Brechtian social picture was originally meant to be). The whole play is rather like one of a delirium sequence in a film: associative, vertiginous, a jumble of figures crowding in around the bedside, gradually pulling into focus and seeing everything clearly. And, in *Great Expectations*, there is the advantage of a particularly strong 'return of the repressed' motif in the shape of Abel Magwitch, the terrifying childhood bogeyman who returns from New South Wales as Pip's benefactor and 'second father'.

Nevertheless, there are two difficulties with this approach as an alternative to the large-cast, RSC-Dickens style. One is that, as I have been arguing, an approach based on psychological realism does not necessarily bring out the best in Dickens. In this respect it is significant that Shared Experience chose to adapt *Bleak House*, one of Dickens's later, more realist 'dark', novels, and one with few groups of purely comic characters. Dickens's other novels, while perhaps attractive because they are shorter and feature on school curricula, can raise their own problems. B.A. Young, reviewing the Royal Exchange *Great Expectations* in the *Financial Times*, argued that 'The story, shorn of its literary adornment, comes out terribly melodramatic, and is played so.'[63] If an adaptation of Dickens does not acknowledge the melodramatic framework of the stories, and yet condenses the narrative so that it is a rapid-fire series of perilous incidents, then the adaptation may end up suggesting precisely what it wishes to avoid, by condensing the story with such furious intensity that it begins to look silly. The second difficulty is that by making adaptations more austere, with small casts that have to transform themselves constantly, companies are really only returning to the 1970s Shared Experience model, but in an edited form that fits more easily into presenting-houses' schedules: less shared, less of an experience.

*   *   *   *   *

Turning points in television drama

In the second part of this chapter, I want to show how television has attempted, in different ways from theatre, to appeal to a 'notional community' through Dickens adaptations. This section aims to demonstrate, more widely, the 'structures of feeling' that have embedded themselves in Dickens on TV over the last four decades. It is harder to find a single moment in television broadcasting, or a series from the 1980s, that affected representations of Dickens in such an important way as *Nickleby* affected theatre. The change was rather more indirect, and spread into adaptations of Dickens from other sources. One very significant turning-point was the huge success of Granada's adaptation of Evelyn Waugh's *Brideshead Revisited* in 1981. Robert Hewison uses this moment as the point of departure for his argument about the rise in 'heritage' and conservation movements in the 1980s: 'The Bridesheads of England were again under threat, just as they had been in 1944 when Evelyn Waugh completed the novel.'[64] It was also a significant coup for ITV in its continuing struggle to outdo the BBC in terms of innovative programming. *Brideshead Revisited* was not only a domestic success but also projected a vision of England – nostalgic, elegiac, class-bound and in decline – that was highly saleable abroad. In 1983, British TV and film earned a surplus of £101 million from overseas sales, which was the highest figure ever recorded; by the late 1980s, the DTI reported that sales were running at ten times the level of the 1970s.[65] *Brideshead*'s timing was also fortunate in that it tied in with a number of commercially and critically successful, and Academy Award-winning, British films of the period, chief of which were Hugh Hudson's *Chariots of Fire* (1981), Richard Attenborough's *Gandhi* (1982) and David Lean's *A Passage to India* (1984). Each of these had in common with *Brideshead* a view of the British in the early twentieth century struggling with modernity, and the strains on the empire and the attitudes thereby engendered.

Another incident that could be seen as a turning point, according to John Caughie in his book on television drama, was the minor 'scandal' in 1984 when Granada produced its own Raj epic, *The Jewel in the Crown*, when all the BBC could offer as competition in the broadcast schedules was an imported mini-series, *The Thorn Birds*. Not only this, but Granada announced that it had already recouped production costs through overseas sales before transmission.[66] Caughie also alludes to the slow fading of the single play from television screens during the 1980s since it was becoming uneconomic; however, serial scheduling was still very attractive since it offered economies of scale.[67] A 1988 interview with Terrance Dicks, then script editor and later producer on BBC1 Classics, captures the way in which such successes were affecting the production of Dickens serials. As Dicks's job title suggests, up until the late 1980s, the BBC had its own in-house Classic Serials department, producing a regular stream of adaptations for broadcast at Sunday teatime. He said of the Classics strand: 'Dickens is our bread and butter and jam and that's basically what people expect.'[68] On the other hand, he acknowledged that such serials were coming into competition with another BBC production wing, the 'flagship' serial, which was placed more prominently in the evening schedules and was 'in a sense a showpiece, whereas we are, I think, much more a part of a routine programming strand'.[69] The example Dicks cites is BBC2's *Bleak House* of 1985, a co-production with the American Arts and Entertainment Network.

Since that time, the funding of BBC drama has changed considerably, in line with the Thatcherite preference for deregulation and competition over state subsidy. The 1990 Broadcasting Act required both the BBC and ITV to commission 25 per cent of its programmes from independent production companies, and the BBC in the 1990s introduced 'producer choice', where producers were required to put together production teams from any source rather than having an in-house group. Another of John Birt's initiatives was a cost-cutting exercise that aimed to reduce expenditure by £70 million within four years.[70] From that point on, all Dickens adaptations would have to start from scratch and would have to guarantee their bankability.

One element of continuity between the 1980s and the present day, however, is that Dickens is still primarily associated with the BBC, which now describes itself in press releases as 'world leaders in classic, period adaptation'.[71] Of the twelve major adaptations of Dickens on television since 1985, only 1999's *Oliver Twist*, 2000's *Nicholas Nickleby* and 2007's *The Old Curiosity Shop* have been shown on ITV. Particularly during the late 1990s, ITV would tend to schedule a Brontë or Hardy adaptation to compete with a BBC Dickens or Andrew Davies adaptation. In addition, the co-production and overseas rights deals that were considered innovative and bold in 1984 have become the norm, and 'flagship' Dickens is the only variety available. As I will show, the style, look and direction of adaptations has changed significantly under the influence of writers such as Andrew Davies: acting, casting, music, shot length, composition and notions of character have all evolved in a different direction from theatre, and from the days of three- or four-channel terrestrial television.

Bleak House (1985) and *Bleak House* (2005)

A comparison between the two 'flagship' *Bleak House* adaptations, 20 years apart, might illustrate some of these changes, as well as the continuities. To begin with, Arthur Hopcraft's adaptation of 1985 shows a clearer connection with the David Lean traditions of 'shadows, darkness and menace' than the 2005 version. Figures like Tulkinghorn and even Guppy are followed down backstreets in silhouette, and they cast long shadows on the walls.[72] Although both versions cut the action of the opening chapters into many more, short scenes lasting from a few seconds to four minutes or more, the earlier version has several long monologues that are either cut or broken up in the Andrew Davies version. Most strikingly, Harold Skimpole is allowed to speak virtually uninterrupted for over three minutes in his introductory scene.[73] In addition, much of the acting appears, in comparison with the 2005 version, 'theatrical' in its very precise diction, long pauses (noticeable in characters like the Lord Chancellor) and rolled 'r's (a particular feature of Skimpole's diction). Krook even seems to be presented in a Brechtian/*Nickleby* style, with a 'quotable' and oft-repeated, wheezing laugh.[74] It is notable that the 1985 *Bleak House* is already using tracking shots to give the impression of thoroughly exploring the grime of London, but does not use dynamic shots overall (pans, zooms, whip-pans) as much as the 2005 version. Davies's version has been described as 'edgy', and this is an interesting term in that it is frequently used to mean 'cutting edge', yet it can also mean 'on edge, unsettled'.[75]

This describes very well the shifting, glancing voyeurism of the series' direction, where we often follow groups of characters from one room or location to another, collapsing strict divisions between scenes, and appear to be tracing their movements on a hand-held camera. This technique, as Jonathan Bignell remarks, semiotically hints that the action has been captured naturally and spontaneously, as in a documentary.[76] This can be taken as an attempt to conjure the 'real' Victorian England in all its detail and with a sense of intimacy and immediacy.

The 2005 *Bleak House* also proclaims its supposed closeness to Dickens's authentic vision of London life through its half-hour, episodic form. Just as theatre has its claim to being the authentic repository of Dickensian feeling via adaptation, and the author's public readings, so the claim is often made for television that it is a medium 'naturally suited' to Dickens. One 2005 *Bleak House* review asserted that 'this glorious adaptation transforms soap opera into art', while a columnist on the BBC's website calls Dickens's serials 'very much the soap operas of their day' and Andrew Davies alludes to the similarities of the two forms, with their 'criss-crossing plots' and use of the 'cliff-hanger ending'.[77] But, as Giddings, Selby and Wensley point out, the assertion 'easily made and readily accepted' – that because Dickens published in serial form, his novels are ideal broadcasting material – 'needs serious qualification'.[78] As they go on to argue, specific textual effects, such as the avoidance of describing Mr Jaggers's appearance in *Great Expectations*, are forced into different forms by screenwriters and directors, who must offer visual referents for things only hinted at in the text.[79] Furthermore, as Caughie notes, adaptations, if they eschew the voice-over, tend to place ironic narrative comments in the mouths of characters who, if the original plot is to hold together, cannot be permitted such a detached view.[80] Structurally, too, the correspondence is far from natural: half-hour episodes, soap-style, generate many short scenes for modern television. By contrast, Dickens's novel devotes entire serial numbers to single character groups and even a single scene. In the first serial number of *Bleak House*, for instance (Chapters I–IV), we are introduced to the Jarndyce case, to Mr Tulkinghorn visiting Sir Leicester and Lady Dedlock, to Esther's new position as an honorary ward in Jarndyce, and to the Jellybys' household.[81] An entire chapter is devoted to each narrative strand. In the Andrew Davies adaptation of 2005, these events are covered in some 40 scenes, none of which is longer than 4 minutes 10 seconds and one of which, Nemo in the opium den, is only 22 seconds. Although there are, as Amy Hayward argues in her book *Consuming Pleasures*, important correspondences between Dickens's serial fiction and modern soap opera, it does not follow that retelling Dickens as soap opera is a natural, neutral or transparent process.

The 'notional communities' of television

So in what ways are 'notional communities' important to television? Compared with theatre, television viewing is almost always (with the exception of, say, a football match in a pub) a more solitary viewing experience. However, the availability of digital television and internet-based entertainment – distracting audiences from its 'flagship' dramas that it hopes will get the whole nation talking – is one of the problems that the BBC faces that was not a consideration 20 years ago. To address this, the BBC has a strong internet presence and digital-only television channels. Its programmes, from BBC1's *Watchdog* to Radio 4's *Today*, solicit audiences to 'interact' by emailing comments that are read out on air before the programme has finished, and the corporation's website encourages feedback in the form of message boards, 'Talking Points', a 'Rant-Cam' video report and emails regarding continuity errors.[82] It also attempts to create 'notional communities', as the 'world on a stage' adaptation style does. It creates narratives between adaptations and other programmes by cross-casting, occasionally against type, either established stage and screen actors or comedy and light-entertainment stars whose careers have been developed on the BBC. In doing this, it seeks to highlight what is unique about terrestrial, home-grown and publicly funded television viewing, in a manner comparable to how theatre sought to highlight what was human and communal and vibrant about itself with its 'community'-themed productions.

For examples of how terrestrial TV encourages this meta-televisual viewing, we might first consider the roles given to Keeley Hawes and Alun Armstrong. Hawes appeared in an adaptation of Wilkie Collins's *The Moonstone* in 1996, then played Lizzie Hexam in 1998's *Our Mutual Friend*, followed by Tess in ITV's *Tess of the D'Urbervilles* (1998), Cynthia in Andrew Davies's *Wives and Daughters* (1999), Kitty Butler in Andrew Davies' adaptation of *Tipping the Velvet* (2002) and Fancy Day in an adaptation of Thomas Hardy's *Under the Greenwood Tree* (2005). While her roles in *The Moonstone*, *Tess*, *Greenwood Tree* and *Our Mutual Friend* were similar (innocent local beauty in danger of being wronged), her role as Kitty in *Tipping the Velvet* seems part of the calculated shock of that series, which took the period-drama's most famous screenwriter, and the Victorian age, its favourite period, and told a story of cross-dressing, lesbianism and prostitution. Kitty seems to be the romantic lead but is characterized as knowing, then heartless and calculating after the first episode. By contrast, Armstrong's stern features keep audiences guessing, never more so than when he played the inscrutable Inspector Bucket in *Bleak House*, where the question of his level of knowledge is part of the serial's suspense. Regular viewers of Dickens adaptations will have seen him rough and imposing as Fleming in ITV's *Oliver Twist*, affable and then heartbroken as Dan Peggotty in BBC's *David Copperfield*, and possibly as the pompous magistrate Fang in Roman Polanski's film of *Oliver Twist* (2005).

Still further comparisons are invited when BBC stars from other genres infiltrate the world of the costume drama. Nicholas Lyndhurst's Uriah Heep in the 1999 *David Copperfield* seemed an attempt to play against type, with a sinister, whispered, reptilian performance rather than the comic acting for which he is famous. Paul Whitehouse's pawnbroker in the same adaptation suggested both his 'cockney thief' and 'suggestive shop assistant' characters from his contemporary sketch vehicle *The Fast Show*, while Johnny Vegas's casting as Krook in *Bleak House* could be seen as drawing parallels with his seedy character in the BBC3 sitcom *Ideal*.[83]

If we were to take these examples of cross-casting from other costume dramas beyond Dickens, then the numbers would multiply. It is a development that troubles neo-Victorian scholars concerned to engage in discussion of the particularities of the Victorian age and our fascination with it. Heilmann and Llewellyn point out, for instance, with reference to the BBC's recent adaptations of *Cranford* and *Lark Rise to Candleford*, the similarities between the themes, scheduling, presentation and casting of the two dramas, which 'almost allowed for a seamless segueing between what are really aspects of the same cultural, hegemonic and homogenous themes'.[84] Hence, it could be argued that the connections we are being invited to draw are not only between Dickens adaptations and non-dramatic or non-historical programming but between the generalized 'past-ness' of the BBC's Dickens-world, its Austen-world and its Hardy-world.

Nevertheless, such cross-programme connections, observed with a critical eye, can offer more than straightforward surprise, the satisfaction of recognition or indeed undifferentiated comfort-viewing. They can be linked to Sarah Cardwell's notion of the simultaneity, the ongoing 'nowness' of television: the stream of entertainment, mixing past and present, news, drama and advertising, never stops.[85] Moreover, Cardwell argues, television programmes often build in elements of performativity, referring to the conditions of their production by, say, cameras panning to the studio audience in live programmes, out-take shows, and 'making-of' programmes about drama and films.[86] We watch adaptations with a degree of awareness that the actors are performers, often celebrities, as well as characters; we might also be aware of adaptations commenting on or paying homage to other adaptations of the same source novel, or to other works in that genre.[87] A network of associated meanings is generated, with no watertight division – for viewers in the UK particularly – between text and context.

In noting these connections, Raymond Williams was prescient as a television critic during the 1970s. He defined his idea of televisual 'flow' thus:

> What is being offered is not, in older terms, a programme of discreet units with particular insertions, but a planned flow, in which the true series is not the published sequence of programme items but this sequence transformed by the inclusion of another kind of sequence, so that these sequences together compose the real flow, the real 'broadcasting'. Increasingly, in both commercial and public-service television, a further sequence was added: trailers of programmes to be shown at some later time on some later day.[88]

He added that programmes increasingly began with prologues that were advertisements for themselves, that they aimed to perpetuate a kind of 'brand loyalty' and that there had emerged a 'mutual transfer' between the formulas of programmes and advertisements.[89] This process has clearly gone much further since the period when Williams first noticed it; we are now living in an age of 'synergy', a cross-flow of advertising between different media 'platforms' (videogames, websites, cinemas and magazines), of which television is only one. Having said this, Williams seems to regard 'flow' as an instrument of hegemonic domination by broadcasters; perhaps, in recent years, the advent of the remote control, then multichannel television, then downloadable programme content and podcasts has made viewers more able, and likely, to be selective about their viewing, and thus to 'screen out' messages they regard as irrelevant.

So costume drama on television, particularly on the BBC, makes the offer that if the viewer invests time in the channel's output, they will be rewarded by a sense of community, of family even (the BBC is often referred to by its nickname, the Beeb, and by the older Reithian moniker 'Auntie', as well as the curious tabloid term 'Auntie Beeb'). Only the BBC can create drama of this standard, the intertextual castings and cameos argue, because only the BBC commands this kind of cultural reach and persuasive power, just as only the BBC could persuade its national news-readers to dress up and perform comedy or show tunes on *Children in Need* night every November. Of course, as with the notional community of theatre, this bond is insubstantial since it demands little from the viewer and is easily broken without consequence. The only 'settlement', to borrow a Williams keyword, that has to be reached with the BBC is our annual licence fee. The idea of a community of viewers here has much in common with the use of the word 'loyalty' in advertising, where a consumer choice is dressed up in the language of moral allegiance and sacrifice.

Making the connections

What Dickens adaptations do not themselves do, however, is attempt to create a sense of 'community' in Dickens's London itself. Marshall McLuhan famously labelled television as a cool medium in comparison with the 'hot' media of the mechanical age that, for him, had just finished. He compared television to the 1960s dance, the Twist, in that both are 'cool, chatty and improvised'.[90] Hence, television Dickens, instead of community, offers connection: an affirming knowledge of how individual lives in the city are interconnected, but a detachment of manner that can border on the voyeuristic, as when we are taken through the police station in *Our Mutual Friend*, or are positioned behind objects or windows to hear secret conversations in *Bleak House*. Facts, intelligence and people's true dispositions are 'knowable', but that knowledge is one that allows the viewer to put the pieces of the puzzle together, not to undergo a spiritual transformation. In Alan Bleasdale's *Oliver Twist*, for instance, we are often shown the meetings that have just been missed, the coincidences that did not take place and that would have placed the groups of characters on the same level of enlightenment as ourselves. Monks visits Sowerberry's funeral parlour just as Oliver runs away.[91] In this version, the story of Oliver's mother and father, and hence his half-brother Monks, is presented chronologically, so the viewer always knows everything and does not have their perspective altered by the revelation of Oliver's parentage, which occurs close to the end of the novel.

Moreover, this need to make everything explicable and known, in contemporary televisual Dickens, extends to frequently altering character histories and relationships. In *Oliver Twist*, Monks's mother (Lindsay Duncan), who is barely mentioned in the novel, becomes the wicked stepmother figure whose murderous greed both motivates her son's criminality and leaves him a pale, contorted, fragile being. The uncanny effects of thunder on him are explained by epilepsy in this version. In the BBC's 1998 *Our Mutual Friend*, Eugene Wrayburn (Paul McGann) is presented in a much more ambivalent light, where the novel arguably represents him as a cad whose near-drowning engenders his transformation into the romantic hero he had previously been posing as. Similarly, Bella Wilfer (Anna Friel) is truculent and distrustful, but far from the petulant and silly girl that Dickens described in the early chapters. Her transformation, too, in the later episodes must be seen to be only a flowering of what was already there, not a transformation into a new way of relating to the world. Perhaps this is a result of the pressure on time in 1990s Dickens adaptations, which usually run to only 3 or 4 episodes, far fewer than, say, the 11 episodes of the BBC's 1981 *Great Expectations*, a format which would allow much more time for character development instead of the characters operating at a similar pitch throughout.

Star performances in Dickens adaptations

As well as rationalizing behaviour and signposting motivation, television Dickens also seems to encourage a peculiar style of acting from a select group that is somewhat at odds with the naturalism of the rest of the cast. As television's status as a 'cool' medium would suggest, high emotion presented in a manner that may be effective on the stage will seem silly, overblown or camp on the small screen. As a consequence, actors in Dickens adaptations produce toned-down performances full of twitches and tics. Examples include Robert Lindsay's Fagin and Marc Warren's Monks in the 1999 *Oliver Twist*, David Morrissey as Bradley Headstone and David Schofield as Gaffer Hexam in *Our Mutual Friend*, and Trevor Eve as Murdstone and Nicholas Lyndhurst as Uriah Heep in *David Copperfield*. Their common features correspond to Colin Counsell's reading of Lee Strasberg's Method and its effect on American screen acting, where the inability to communicate is read as 'psychological "intensity" '.[92] As with American method performances, these actors deliver lines full of pauses, breaks and mutterings (Lindsay, Morrissey, Warren), smile at inappropriate moments (Lyndhurst, Eve, Lindsay) and adopt 'personae of impenetrable passivity' using silences, stillness and blank expressions (Schofield, Eve, Lyndhurst, Morrissey).[93]

One explanation for the recurrence of this style is that, tending to be limited to actors who are already well known, it is one way of turning in a recognizable 'star' performance for the benefit of the international market, since the method style is perceived as a marker of quality and actorly commitment in Hollywood films. Another explanation is the notion that Dickens's characters must have interior lives, childhoods and psychological traumas that explain their eccentric or sinister behaviour. John Gardiner cites the enthusiasm for applying Freudian analysis to Dickens's characters as one reason for the resurgence in the author's popularity since the 1940s.[94] The Bleasdale *Oliver Twist* could certainly be read as Freudian: a castrating mother, Elizabeth Leeford, encourages her son to kill his father; as a result of her behaviour, the son is unable to even mount a female horse. Sent to kill Oliver's mother Agnes, he tells her as he holds her down: 'I can't. It isn't in me... there's no point in biting my hand. I like it.'[95]

There are some things that television can do that theatre plainly cannot: zoom, pan and cutaway, study small items in detail, pick up an actor's whisper or a twitch. There are obviously medium-specific reasons for Dickens being adapted differently across the two forms. Nevertheless, if two 'structures of feeling' can be identified in this section, it is the contrast between one set of aesthetic and representative choices, felt to be 'natural' for television, and one set felt to be equally 'natural' for theatre. As I have shown, these choices did not appear spontaneously or develop without thought: they were tied to economic and political objectives both from within, and brought to bear on, the two art forms. Even when these economic and political contexts changed, the styles of adaptation retained their mark, so that they became a structure of feeling, a groove that somehow feels 'right'. And it is a structure of feeling of a period of television and theatre history, of the 1970s, 80s and 90s, rather than a structure of feeling belonging to Dickens's own period.

* * * * *

'Self-Help' and 'Hard Times' revisited

What, then, can explain the continuing popularity of Dickens on stage and on television? As was suggested earlier, the two rival structures of feeling for thinking about Britain in the 1980s both related to the Victorian past in different, and somewhat self-contradictory, ways. The 'Hard Times' view of Britain looked back with horror at the injustices of Victorian times, a view typically expressed by Neil Kinnock, then shadow education secretary, when he said: 'Victorian Britain was a place where a few got rich and most got hell. The "Victorian Values" that ruled were cruelty, misery, drudgery, squalor and ignorance.'[96] On the other hand, the 'Hard Times' view stressed certain continuities between the nineteenth and twentieth centuries in terms of the workers' struggle for rights, representation and a welfare state. Raymond Williams expresses this sense when discussing a 1968 adaptation of Elizabeth Gaskell's *North and South*: 'It is as if some part of the BBC, some part of England, turns with particular readiness to the years before 1900: with nostalgia, of course, as we shall see in *The Forsyte Saga*; but also with interest, with a connection to that history of the industrial revolution, the class war, the struggle for democracy, which is so clearly unfinished but which can be looked at, carefully and seriously, if there is a bonnet or two about.'[97]

Both 'Self-Help' and 'Hard Times' have left their mark on British society, and on the way Dickens, and the Victorians more generally, are adapted; this is why I have termed them 'structures of feeling', for they are the ghosts in the machine, the habitual way that stories are presented, whether their source is acknowledged or not. The 'Hard Times' view is evoked especially in large-cast, world-on-a-stage Victorian drama where the audience is encouraged to witness oppression, and join emotional forces with the cast in order to challenge it. The after-effects of the Thatcherite, 'Self-Help' view can be felt in the way that adaptation is now treated as a commodity, theatrical adaptations of Victorian novels being expected to 'tell the story' without taking too many liberties, to keep costs low and be amenable to touring, and to fit educational remits in order to secure funding.[98] Meanwhile, television drama, following the 'Self-Help' outlook, is now produced and marketed as a worldwide brand and signifier of Britishness and 'quality', its costumes and locations expensively recreated in the Dickensian equivalent of the Raj epics of the early 1980s. All this is far removed from the much more modestly budgeted, mostly studio-bound, slow-burning adaptations on offer during the BBC's own 'Hard Times' of the 1970s and 1980s.

Dickens and nostalgia

There may be something else, however, peculiar to Dickens, that keeps him as the focus for so many contradictory feelings about the Victorians. As Chapter 1 argued, the set pieces in Lionel Bart's *Oliver!* suggest that a nostalgia for the idea of a Victorian 'community' has existed since at least the 1960s; perhaps this longing has become more acute since the election of three Labour governments in 1997, 2001 and 2005, when the language of 'community' developed a free-associative usage, yet was unaccompanied by any structural change to make such notional communities a reality. Then again, perhaps, Williams's idea of a 'knowable community' within the industrialized city has always itself been a myth, rather like the concept of a bucolic golden age that Williams traces ever further back in time at the beginning of *The Country and the City*.[99]

And yet if we look at the final scene of Edgar's *Nicholas Nickleby*, we notice there has been a change from Dickens's novel, as Nicholas leaves the party to rescue another Dotheboys Hall boy who is sitting in the snow – a change that functions, Edgar has commented, as 'a reminder that for every Smike you save there are thousands out there, in the cold'.[100] Edgar writes that he was dissatisfied with the novel's ending, and wanted to suggest that mere decency alone could not change the world.[101] In making this change, Edgar argues that he has constructed 'a play of which Dickens himself was the subject-matter', and this is certainly the exception in the adaptation process, where endings are usually reproduced as in the novel, often word-for-word. The usual ending for a Dickens novel is one in which family members are reunited, some misunderstanding or question of identity having been resolved, whether this is the happy adoption of Oliver Twist by Mr Brownlow, or the more bittersweet reunion of the Nickleby family (with Smike and Ralph dead), or Joe Gargery and Pip in *Great Expectations*, or Esther and Lady Dedlock in *Bleak House*. As Ronald R. Thomas has argued, 'almost every Victorian novel has at its heart some crime that must be uncovered, some false identity that must be unmasked, some secret that must be revealed, or some clandestine plot that must be exposed', meaning that detection was a consistent trope, and that *Bleak House* has been claimed by some as the first detective novel in a period when the legal construction of 'identity' was coming to replace the notion of 'character', a natural inheritance of class.[102]

Family versus community

In the light of these reflections on identity, detection and connection, I propose a hypothesis: what if, rather than simply a fantasy of community life, what we find in Dickens is a fantasy of a clear and stable identity? As Chapter 6 of this study explains in detail, identities linked to region, class and occupation (and arguably gender) have been placed under increasing strain over the last 30 years. At the same time, the white-Caucasian sector of British society has become increasingly secular. Although a friendly, close-knit neighbourhood might provide a social structure and sense of identity while one is alive, it cannot guarantee to do so after death, where a plaque on a park bench, theatre seat or church pew are often the only ways of commemorating a person's involvement in a community. Family, however – passing on identity through blood – seems to displace this fear of a disintegrating self; and so perhaps when we praise the idea of 'community' we, like Dickens, actually mean finding a place where we belong by finding our 'true' family. As Maryanne C. Ward has shown, many of Dickens's main characters retreat into what she calls 'enclaves' at the end of their stories, so that they may live happily without society being threatened.[103] Yet such enclaves contradict the spirit of the novels, since they cut the characters off from 'the society which needs its good people so desperately'.[104] Hence, in *Bleak House*, with Esther's move to Yorkshire and marriage to Alan Woodcourt, 'The conclusion destroys the community which had Esther as its center'.[105] As in real life, family and community do not go hand in hand, but compete with each other as primary definers of identity. With the increasingly popular hobby of genealogy, again investigated further in Chapter 6, people aim to get in touch with their 'roots' and (re)construct family and community origins, but the ultimate aim is to find evidence of individual blood-relative ancestors, in order to, in Paul Basu's words, 'relocate the self in time and space' – a point that is supported by a barrage of evidence from Basu's online correspondents.[106]

The lost child and belonging

Perhaps this explains why *Oliver Twist* is easily the most popular of Dickens's novels for adaptation. Since the more adult 1999 Alan Bleasdale adaptation for ITV, there has been the Roman Polanski film (2005), a BBC adaptation, screened in December 2007 on consecutive nights in the style of 2005's *Bleak House*, and the intertextual event that has been the television talent show *I'd Do Anything* (2008), where young women compete for the chance to play Nancy (and boys compete to be one of the Olivers) for a Cameron Mackintosh revival of Lionel Bart's musical *Oliver!*.

As Samuel observes, *Oliver Twist* reproduces the evangelical theme of the little boy lost, and it does so, in these adaptations, for a secular age in which the real fantasy is of a reunited family, and of a narrative that will explain and fix identity, guarantee a secure domesticity, and put paid to the dangers of the community (which, in *Oliver Twist*, is constantly interpenetrated by thieves, kidnappers and would-be murderers, even in the isolation of the countryside).[107] It can also be considered as a manifestation of anecdotalism, as discussed in the introduction: Oliver's exceptional story, full of coincidence, is given exemplary significance,

implying that no one will be truly lost (we do not follow the workhouse children who do not find kindly relatives).[108]

Viewed from the point of view of the ending, then, Dickens's stories provide a sketch of just enough of a 'community' to make coincidence less extraordinary and to provide the connections to enable the lost child to be returned to the domestic world, where he 'belongs' – a far more Thatcherite, 'Self-Help' solution than the 'Hard Times' belief in society's ability to redeem the waif. In this sense, then, Edgar's adaptation of *Nickleby* has become the stylistic rule, but the conceptual exception in reaching out of the narrative to argue with Dickens's domestic idyll.

Perhaps, finally, what we find so satisfying about the Dickensian ending is that its security offers a future, not just in terms of descendants, but a national, historical future that we know took place, and that links us to the present day in only four or five generations. With the fear of Cold War nuclear annihilation giving way, at about the same time as the disintegration of the Soviet bloc, to contemporary fears of environmental catastrophe, the nineteenth century (in its bourgeois manifestation) seems an age of optimism and progress, because we are outside the age, filtering it through fiction, recreating it with detailed costumes and sets, and then labelling the happy result 'Victorians'.

4
Staging Life Stories

Ann Heilmann and Mark Llewellyn's recent book *Neo-Victorianism* uses the Christopher Nolan film *The Prestige* (based on the novel by Christopher Priest) to superb effect in the chapter 'Doing It with Mirrors', discussing it alongside Neil Burger's *The Illusionist* and a clutch of neo-Victorian novels.[1] Their use of the three-part trick, highlighted in the film, as a framework for a neo-Victorian return is one to which I am indebted in this chapter. However, as the process I will be describing takes place in a theatre, the connection with Victorian stage magic becomes less of a striking metaphor in the present study and more a way of attempting to account for the uncanny audience experience of stage impersonation. Where Heilmann and Llewellyn's neo-Victorian novelists depart from stage magic by allowing the reader 'insight into how the illusion is produced', the biodrama genre that I will be discussing is already in many ways an anti-illusionist style of modern theatre, with stripped-down staging, direct address to the audience and occasionally the actor stepping out of role.[2] Nevertheless, biodrama's convention of making the dead speak to a modern audience offers a 'double vision' where the interaction between actor and role becomes an important part of apprehending and historicizing the performance event.[3]

The Prestige is a 2006 neo-Victorian film set in 1890s London and, briefly, Colorado. Two stage magicians, Angier and Borden, are engaged in a bitter competition to perform the most sensational magic trick in front of an audience. In particular, they try to outperform each other with variations on an illusion called 'The Transported Man', where the magician leaves the stage and then reappears somewhere else in the theatre. Borden, we discover at the end of the film, had achieved this feat because he is an identical twin, and he and his brother had carefully arranged their lives and appearances in order to make themselves appear to be one person. Angier, in attempting to replicate the trick, had enlisted the help of Nikola Tesla, the 'father of electricity', who had built him a machine that duplicates matter. Thus, every night he performed the trick, a new double was created and then killed off after the show.

I want to use the idea of a 'Transported Man' stage illusion in this chapter in order to discuss the popularity of Victorian biographical dramas during the 1980s, and especially the popularity of monodramas and two-handers. *The Prestige* is a useful starting point because, first, it is an example of a drama set in Victorian times that, like many of the plays under discussion here, uses the key discourse of emergence in order to facilitate the diegesis (see the Introduction). As Nigel Morris has argued, *The Prestige* is set around the time of the birth of two technologies that help to define modernity: electricity and the film's own medium, cinema.[4] The audience for *The Prestige* is invited to take a view of modernity that corresponds with that of either the fascinated girl or the boy who knows that a bird has been killed in order to create the illusion.[5] Electricity and the cinema have enabled illusion to become more 'real' than reality, the film can be read as arguing, and there is always a price that must be paid (the crushed bird, the replicated Angier, or Borden's wife, who commits suicide, unaware that her husband is a twin).[6]

Secondly, the film's theme of doubling is a useful one with which to think about the performative practice of biodrama. This chapter will argue that, as in the 'Transported Man' trick, whenever an audience watches a biodrama performance, it sees not only an evocation of the original but also a double, a *Doppelgänger*, the presence of which is usually only made manifest at the final curtain, when the actor returns for a curtain call, having 'killed' their original. So, no matter how impressive a biodrama performance, there will always be at least two sets of performative signals being created or reproduced: those of the Victorian being impersonated, and those of the present-day performance. It is these traces of performance conditions and attitudes to the Victorians during the 1980s that I wish to bring to the fore in this chapter. The argument draws on some ideas proposed by Nick Ridout in his book *Stage Fright, Animals, and Other Theatrical Problems*. I intend to use his analysis of the final, liminal moments of performance, the curtain call, where the 'residue of the role' still clings to the actor, in order to analyse the paradoxes of representation.[7] Furthermore, as Ridout argues, the audience's applause comes 'just as the division of labour appears at its most intense', since the economic foundations of the theatre – with the actor as worker – are made manifest at this point.[8] It is the connection between the representation of a stage or literary legend, supposedly a transcendent talent, and the real economic and cultural conditions of 1980s British theatre that I wish to explore further in what follows.

I want to begin with a definition of the term 'biodrama' as I am using it here, and then to consider some important antecedents to the biographical monodramas of the 1980s. Building on the previous chapter's exploration of the change in the focus of representations of the Victorians during Margaret Thatcher's time as prime minister, I will go on to argue that biodrama in general was a response to the apprehension of 'Hard Times' by theatre-makers, allowing new plays to be produced that had name recognition but could be made on a limited budget. However, biodrama also, along with the growth in adaptations in this period, was reflective of a crisis of confidence within the theatre industry under new economic conditions, and of the growing expectation that theatre measure its success through its performance in commercial markets. In going on to investigate the circumstances surrounding the success of the monodrama *Kipling* in 1984, I will consider the influence of such contexts as the growing prominence of the individual actor and the one-person show (Simon Callow, Ian McKellen), and the Falklands Conflict of two years earlier, which allowed Mrs Thatcher to add a neo-imperial dimension to her praise of Victorian values.

The second part of this chapter investigates the popularity of Marie Lloyd as a subject for biodrama, and places this within the context of a nostalgia for working-class life and popular culture that, as Chapter 1 explains, had been evident since the 1960s; it also examines the Marie Lloyd-revival phenomenon as a continuation of left-wing social-realist practices in theatre-making during the 1970s. Placing both Kipling and Lloyd in the tradition of Victorian biodrama that stretches to the present day, I argue, using Ridout's book, that one of the peculiarities of biodrama is that the impersonation both shields and draws attention to the impersonator. The chapter also argues that the genre has a particular attraction to figures whose lifespan included the late Victorian period as well as the Great War, the better to chart (in a similar way to the 1970s television serials discussed earlier) the emergence of modernity, to 'tell the story' of the twentieth century. The biodrama, in this analysis, functions as a 'body of evidence' that, by analogy with the body in the detective story genre, provides clues through its writings, performances and death towards an explanatory narrative of how we arrived at modernity. Finally, the chapter attempts to explain the relative contemporary scarcity of Victorian stage biodrama by considering the elements of the genre that are reproduced in television dramatized biography and 'heritage performance' or 'live interpretation' at museums, galleries and sites of historical interest. In the latter case, I argue, the theatrical 'doubling' that sends out such mixed messages in Victorian biodrama is, in many ways, still present.

The rise of biodrama

Plays using the biographical details of a historical (or mythological) individual's life are, of course, as old as drama itself. However, this section will attempt to trace the development of the self-narrated, pseudo-autobiographical, small-cast play, which I have termed in this chapter 'biodrama'. During the 1980s there were plenty of plays that dramatized an episode from the life of an eminent Victorian. Often these were what might be classified as 'epiphany' plays: the historical figure is shown undergoing a life-changing experience, often actions for which the audience know the character subsequently became famous. Examples of these include David Pownall's *Livingstone and Sechele* (discussed in Chapter 2), Frank McGuiness's 1988 play about Marx and Engels, *Mary and Lizzie*, and Nigel Williams' play about Cecil Sharp, *Country Dancing*. However, in using the term 'biodrama', I refer specifically to a type of play that aims to tell the life story of a historical individual from birth (or early youth) to death, supposedly narrated by that individual, and featuring him or her stepping into role as protagonist as well as narrator. Such biodramas are often one- or two-person shows, weaving together documentary evidence from letters and other writings with direct audience address and, usually, a self-conscious theatricality. Between the years 1976 and 1979, there were seven plays produced in London that were, in some sense, biographical portraits of Victorians.[9] Among these are *Tribute to a Lady*, a celebration of Lilian Baylis at the Old Vic (her career begins just at the end of the Victorian age), and *Fearless Frank*, a musical about Oscar Wilde's friend Frank Harris. Between 1986 and 1989, however, there were 23 biodramas reviewed in national and metropolitan newspapers.[10] These included one- or two-person shows about figures such as Mary Seacole, Lewis Carroll, Queen Victoria, Dr James Barry, the painter Simeon Solomon, Ellen Terry and Fanny Kemble.[11]

What were the reasons for the popularity of this theatrical form, and what were its antecedents? As mentioned in Chapter 1, the 1968 Theatres Act had removed the Lord Chamberlain's powers to refuse a play a licence because its representation of a historical figure was not sufficiently serious; nevertheless, as we have seen, the Victorian plays that followed in the wake of the act tended to be pieces with large casts, and to take a kaleidoscopic or dreamlike approach to history, as in *Early*

Morning or 'H'. Nevertheless, during the 1970s, at least two plays pointed towards the 1980s biodrama form: John Bowen's *Florence Nightingale*, which was performed at the Marlowe Theatre, Canterbury, in 1975, and David Horlock's Lewis Carroll biodrama, *Crocodiles in Cream*, at the Mermaid Theatre, London, in 1976. Bowen's play is significant in that it treats theatrical biography as a problematic genre: the play is presented as the dress rehearsal of a group of actors who are putting on a devised work called *Florence Nightingale: An Exploration*, but each has reservations about their character and brings in their own research on Nightingale, which contradicts the impression that the director wishes to make, conveying the impression of what might have happened had a Joint Stock or RSC *Nicholas Nickleby* rehearsal gone horribly wrong. Horlock's biodrama, meanwhile, is an example of a play that uses original letters and documents to tell a life story yet is ambiguous in tone, exploring Carroll's predilection for prepubescent girls and the effect that this had on the families with which he formed friendships. At one point, he reads out a letter to Mrs Aubrey-Moore, asking if her daughters are 'kissable', and then Horlock juxtaposes this question with Humpty Dumpty's assertion in *Alice in Wonderland* that 'When I use a word, it means precisely what I choose it to mean.'

Other representations of the Victorians in the late 1970s and early 1980s may well have been an influence on the development of this biodrama style. Bernard Pomerance's *The Elephant Man* was a huge international success, premiering at the Hampstead Theatre and later running in the West End and on Broadway. Pomerance tells Joseph Merrick's life story using a series of short scenes, frequently where two characters are pushing for opposite outcomes, to which Robin Davis's *Up in the Gallery*, where the caller and Marie Lloyd narrate Marie's life from different perspectives, certainly seems to owe a debt (as does Stewart Parker's *Heavenly Bodies*, with its sparring between Dion Boucicault, who is the play's protagonist, and the Irish clown Johnny Patterson). *Nicholas Nickleby*'s technique, borrowed from theatre company Shared Experience, of having the characters 'step out from themselves and narrate their own feelings about themselves or other people', furnished the biodrama genre with a means of covering a great deal of biographical material with a very small cast.[12]

Funding and theatre's crisis of confidence

Looking back on the 1980s theatre climate from the 1990s, both David Edgar and Roland Rees seem certain of the negative effect that the withdrawal of local authority and Arts Council funding had on theatre repertoires, and this suggests a set of reasons for the popularity of biodrama with theatre producers. Edgar claims that 'by the end of the 1980s it was hard to tell rep programmes apart. There was, for a kick-off, a nationwide epidemic of adaptations', while 'the late 1980s saw a precipitate decline in the amount of new work presented'.[13] Rees notes the tendency of theatre in the period to become more inward-looking, while in interviews with Rees, playwrights Nigel Gearing and Bernard Pomerance speak of theatre concentrating on a smaller number of specific skills and becoming more self-referential.[14] Edgar quotes Anthony Minghella's complaint that studio theatre spaces have encouraged the writing of 'mumble plays'.[15] All of these descriptors apply to biodrama to some extent. Many biodramas, such as Richard Osborne's *Our Ellen* (Battersea Arts Centre, 1989) and Christopher Godwin's *The Guv'nor* (Young Vic Studio, 1990), about Ellen Terry and Sir Henry Irving, respectively, are designed for studio spaces and require the singing and/or acting skills of only one performer – an actor playing a Victorian actor. Such plays, while qualifying as 'new work', might be seen as less of a risk for the theatre than a play with a contemporary setting. Certainly Melvyn Morrow's *A Song to Sing, O!* (Savoy, 1981) – a one-person show about the Savoy Operas' George Grossmith – and the four plays featuring Marie Lloyd produced or revived in this period (*Marie, Our Marie, Up in the Gallery* and *A Star is Torn*) contain a large proportion of musical material already familiar to the public.

The self-referentiality of theatre at the time might be interpreted as a crisis of confidence, as expectations of state subsidies at 1970s levels gave way to the requirement for theatre to justify its place in the market. One way in which theatre responded was with celebration or gala evenings in which a strand of theatrical history could be followed and enjoyed, and money raised for the relevant theatre or organization in the process. *The Undisputed Monarch of the English Stage*, 'A Recital in Praise of David Garrick' (Old Vic, 1979), was performed to highlight the theatre's historical connections with the actor, and *A Song to Sing, O!* is linked in Antony Thorncroft's review in the *Financial Times* with the Savoy's 'Save D'Oyly Carte' campaign.[16] Another way of theatre justifying its existence was through education. By 1990 the Theatre Museum, then based at Covent Garden, was hosting biodrama performances itself, such as Andrew Powrie's *Vivien* (the life of Vivien Leigh), and John Swift and Peter Gee's *Brel*.[17]

The funding pressures, Edgar, Rees and many of those they have consulted agree, also made theatres, and actors, think much more in terms of marketing. Edgar, in particular, sees Thatcherite market values as an ingenious way of restricting radicalism in art by making it behave like any other consumer product: 'Under the discipline of the market-place, the producers of art would be forced to provide what its consumers wanted, which was that which would be least likely to disrupt and disturb.'[18] In *The Heritage Industry*, Robert Hewison argues that the Arts Council was biased much more towards the preservation of traditional art forms than the evolution of new ones, since it had so many long-term clients that most of its fund was already committed at the beginning of each year.[19] Furthermore, in response to the Thatcherite 'Self-Help' argument that corporate sponsorship should be found to fill the funding gap, Hewison asserts that 'The arts which do attract sponsorship are those which are the most prestigious, the most conventional and the most secure: the heritage arts.'[20] Despite biodrama's promise as a mode that can encourage the audience to reflect on the past in a new way, biodrama is itself caught in the nexus of heritage culture, trading on name-recognition and generic expectations long before opening night.

Biodrama and identity politics

Another trend influencing biodrama was the developing concern with the politics of identity in the 1980s. In terms of the writing and selection of material, Edgar notes that 'in the early 1980s the ground shifted once more, as women, black and gay playwrights confronted the question of difference and identity which emerged in the 1960s and 1970s'.[21] Chapter 2 has already considered the growing prominence of black and Asian playwrights, companies and venues, and it could also be argued that Mrs Thatcher's preference for 'Victorian values' implicitly favoured a view of the British as white, male (Thatcher does not appear to have praised any Victorian women's achievements) and heterosexual. The changing times, Edgar asserts, had an influence on how companies worked: the coalition of theatre interests in the 1970s had begun to dissolve by the 1980s, as companies became more specialized in their concerns and techniques.[22] The individual biodrama might be seen as the opposite of the devising, collective aesthetic of the 1970s: the ultimate celebration of the individual, the subjective view, the celebrity who did it their way.

Alec McCowen as Kipling

I have chosen to begin with Brain Clark's *Kipling – East and West*, starring Alec McCowen, which premiered at the Mermaid Theatre, London, in May 1984, and was eventually filmed for Channel 4 television in December of that year. I chose the play because, first, it serves as an example of the one-person biodrama, with no foil, chorus or antagonist to provide context or contestation for the subject's views. Secondly, it is an example of the literary biodrama, the lineage of which can be traced back at least as far as *Crocodiles in Cream*, in which an author relates their life story and performs extracts from their work; usually, the life and work become entangled in interesting ways. Such author plays had continued to be popular in the 1980s, with Clark's play being preceded on British stages that year by *My Dearest Kate*, a one-woman show based on the letters of Dickens's wife, a one-man version of *Heart of Darkness* and a life of Gerard Manley Hopkins.[23] My third reason for choosing *Kipling* is as a demonstration of how biodrama's ambiguity – its determination to tell truths by creating an impossible situation – can have unexpected consequences, giving insight into what the Victorians and their empire-building attitudes meant to audiences in the 1980s.

The first thing to note is that, with the author-biodrama being by this point such a well-established genre, the Kipling presented to us in Clark's piece seems to be wary of the biodrama format. He has been expecting us – 'it had to happen, I suppose', he remarks to the audience – but he does not want to give anything away in telling his life story: 'you won't get anything out of me'.[24] Throughout the play, rather than showing a dreamy lack of awareness that he is being watched (as, judging from the scripts, Carroll had in *Crocodiles*, and as the poet had in *Hopkins!*), Kipling is on edge, defensive, suspicious of the audience's motives and confrontational. He 'stares' and 'looks balefully' at the audience, as if daring them to snigger or smirk as the Union Jack is projected during a recital from *Stalky and Co*.[25] He claims to hate biography, referring to it as 'the Higher Cannibalism', and even advises the audience not to come back after the interval.[26] However, Kipling's superficial refusal to play up and play the game of the biodrama genre does not actually affect the structure of the piece. We expect the subject of a biodrama, if he appears initially in control, or angry, to reveal the reasons for that authoritarian behaviour or anger, to strip themselves bare; and, as there is no foil in solo biodrama, the change has to come from within, from the act of telling the life story itself. Kipling is no exception to this requirement. He 'struggles to control himself' at the memory of his favourite child, Josephine, and becomes 'totally enervated' as he reads the First World War poem 'The Children'.[27] This is despite his insistence that we find out no more than what was in his books, and his praise of the corporal punishment at school which gave him the 'Anglo Saxon discipline' to maintain the empire.[28]

Speaking from beyond the grave

Yet there is still something odder than usual about this act of biographical ventriloquism, where the public figure who hated public speaking is made to defend himself by performing a patchwork of his poetry and prose to generations yet unborn. The play also resurrects Kipling with the political outlook – we might say, borrowing the term in its restricted sense, used in the previous chapter, the structure of feeling – of someone who died in 1936. He seems to know, in factual terms, of the major events in British political history in the 48 years since his death, but has no feeling for what it means to live in a Britain, a world, that is post-Holocaust, post-Atlee, post-Suez, post-decolonization.[29] Partly this is a practical consideration on the part of the playwright: Clark had information available to him on Kipling's response to the Great War, but would have had to invent his feelings about its sequel. Nevertheless, in presenting these preoccupations to an audience in 1984, it seems likely that the effect would be one of emotional distancing, rather than the closeness – the humanist connection to another person despite the distance of years – that biodrama usually strives for.

Kipling seems to speak to us from beyond the grave, addressing us directly to warn and admonish us ('If your fathers and grandfathers had listened to me ...').[30] His strangeness is further magnified by his inability to understand why, after imperialism and Nazism, his audience might be so suspicious of militarism. Furthermore, Kipling is unable to abide by his own rules (he insists on a self-governing, emotion-suppressing discipline and yet cannot so discipline himself). Nor is it necessarily the case that his poems mean to a modern audience what he thinks they do.

For instance, Kipling chooses to end on 'The Children's Song' from *Puck of Pook's Hill*. Its pledge of allegiance and rhymed association between 'place' and 'race', and its wish for an 'undefiled heritage', are very hard to accept for generations who are aware of the Nazis' eugenics experiments and used to multiculturalism. Its lines about controlling ourselves to avoid any 'maimed or worthless sacrifice', loving 'all men 'neath the sun' and never using strength 'By deed or thought, to hurt the weak' are values that are more likely, in contemporary Europe at least, to be associated with democracy and national self-determination rather than imperial ideals.[31] It is precisely these delusions of empire, the notion that Britain was intervening in world affairs selflessly to protect the underdog, that became the subject of mockery, at least in left-wing circles, after the First World War. In this sense, as in our attitudes to universal health care and the welfare state generally, the ground has shifted decisively to the left since Kipling's day. Hence, although to him these values represent an unchanging bedrock, to an audience that came to adulthood after 1945 they can sound quite alien.

We are effectively presented with a choice between the lost empire that Kipling decries and the alternatives that he suggests. Some in the audience may indeed have mourned the loss of the British Empire, and argued that it led to some good – stability, modernization – in some parts of the world. But Clark's Kipling asks us to subscribe, in addition, to the scrapping of old-age pensions and representative democracy, the continuing British occupation of South Africa, and militarization on a scale greater than in the build-up to the First World War.[32] Again, it is hard for a modern audience member to hear this prescription and not wonder if, had Britain followed Kipling's path, the nation would have been able to put less distance between its own expansionist activities and atrocities, and those of Nazism during the mid-twentieth century.

Critical responses to *Kipling*

In performance, these discrepancies in the script might be harder to spot. Nevertheless, the critical reception of the piece is notable for its widely divergent readings, suggesting considerable confusion over Clark and McCowen's intentions. So, for Christopher Hudson in the *Evening Standard*, McCowen's triumph as Kipling is to 'resolve these contradictions by portraying a man who was always true to himself and what he saw'; furthermore, he opines, 'About India, about the Empire, about the 1914–18 War, he rarely struck a false note.'[33] Similarly, Colin Shearman in *Time Out* sees Clark's script as 'strangely persuasive' and the play as a 'much-needed re-evaluation' of Kipling.[34] By contrast, Martin Hoyle in the *Financial Times* thought that much of the Kipling philosophy displayed here 'leaves one deeply uneasy', and Giles Cardon in *The Spectator* called McCowen 'the Enoch Powell of contemporary actors, dry, taut, mannered, calculating', and found his performance 'scary and jingoistic'.[35] In the most considered review, David Trotter in the *TLS* compares this Kipling to 'a cheery old bigot' in the Alf Garnett vein.[36] Michael Billington insists that 'what McCowen brings out, above all, is Kipling's anger', while Ian Stewart in *Country Life* states that, on the contrary, 'When Alec McCowen first emerges, we are at once alerted to the clownish, button-holing vein that runs through his performance. Direct address is taken to the point of urgent appeals to imaginary children in the audience...'.[37] Both David Trotter and John Peter, in *The Sunday Times*, note the irony of Kipling saying in the play (with reference to the cliché 'East is East, and West is West'), 'Don't you half-quote *me* to reinforce your prejudices!' when the passages of Kipling that McCowen recites are often misleadingly edited to present a less troublingly racist image – 'an identikit Kipling', as Trotter has it.[38] In terms of audience response, the *Evening Standard* reported a standing ovation on the opening night, while Rosemary Say in the *Sunday Telegraph* noted that McCowen 'has the audience cheering to the high rafters of the Mermaid Theatre. Once again this genial actor has achieved a feat of memory and expertise.'[39]

The solo show and the actor as personality

It seems that much of the reason for the success of this equivocal portrait of Kipling is down to McCowen's performance. In the late 1970s, he had toured his one-man show, in which he recited the whole of St Mark's gospel, across Britain and America, where it achieved immense success. Although not a Christian himself, the recital seems to have proved popular with Christian groups, and his close personal identification with the show led to the publication of a book on its creation and reception, *Personal Mark*, to complement his earlier memoir, *Young Gemini*. Hence, McCowen was very much part of the modern movement towards considering the actor as independent creative spirit, the main feature of the night out rather than simply the servant of director or text. He spoke of his inspiration for the gospel recital as having come from comedians like Sid Field, Max Miller and Jack Benny, 'entertainers turning an auditorium into a living room of friends', as he put it.[40] For the Kipling play, Brian Clark was very much the journeyman who had been given the task of editing Kipling's work into something that McCowen could perform as a follow-up solo show, as interviews with both men confirm.[41] Hence McCowen's presence at the Mermaid Theatre carried a good deal of theatrical baggage that implied the actor's personal investment in Kipling, and his sincerity in presenting the writer's views and work. Precisely what it was that 'ha[d] the audience cheering to the high rafters' we can never properly know, but it seems more likely to have been at least as much an appreciation of McCowen's performance as an appreciation of Kipling the man.

To understand this phenomenon better, it is necessary to take a wider view of the one-man show and its relationship with biodrama. McCowen's success and renown for one-man shows had at least two important precursors. Emlyn Williams achieved enormous success over 28 years with his solo readings from Dickens, in the style and costume of the author. One of the plays following on from this success was *Emlyn Williams as Saki*, which ran at the Apollo Theatre in 1977. Despite the fact that there was an age gap of around 30 years between Williams at the time and Saki when he was killed in the First World War, Williams again went for impersonation rather than simply readings of Saki's work. Michael MacLiammóir also achieved great success with his Wilde solo show, *The Importance of Being Oscar*.[42]

In the 1980s, however, many other actors – including those who had trained and worked in the radical theatre of the 1970s – were taking the opportunities that the one-person show offered to develop their relationship with audiences, to show off their range and technical virtuosity, and to celebrate the actor as exceptional individual rather than company member. McCowen was an early innovator and beneficiary of this trend, though he was not of the post-1968 generation, having had a classical acting career stretching back to the 1940s. A younger actor like Ian McKellen, though, is an example of someone having taken the actor-as-personality tendency to new levels. His solo show *Acting Shakespeare* toured on and off for nine years during the 1980s. After 'coming out' as gay in 1988, and being awarded a knighthood in 1993, his follow-up (which toured from 1994 to 1997) was self-consciously titled *A Knight Out*. McKellen described the format as 'candid reminiscence of my parallel lives as an actor and a gay man, illustrated with the words of poets, novelists and playwrights'.[43] Similarly, the degree of self-revelation offered by actors to their public in print seems to have increased considerably in the 1980s. Simon Callow's 1984 autobiography *Being an Actor* is notable not only for the author's 'outing' of himself (Callow has since claimed to have been 'the first actor to come out as gay' in writing the book) but also for the polemic of its final chapter, 'Manifesto', where he argues that 'the important thing is to restore the writer – whether dead or alive – and the actor to each other' without the colonizing intervention of the director.[44] Callow, too, foregrounds his artistic relationship with Shakespeare, and gave his own one-man performances of the sonnets, as well as a solo show on Juvenal.[45] Antony Sher's book *The Year of the King*, a diary of the actor's preparation and performance of the role of Richard III, was published the following year, and it popularized the genre of the rehearsal journal.[46] All three actors could be said to be using an autobiographical format to make revelations about their homosexuality, strategically 'outing' themselves to the general public at a particular point in their careers. McCowen 'outed' himself in 1989 in an edition of the television programme *This Is Your Life*.[47]

McCowen's personal attachment to the Kipling project was treated sympathetically by the press. The *Evening Standard* reported uncritically his view that Kipling's 'great love for ordinary people' would be a 'revelation' to theatre audiences, and was pleased that the try-outs of the play in Chichester were so well received: 'people have become so used to satire and sending [patriotism] up it seems to come almost as a relief to find anyone expressing these views'.[48] Elsewhere, McCowen talks of the accusations of imperialism against Kipling being 'almost a reason for giving Kipling this recital – to set the record straight'.[49] It is interesting to note that an unavoidable fact – Kipling's belief in the moral and military necessity of a British Empire – is here diminished to a petulant-sounding 'accusation', and that he described the play not as a work of fiction but almost as a pure show-business tribute, 'giving [him] this recital'.

The reception of the play could also have been influenced by a particularly fertile period for publications on Kipling, with Angus Wilson's *The Strange Ride of Rudyard Kipling*, published in 1977, being considered a landmark biography. This was followed by a revised edition of Robert Carrington's authorized biography, *Rudyard Kipling: His Life and Work*, and Lord Birkenhead's *Rudyard Kipling*, both published in 1978. In 1983, *Kipling: Interviews and Recollections* was issued by Macmillan in two volumes, collecting further autobiographical insights from this very private man. The interest in Kipling may also, of course, have been a symptom of the taste for pre-war nostalgia noted in Chapter 3. Brian Clark has acknowledged that the Kipling play was part of a wave of nostalgia for the British Raj,[50] and indeed 1984 was the year of the mini-series *The Jewel in the Crown* and David Lean's film of *A Passage to India*.

Thatcher, Kipling and the new patriotism

More important than this broader context, however, is Kipling's status as Britain's imperial poet, author of 'If...', at a time in British history when the Conservative Party had just been returned to government after the successful recapture of the Falkland Islands. None of the publicity surrounding *Kipling* makes explicit reference to the Falklands War, but McCowen's comments above about this play allowing the people of Chichester to express patriotism without embarrassment, and his observation that 'There's a change of mood now' that has allowed Kipling to be reconsidered, imply that a post-imperial liberal consensus had, for some decades, made sniggering at patriotism acceptable, and that just recently someone or something had put the pride back into being British. Clark, too, sounds almost Thatcherite when he asserts that Kipling 'deserves due credit for the fact that the empire was run on a sense of values, and wasn't just a squalid story of economic exploitation'.[51] Leaving aside the point that many would argue, as Orwell did, that empires were and are precisely about economic exploitation, this quotation is interesting for its implication that Kipling was somehow responsible for the empire, and a creator rather than a reflector of its values.[52] We might note, also, the Thatcheresque use of 'values' as an all-purpose term of approbation, as if there were only one proper set (presumably the 'timeless' Victorian ones), and as if a 'sense' of them would suffice to make palatable the effects of globalized capitalism.[53]

All this would be circumstantial conjecture were it not for the fact that recapturing a sense of Victorian imperial greatness (rhetorically, at least) was very much on the Conservative agenda under Thatcherism. Mrs Thatcher was fond of quoting Kipling in speeches, so much so that by 1987 it had become a cliché; she stated at the Conservative Party conference: 'Mr President, you may perhaps have heard that I'm a faithful student of Rudyard Kipling. Occasionally, I've even been known to quote him. So it won't come as a complete surprise if I refer to his poem "Recessional"...'.[54] As we have seen in the previous chapter, Thatcher regarded her self-selected group of Victorian values as the ones in operation 'when our country became great'. In 1983, with the general election approaching, Thatcher made a direct link between the Falklands victory and the British Empire when she summarized the war's lessons as follows:

> When we started out there were the waverers and the faint-hearts, the people who thought we could no longer do the great things we once did, those who believed our decline was irreversible, that we could never again be what we were, that Britain was no longer the nation that had built an empire and ruled a quarter of the globe. Well they were wrong.[55]

It is interesting that here Thatcher is expressing the sense of national decline discussed in Chapter 2 as a hallmark of the late 1960s and 1970s, and presenting military expeditions like the Falklands (including its highly controversial attack on the Argentine battleship the *General Belgrano*) as the way to turn this decline around. Interesting, too, is that Clark's Kipling uses the same phrase, 'faint-hearts', to describe those who wanted the British to withdraw from South Africa.[56] Of course, Thatcher's rhetoric, like Kipling's verse, does not stand up to scrutiny, especially removed from the euphoric heat of the moment: she cannot, surely, be suggesting that Britain return to ruling a quarter of the globe, or that recapturing the Falklands is comparable to Britain's vast territorial acquisitions up to the nineteenth century. Her intention seems rather to have been to give a sense of this former imperial glory without the necessity of further unilateral military action.

Clark and McCowen's *Kipling* exposed a fault-line, certainly among British theatre critics, and quite possibly among its audience too – a fault-line that might bear traces of the difference Hall noted between the cosmopolitan elite and the resentful lower-middle class (see Chapter 2). Despite, or perhaps because of, the supposed revival of the 'special relationship' between Britain and the US under Ronald Reagan, there had been no post-Falklands revival of Britain's superpower status, no lasting boost to British self-esteem. To those on the left, the war must, by the time of *Kipling* in 1984, have seemed to have been cynically exploited by an unpopular prime minister in order to ensure re-election (Neil Kinnock's outspoken summary of this view being one of the most memorable).[57] Those who felt that way could hardly have left the Mermaid Theatre without feeling uneasy. Just as Kipling's inability to feel anything after 1936 makes his seem a distant, archaic voice even as he stands embodied before us, so the shadow of the Falklands Conflict illustrates how distant that world of massive global influence really is from present-day realities: we can indeed 'never again be what we were'. Hence, despite McCowen and Clark's intentions for the piece, and their belief that it remodels Kipling as a man with something to say to our times, its effect could be quite the opposite – unless, like many seem to have done, one has fallen under the spell of McCowen's personality. While the show's popularity, its press coverage, the other Raj epics of the same year (see Chapter 3) and Thatcher's pronouncements indicate how profoundly the sense of lost empire resonates in the British psyche, the idea of resurrecting the empire on the back of the Falklands victory was Mrs Thatcher's own piece of anecdotalism (see the Introduction), suggesting a global application for a partial view of a single campaign.

*   *   *   *   *

Commemorating music hall

As Andrew Rutherford pointed out in his select Kipling bibliography of 1987, which accompanied the reissue of several Kipling works in the Oxford World's Classic range, reassessment of Kipling had begun shortly after his death, with influential essays being written by W.H. Auden, George Orwell, C.S. Lewis and Edmund Wilson during the 1940s.[58] By contrast, interest in Marie Lloyd seems to have waxed and waned during the middle years of the century. Although the first full biography of Lloyd appears to have been broadcast on BBC television in February 1953 (starring Pat Kirkwood), *The Guardian* reported in 1961 that an auction of the contents of the Manchester Hippodrome failed to fetch large sums, with what was rumoured to be Marie Lloyd's dressing table included in a job lot for £7 10*s*.[59] Nevertheless, if there had been a period of 'little sentiment' for turn-of-the-century music hall (as the article stated), this had begun to turn around by the late 1960s, the very point, as Chapter 1 argues, when the clearance of Victorian 'slum' neighbourhoods and the rise to cultural prominence of pop music were consigning the geographical and cultural place of music hall to history. Daniel Farson and Joan Littlewood's *The Marie Lloyd Story*, starring Avis Bunnage in the title role and telling the story in a series of music-hall-style back-stage vignettes, opened at the Theatre Royal, Stratford East, in 1967. However, it was prevented from transferring to the West End by a rival production, Ned Sherrin's Marie Lloyd musical, *Sing a Rude Song*, starring Barbara Windsor.[60] Also in the mid-1960s, Charles Lewson performed a long-running 'music hall pot-pourri', including the songs of Dan Leno, George Robey and Marie Lloyd.[61]

After a revival of Farson's Marie Lloyd play in 1969, 1972 (the fiftieth anniversary of Lloyd's death) brought the publication of his biography of Lloyd, another revival of his play and the unveiling of a memorial plaque on the site of the old Tivoli Theatre in the Strand.[62] In 1970 a plaque was unveiled in memory of Lloyd at St Paul's Church, Covent Garden, and in 1977 Hackney Council placed a plaque, later taken over by English Heritage, at her house at 55 Graham Road. Also in the 1970s, the National Museum of Music Hall opened in part of the Empire Theatre at Sunderland, with money from the local corporation as well as the English Tourist Board,[63] and articles in the *Guardian* marking the seventieth anniversary of Dan Leno's death, and on the lost connections between pantomime and music hall, indicate that the form was acquiring more of a historical-critical appreciation.[64] There is also a record of a Marie Lloyd biodrama, *Our Marie*, devised by and starring Margaret Dent, at the Traverse, Edinburgh, in 1975.[65]

By the end of the 1970s, then, the decade that Robert Hewison sees as crucial in establishing the current British mood of heritage and nostalgia, Lloyd was being proudly commemorated as part of London history. Robyn Archer's 1981 revue *A Star is Torn*, which ran from 1981 to 1982 at the Theatre Royal, Stratford East, and at the Wyndhams Theatre, also featured a Marie Lloyd segment. There, she was presented as the first in a twentieth-century line of strong female performers – among them Judy Garland, Bessie Smith and Janis Joplin – who suffered in a patriarchal world. As the notes on the manuscript assert, 'Two of the [eleven] women under discussion tonight never married two of them were raped and [crossed out] 2 of them were raised in brothels. + Between them these eleven women had 31 husbands.'[66] From the early 1980s to the early 1990s, the interest in Marie Lloyd as a music hall star and the fashion for biodrama were to intersect on several occasions. Daniel Farson's *Marie* was revived again in 1985, Steve Trafford mounted and toured his Marie Lloyd biodrama in 1987 and 1988, Robin Davis's *Up in the Gallery* toured in 1989, and then Trafford's play was revived in 1991, 1995 and 2000 (and several subsequent times since). Marie Lloyd also features prominently in a 1993 Vesta Tilley biodrama called *Bertie*, where she is one of a troupe of theatrical ghosts haunting a music hall.[67] There was also a 2007 BBC4 biodrama, *Miss Marie Lloyd: Queen of the Music Hall*, starring Jessie Wallace. What is remarkable about the film is how similar it is to the theatrical versions of twenty years earlier, in the incidents it chooses to dramatize, the songs it uses, and the framing devices.[68]

This chapter uses as its main example Steve Trafford's play, the most successful of these Marie Lloyd biodramas, which has been variously titled *Marie*, *Marie: The Story of Marie Lloyd*, *Marie: The Marie Lloyd Story* and *Marie Lloyd: Queen of the Halls*, as it has evolved from its 1987 Edinburgh production through a series of revivals. References are to the manuscript deposited in the British Library, dated July 1987. Trafford's play also stands out because in many ways it is the most stripped down and stark: it is just the actress playing Marie (Elizabeth Mansfield) and a pianist. It begins with Marie singing her most well-known songs ('A Bit of a Ruin', 'When I Take My Morning Promenade' and 'Don't Dilly Dally'), but it soon becomes clear that exhaustion is taking over, and she is telling us the story of her life while on the point of death.[69]

Marie Lloyd may have been an attractive subject for biodrama for several reasons. First, she lived a genuinely dramatic life, married three times, was generous, gregarious, a supporter of the unions and the artistes' strike, and a fixture in newspapers and public gossip. This in turn provides a *tour de force* opportunity for an actress seeking to make her name and demonstrate an ability to cavort, to sing and to age convincingly. Reviving Marie Lloyd can also be seen as a 1980s feminist statement: with her clashes with the censors, and her overt sexuality, she comes across at times in these plays as a prototype for Mae West, or even Madonna, who of course rose to global stardom in that decade. Lloyd could also be seen as emblematic of the transition from a Victorian notion of being famous to a modern one, a claim further examined in the section on theories of emergence. However, what I want to argue at this point is that Marie Lloyd in the 1980s represented an attempt to re-contextualize music hall as the gritty product of the Victorian streets, stripped of the cosy trappings of the long-running television music hall recreation, *The Good Old Days*, to reposition the comedy within the frame of social documentary with which fringe theatre in the 1970s had become comfortable.

Documentary theatre and music hall

Documentary theatre, as a way of representing the experience and concerns of a particular group or region (a notional community), has a history stretching back at least as far as the mid-1960s, with Peter Cheeseman's work at the Victoria Theatre, Stoke on Trent. In 1964, the theatre company produced a documentary on industrial unrest in the 1840s called *The Jolly Potters*, and this was followed in 1966 by *The Knotty* (subsequently revived in 1967 and 1969), a history of the North Staffordshire Railway from 1845 to 1923, and built from documentary materials such as tape-recorded oral testimony and newspaper reports.[70] Other documentary dramas that followed in Cheeseman's wake included Alan Plater's *Close the Coalhouse Door* in Newcastle (and subsequently at the Fortune Theatre, London) in 1968, and Alan Cullen's *The Stirrings in Sheffield on a Saturday Night*, a documentary drama about industrial unrest in the 1860s, at the Sheffield Playhouse in 1966 (revived at the Sheffield Crucible in 1992).[71] Interestingly, Cheeseman asks if the documentary drama style can be seen as 'part of our response to the evasion and humbug of Victorian social morality, one of our answers to our grandfathers who draped piano legs for decency's sake'.[72] In 1970, Peter Terson, resident dramatist at

Stoke-on-Trent, went on to write *The 1862 Whitby Lifeboat Disaster*, a play with a documentary slant that uncovered layers of 'evasion and hypocrisy' about a Victorian legend in Edwardian Whitby.[73]

The use of music was also important to the documentary theatre style from the outset. Cheeseman writes of the difficulty of finding 'talented and inventive variety artists' to match those in Joan Littlewood's *Oh What a Lovely War!*, another important and influential piece of documentary drama.[74] Cheeseman used Jeff Parton, a local folk singer and instrumentalist, for *The Knotty*, and Plater's *Close the Coalhouse Door* was built around the songs of Sid Chaplin. One of the most influential documentary-dramas of the 1970s was John McGrath's *The Cheviot, the Stag and the Black, Black Oil*, a history of the Scottish Highlands from the time of the Clearances to the 1970s, produced for the Scottish wing of 7:84 Theatre Company (and broadcast on BBC1 in June 1974). As Catherine Itzin records, the play was structurally based on the Scottish *ceilidh*, a form dating from the nineteenth century – a means of 'reinforcing the Gaelic culture and of a political getting together'.[75] The form allowed for songs and sketches, as with the appearance of Queen Victoria in drag singing, 'These are our mountains/And this is our glen', and the two English aristocrats claiming to be, as the song title has it, 'More Scottish than the Scotch', who then turn their guns on the audience and warn, 'But although we think you're quaint,/Don't forget to pay your rent . . . You had better learn your place,/You're a low and servile race'.[76] This style of presentation was called in one newspaper interview with McGrath 'Marxist music hall'.[77]

In fact, despite documentary-drama's preference for 'just the facts', it seems to have been enthusiastic about imitating Victorian music hall to communicate its view of political realities. Perhaps this was because music hall was considered a demotic, 'unofficial' form of entertainment and thus allied with the working class; or perhaps it was because Victorian entertainment styles provided a stock of instantly recognizable stereotypes to enable a point to be made with maximum impact. Itzin reports on the Agit Prop Street Players (the forerunner of Red Ladder Theatre Company), which had a play called *Rose-Tinted Spectacles*, a tenants' play 'written in a music hall style' in the late 1960s, where 'There were two stock characters. Joe and Lil, the archetypal tenants who appeared in all the plays.'[78] This seems to belong to the former category suggested above; Itzin quotes company member Kathleen McCreery recalling 'They laughed partly because the whole thing was so gross and far-fetched and silly, partly because the form of music-hall and drag was part of the tenants' cultural heritage'.[79] A few years later, one of David

Edgar's plays for the General Will Theatre Company was *Rent, or Caught in the Act* (1972), a show devised for tenants' groups which explained the various repercussions of the Housing Finance Act. As Itzin describes it, 'They felt that this was impossible to do naturalistically, so they decided on the form of Victorian melodrama, with music hall acts', a decision of which Edgar remarks, 'Not because it was a popular cultural form, but because it was funny, and because it was a very good odyssey form'.[80] *Rent* would seem to belong, therefore, to the latter category, using music hall to communicate a point more clearly. In fact, it could be argued that *Rent* and *Rose-Tinted Spectacles* are more agit-prop than docu-drama, since they took a contemporary situation and agitated the audience to resist official explanations (of the Housing Acts) and know their rights.

Red Ladder also devised and performed *Taking Our Time*, which lies somewhere between the docu-drama and agit-prop formats, since it deals with the 'plug-plot' industrial action by the weavers in the 1840s, and features a clown (who acts as an induction figure, commenting on the action) and songs sung directly to the audience. However, it also ends with a challenge to the audience: 'Will you wake and take this world and turn it upside down/Twentieth-century dreamer? . . . take your time and live before you die/Wake up from the dream'.[81] As mentioned in Chapter 1, *Mary Ann: An Elegy* is also an example of a play based on real events that seeks to bring home its points about the legal system and the press through the use of melodrama and music hall. Both *Mary Ann: An Elegy* and *Taking Our Time* (and, indeed, the earlier Red Ladder play *A Woman's Work*, set in the present day) also addressed the influence of patriarchy and sexism on society, with one of the main characters in *Taking Our Time* being John and Mary Greenwood's rebellious daughter Sarah, who objects to being treated as the servant of the family.[82]

In this context, the choice of music hall star Marie Lloyd as a subject for biodrama is not a neutral one, but can be seen as bearing traces of the docu-drama and agit-prop styles of the previous decade. This seems especially likely when it is realized that Steve Trafford, the writer, and Elizabeth Mansfield, the star, were both members of Red Ladder in the 1970s.

Marie as documentary drama

How, then, might the traces of the concerns of agit-prop and docu-drama be present in Trafford's play? First, it emphasizes Lloyd's place in the class system of Victorian England; her ordinariness is made a virtue (Figure 1). This is captured in Trafford's *Marie* by her opening

Figure 1   Elizabeth Mansfield in *Marie* at York Theatre Royal (photo by Nao Nagai)

song 'My Old Man', with its tale of moving house under cover of night because the family could not pay the rent, and by her reflections on her childhood with an alcoholic father, where she would sing to him in an attempt to coax him home from the pub.[83] Perhaps most importantly, the ordinariness of Marie is underlined by the biodrama's performance of her song 'Up in the Gallery'. The song's lyrics point out 'the boy I love' who is 'up in the gallery', where the performer herself is both holding the stage and yet ordinary enough to be in love with a member of the audience: worldly yet innocent, special yet, at heart, ordinary.

Secondly, Lloyd's life is shown to be a mirror of her times; for instance, her involvement in the union activities of her second husband, Alec

Hurley, and the first artistes' strike, is given due attention.[84] She is also shown to have battled with the patriarchal assumptions and censorious-ness of the late nineteenth and early twentieth centuries; in addition to her battle with Mrs Ormiston Chant's Purity Party over her supposedly lewd lyrics, the Crown refused to grant Hurley and Lloyd a divorce and, on their visit to America, Lloyd and her paramour Ben Dillon were held on Ellis Island under the Immorality Act for not being married, and when released had to keep a 'respectable' distance from each other.[85] We are shown her anomalous position as a self-made, wealthy woman who suffered at the hands of a violent, abusive man, Ben Dillon. By the end of Trafford's drama when, having told us of her rise and fall, she sings again her final signature song, 'It's a Bit of A Ruin That Cromwell Knocked About A Bit', the audience is now aware of the socio-political factors that have brought her to this pass.

Dying on stage and 'the prestige' of resurrection

The song is indeed a startling one, in which Lloyd takes on the public perception of her as an alcohol-raddled, ageing woman, fond of public scenes and involved with a violent man, and uses it to transform her-self into a piece of history, an Ozymandias-like pile of stones indicating vaulting ambition and folly:

> I'm one of the ruins that Cromwell knock'd about a bit,
> One that Oliver Cromwell knock'd about a bit.
> In the gay old days there used to be some doings,
> No wonder that the poor old Abbey went to ruins.
> Those who've studied hist'ry sing and shout of it,
> And you can bet your life there isn't a doubt of it.
> Outside the Oliver Cromwell last Saturday night,
> I was one of the ruins that Cromwell knock'd about a bit.

After one such performance at Edmonton in 1922, Marie Lloyd collapsed and died, and Trafford's play shows us this happening onstage. So the most extraordinary thing about Marie, in the biodrama, is the manner of her disappearance: she transforms herself into a ruin, announces herself as such, and then disappears, drops dead.

This is the end of Marie Lloyd's life, though not the end of the perfor-mance, since after the curtain comes down, the actress playing Marie, Elizabeth Mansfield, takes her bow and curtain call.[86] Returning to the film reference that opened this chapter, I want to compare this dramatic disappearance and reappearance of 'the one and only Marie' with the three stages of the illusion in *The Prestige*, as outlined by Borden's *ingenieur*, Cutter (played in the film by Michael Caine):

> The first part is called the pledge. The magician shows you something ordinary. A deck of cards, a bird, or a man. The second act is called the turn. The magician takes the ordinary something and makes it do something extraordinary. But you wouldn't clap yet, because making something disappear isn't enough. You have to bring it back. That's why every magic trick has a third act. The hardest part. The part we call the prestige.[87]

In the first stage, the pledge, we are shown proofs of Marie's ordinariness: her poverty, her family background, her love for a boy in the gallery. In the second stage, the turn, we are shown the ordinary girl, then woman, doing extraordinary things: breaking social and theatrical conventions, living her life in public, performing in a state of near-collapse, finally dying. In the prestige, she returns to the stage, unhurt, for the final, liminal moments of performance, where what Nick Ridout calls the 'residue of the role' still clings to the actor, most obviously in that she is still in costume.[88] The Marie we saw die is visibly revealed to have been an illusion (a fact of which the audience, of course, was already pleasurably aware), and Marie, like Angier or Borden, is revealed (if the performance is fine enough) to have had a 'double', the same but different.

Trafford's play is actually the most subtle in this respect, and other biodramas are much more celebratory in their moment of 'the prestige'. In the recent BBC4 film, Marie reappears in her most glamorous costume, looks out at the television audience and repeats her catchphrase: 'Is everybody happy?' In Robin Davis's play, as in Dan Farson's a few years earlier, the curtain rises to reveal 'the MARIE we all wish to remember. Beaming, full of fun', who gets the audience to join in with a final rendition of 'My Old Man'.[89] Dead but full of life, these encore moments, these prestiges, create a transitional zone between the Victorian setting and the street outside, allowing us to join in the valedictory singalong with the express permission of – almost as a way of showing appreciation for – the actress, detached from the role.

However, as noted earlier, Ridout points out the fallacy of the notion that at this point we are meeting face to face with the actor and 'all the pretending has come to an end'; in fact, the 'gift' of the audience's applause comes 'just as the division of labour appears at its most intense'.[90] The actor is revealed to be a worker, theatrical entertainment an economic transaction. The appearance of Marie Lloyd transcending death is actually revealed to be the actress transcending her role and visibly inhabiting something else, her job. This is a strangely contradictory moment. On one level, the socioeconomic traces that Trafford's script has been so careful to weave into the Lloyd life story have now been shadowed by the socioeconomic traces of this particular performance in 1987, say, or 1991. The role of a beleaguered middle-aged music hall performer in the 1920s is being claimed, in exchange for audience acclaim, by a younger actress in a West End theatre in the 1980s or 1990s. On another level, the point at which the Marie character is bereft of life is the point at which the actress inhabiting her role probably reveals the most signs of her live physicality – breathlessness, sweating, physical work done for a paying audience – and acknowledges the audience's real physical presence as a theatre audience, rather than an imagined music hall audience from a century ago.

Furthermore, as Ridout argues, there is 'always something in the way, always something left over from the representation'.[91] The actress Elizabeth Mansfield is not simply 'being herself' onstage, any more than Alec McCowen is 'being himself' after a performance as Kipling; rather, they are performing a version of themselves who has just finished playing the role of a Victorian celebrity. The curtain call cannot escape representation, even when it 'gestures beyond the machinery of representation'.[92] What this means for biodrama is that part of the pleasure will always be in the material itself; as audience member, you would surely have to have no interest in poetry or popular music to not be at least diverted by Kipling's poetry or Lloyd's songs. Nevertheless, the actor who steps into this role onstage becomes caught in the representative nexus of the theatre industry of their own time as much as in the 1890s or 1920s, something that the historicizing interpretations in this chapter have attempted to demonstrate.

The two levels of representation create a further problem within the economies of prestige for solo biodrama, since to give a bravura performance of Marie Lloyd or Kipling would presumably be intended as a tribute to some aspect of their achievement, yet to do so involves receiving rapturous applause, 'cheering to the high rafters', which is received by the actor, and taken as an approval of their virtuosity. So is such a performance original interpretation, or perhaps mere imitation, which carries less prestigious connotations of 'celebrity impressionists'? Can the theatrical biodrama, which seems to offer a platform for the eminent Victorian, ever really escape the suspicion of a sleight-of-hand trick where it is actually the actor who receives the platform, who emerges with the prestige? After all, there is no way in the theatre of communicating applause for the Victorian individual when they and the actor are physically the same person.

Staging the mystery of modernity

As mentioned earlier, there seems a particular bias in Victorian biodrama towards the stories of individuals whose life-spans encompass both the nineteenth and twentieth centuries. The Kipling play does this, as do all the Marie Lloyd biodramas except Farson's, and the Sherrin/Brahms musical; as does the ensemble biodrama *Mrs Pat* (York Theatre Royal, 2006), on the life of *fin-de-siècle* actress Mrs Patrick Campbell, by Pam Gems. In particular, there is a tendency to pick individuals whose stories might somehow encapsulate a sense of the ending of the 'long nineteenth century', through them meeting their end at some time between 1914 and 1918. Richard Osborne's *Our Ellen*, a life of Ellen Terry, has her dying in 1917 (although there is little narrative of consequence in the play after Victoria's Diamond Jubilee); Christopher Godwin's *The Guv'nor* recalls the life of Sir Henry Irving through the eyes of his dresser, Walter Collinson, who is in his attic toasting Irving on the anniversary of his death in 1914, as a sergeant drilling soldiers is heard from the barracks outside.[93] *The Original Chinese Conjuror* (Almeida Theatre, 2006), a musical life of the faux-Chinese stage magician Chung Ling Soo, actually has him die as the result of a botched 'bullet-catch trick' in 1918 (the marksman is a fully dressed First World War officer).[94]

Certainly, in the case of Marie Lloyd, there is an argument for saying that the play traces the development of our modern conception of fame. From being a local star who would play several halls in one night, Lloyd becomes, in the twentieth century, a propaganda tool for the Great War (she is shown singing send-off songs like 'I Do Like Yer Cocky Now You've Got Your Khaki On' in Trafford's play), and an international star whose every misjudged public manoeuvre is reported by the newspapers.[95] The plays are perhaps looking back to a period when songs such as 'My Old Man' reflected the pathos and humour of genuine working-class situations, or when songs like 'Burlington Bertie' or 'Pop Goes the Weasel' contained local jokes and references for a particular 'knowable community'. Indeed, both Farson's *'Marie': The Story of Marie Lloyd* and Sherrin and Brahms's *Sing A Rude Song*, although rival large-cast productions in 1969, are similar in choosing to begin the action in 1909 and 1907, respectively, well into Lloyd's period of excessive spending, national touring and international fame, so that she, too, can look back on her simple roots with a degree of nostalgia.[96]

A further, more general suggestion is that, to return to the idea of the detective story in the previous chapter, and the idea of retelling the story of the century discussed in Chapter 1, the physical body of the character in Victorian one-person biodrama (while inevitably producing its *Doppelgänger*, the actor playing the character) is treated as 'evidence'. That is, its life, writings, performances and the manner of its death supply clues as to how the audience arrived at modernity, why such a time as the Victorian age, with such people in it, is dead and gone. In Peter Brooks's *Reading for the Plot*, he gives an account of Tzvetan Todorov's theory that the condition of the classic detective story is to go over, repeat, the ground covered by his predecessor, the criminal; that the work of detection exists to reveal, to realize, the story of the crime, the important narrative that bears meaning.[97] What is important about this, Brooks argues, using a Sherlock Holmes mystery as an example, is 'the constructive, semiotic role of repetition: the function of plot as the active repetition and reworking of story in and by discourse'.[98] In other words, we are told a story once and it appears inconsequential or nonsensical; once we are retold it with all the pieces in place and the right emphases as the result of detective work, the story acquires new meaning. So it may be that the need to tell and retell the transition from Victorian to modern times is an expression of British culture's sense of dislocation in modernity, and its need to explain where and what Britain is now by appealing to the evidence of those who have 'passed over' from one century to another.

Biodrama on television and in the heritage industry

What, then, has become of Victorian biodrama since the 1980s? One argument is that television has taken over the genre, not in the grand style of *Disraeli* and *Lillie* in the 1970s (see Chapter 2) but in a more intimate, low-budget, confessional style that reflects elements of the 1980s solo biodrama aesthetic. This type of television film is now especially prominent on the BBC's arts and minority interest channel, BBC4, which in recent years has screened *Miss Marie Lloyd: Queen of the Music Hall* (as mentioned earlier), *The Secret Life of Mrs Beeton* (Jon Jones, 2006) and *Florence Nightingale* (Norman Stone, 2008), the first two featuring direct address-to-camera, the third featuring a commentary on the action from a music hall troupe. Beyond the Victorian period, BBC4 has also screened a series of biodramas about mid-twentieth-century comedians, such as *Kenneth Williams: Fantabulosa* (Andy de Emmony, 2006), *The Curse of Steptoe* (Michael Samuels, 2008) and *Frankie Howerd: Rather You Than Me* (John Alexander, 2008). It is significant that again, in these revisionist biodramas, the BBC is invoking the familiar figures of its own 'golden age' (see Chapter 3), and examining their private lives, as it has been consistently doing with the Victorians since the 1970s.

Another explanation for the disappearance of theatrical Victorian biodrama is that it is found in different theatrical venues. Performances of, and in the style of, Charles Dickens are still popular; for instance, Simon Callow in *The Mystery of Charles Dickens* (Albery Theatre, 2002) or Patrick Stewart reading *A Christmas Carol* (Old Vic, 1993) – but note that the actor in each case is now sufficiently well known for there to be little suspicion of using the writer's life as a 'platform', as discussed earlier. At the other end of the scale, one-person biographical plays are still very popular on the Edinburgh Fringe, where a cast of one makes a more financially viable production, and where the close proximity of theatre and stand-up comedy might make 'impersonation', as distinct from actorly 'interpretation', less generically problematic.

A more compelling reason than these two, however, is that Victorian monodrama has now been absorbed into the heritage and education industries, rebranded as 'live interpretation'. There was already something of an educational stake in biodrama, as explained earlier with reference to Theatre Museum performances. As Raphael Samuel argues in *Theatres of Memory*, the idea of 'living history' has much in common with the progressive movement in education of the 1960s, with its emphasis on empathy for a historical character's experience, a practice that, as he says, has become enshrined in school curricula as primary schools' 'Victorian Days', where the children and teachers dress as Victorians and attempt to replicate Victorian educational practice and social mores.[99]

Clearly, for every museum, gallery, stately home or site of historical interest, there will be a slightly different variety of 'live interpretation' (the favoured term within the heritage industry for actors in period costume who play a historical figure and relate information about themselves or the venue in role). Nevertheless, there are a number of ways in which live interpretation adjusts the relationship between actor and audience, and its representative quality (as discussed by Ridout) in a way that may be more satisfying for certain audiences.[100] First, where biodrama by its very nature focuses on the exceptional individual, live interpretation can use historical figures but also composite characters meant to represent the everyday experience of the poor or undistinguished. There is consequently perhaps less of an illusionism about live interpretation, since speech and some information, even if an actor is playing Charles I, for instance, will not be based on documentary evidence but invented on the spot to enhance the impression of verisimilitude. This relative lack of illusionism is furthered by the non-theatrical space of performance in live interpretation; rather than a theatre stage representing some other place – a music hall, say, or Queen Victoria's study – live interpretation often takes place in the actual historical settings mentioned in the performance, or else in significant spaces, such as a museum, where the relationship between the performance and the surrounding artefacts is suggested but there is no attempt to block out the twenty-first century. Live interpretation seems usually to include a pre-rehearsed element, and to that extent it is similar to the conditions of biodrama in that the prepared part of the performance will have an end, where audiences/visitors often applaud. However, there are usually opportunities to question the character, and sometimes the questions and the prepared segments merge, so that the effect is far removed from the solo biodrama's final curtain, followed by the moment of revelation when the actor stands before us, theatrically representing themselves.

As the museum theatre practitioner and scholar Catherine Hughes has pointed out, because of the tension between distance and contact in live interpretation, the relationship between actor and audience should ideally be one of informed consent; spectators cannot be controlled and will produce meetings that are utterly individual (probably to a greater extent than the differences of opinion over *Kipling*, for instance). Nevertheless, Hughes also talks of the hope that the spectators' experience will be one of 'seeing double', of seeing the character in their world while at the same time being aware of the actor playing a role in the present day.[101] This 'double vision' is what this chapter has attempted to delineate in placing *Kipling* and *Marie* in their political and economic contexts, but it is one that, as Ridout claims, is an effect produced in the theatre by the rituals of performance and applause.[102] The 'double vision' that Hughes refers to seems to be a more implicit perception, since the live interpretation actor is expected, for the sake of professionalism, to mask their own personality during and after the performance, rather than placing it at the centre of the one-person show, as Ian McKellen has done, or returning for recognition as 'themselves' at the end.

The development of live interpretation into a contemporary form of biodrama does mean, however, that future attempts to historicize biographical performance will not have had the same starting point as this chapter, which has asked why, of all the biographical choices available, did McCowen choose Kipling at that time, why did Trafford and Davis and Farson and Dent choose Lloyd? In live interpretation, by contrast, the choice of subject tends to be dictated by the period and relevance of the venue. Still, it is hoped that this section has highlighted the similarities between the two forms, and that the chapter in general has demonstrated that Ellie O'Keeffe's demystification of live interpretation practice also holds true for biodrama. O'Keeffe, who represents Past Pleasures, the company that supplies live interpretation for the Royal Palaces, insists that there are limits to what the practice can do. As with biodrama, live interpretation cannot 'communicate the idea of 'maybe', or produce evidence there and then for its claims; it is a mode of creating, rather than 'being' in any authentic sense; it is not biography; and it is a 'vehicle' with which a performer can travel the world, and see the reactions of audiences in different cultures.[103] To this, I would add that solo biodrama is not only a 'star vehicle'[104] but a vehicle that, while it apparently 'imports' a Victorian to perform for a present-day audience, is also importing present-day sensibilities into a Victorian context.

5
Staging the Brontës

In March 2011, it was announced by Arts Council England that Shared Experience theatre company would not be included in its new national portfolio, and would therefore have its Arts Council funding cut completely from 2012 to 2015.[1] The company was in the midst of staging *Brontë*, a revival of its 2005 show by Polly Teale. The adaptation of *Jane Eyre* and its two related plays, *After Mrs Rochester* and *Brontë*, helped to underwrite a decade of successful touring, but, as this chapter will demonstrate, the plays have also absorbed and reflected some of the confusions and contradictions in British cultural attitudes towards the Brontë sisters, and towards their best-known works, particularly *Jane Eyre*. Here I will argue that the move from *Jane Eyre* to *After Mrs Rochester* and thence to *Brontë* is representative of a set of post-1960s cultural imperatives that have swelled audiences for theatre dealing with the Brontës' work, while limiting the terms of engagement with it. In seeking to maintain the Arts Council's funding for its 'highly physical interpretations of classic novels', Shared Experience has had to negotiate these limitations. It would not be uncharacteristic of Arts Council policy history if the theatre company was, cruelly, now being punished for it.[2]

This chapter, then, seeks to show the effect that applications of feminist and, to a lesser extent, postcolonial theory have had on representations of Charlotte Brontë. It traces the development of the Brontë biodrama since the 1970s. In the light of this, it argues that Polly Teale's *Jane Eyre* was overdetermined by these cultural attitudes and anxieties – particularly those associated with gender and colonialism – regarding Charlotte Brontë's novel. I use Erin O'Connor's idea of 'Victorientalism' and combine it with my own notion of 'anecdotalism' to explain why Jane Eyre (and by extension Charlotte Brontë) is now considered a suspect presence in her own novel. I will argue that the success of *Jane Eyre*, *After Mrs Rochester* and *Brontë* reflects our cultural tendencies to champion (and to redefine) the underdog, to read the Victorians through Freud and consequently to interpret *Jane Eyre* as the outpourings of Charlotte Brontë's unconscious.

Why Charlotte Brontë?

This chapter is also presented as an extension of the concerns of both the chapter on biodrama (Chapter 4) and the chapter on Dickens adaptation (Chapter 3). It builds on the tensions I explored in the biodrama chapter with reference to Marie Lloyd and Rudyard Kipling, where a play ushers us into the presence of a long-dead Victorian, creating a doubling effect where Charlotte and Jane are presented as corresponding figures, one 'real' within the stage world and one 'fictional'. The chapter also affords us an important glimpse of an alternative (perhaps the main alternative) to the Dickensian notion of the Victorians, for late twentieth and early twenty-first century audiences. Certainly, in terms of the number of adaptations, there is no one to touch Dickens, as detailed earlier. The Brontë sisters have had far fewer stage adaptations of their works, but there have been 11 plays about the sisters' lives. Here I will, among other things, investigate the relationship between the adapted works and the adapted lives.

As enduringly popular Victorian figures, Dickens and the Brontës have not only inadvertently founded two enormous heritage industries (their chief shrines now at Dickens World in Kent and Haworth Parsonage, respectively) but are also rallying points for sets of modern-day ideas about the Victorians. Adaptations are one of the key circulators of these ideas.[3]

There is no Brontë novel adaptation with a cast of 42, like *Nicholas Nickleby*, that puts the world on a stage and implies 'all human life is here'. Cliff Richard and Tim Rice's musical *Heathcliff* is the exception rather than the rule, as Dickens's novels have been far more widely and (commercially, at least) successfully adapted for the musical stage. Conversely, there is no Dickens adaptation (or novel) that is narrated exclusively by a female character, as Brontë novel adaptations generally are (even in *Bleak House*, many important events are necessarily outside Esther Summerson's purview). Most strikingly, the gregariousness of life in Dickens's fiction, and his many styles of narrating, allows his universe to appear, in a sense, stable and 'ready-made', the fecund creation of an unseen author. By contrast, Charlotte Brontë's sparse single-character focus, and the similarities between her experiences and those of her protagonists, seems to suggest, to adaptors, the writer's hand intruding on the action. And so, as we shall see, there is a proliferation of Charlotte-as-Lucy, Charlotte-as-Jane, Jane-as-Charlotte, novel-as-autobiography hybrids.

Rather than consider each of the Brontë sisters in turn for this chapter, I shall limit my analysis to Charlotte Brontë, focusing on *Jane Eyre* but, in my conclusions, making comparative references to her final novel *Villette*. The sections pp. 130–132 on the Brontë industry will, however, necessarily refer to the joint biographies and myths surrounding the sisters. It is at this stage important to explain more particularly why adaptations of Emily Brontë's *Wuthering Heights*, which has as much cultural purchase as *Jane Eyre*, will not feature directly in this chapter. The British Library's manuscripts collection holds 12 adaptations of the novel; this compares with 8 versions of *Jane Eyre*.[4] However, no single *Wuthering Heights* production has quite achieved the status of a standard work. By contrast, the nine-year development of Shared Experience's 'Brontë trilogy' began with the first run of *Jane Eyre* at the Young Vic in 1997, and it was followed by the 1999 revival, *After Mrs Rochester* in 2004, *Brontë* in 2005, another Jane Eyre revival and West End residency in 2006, and, as mentioned above, a *Brontë* revival in a co-production with Oxford Playhouse in 2011. Hence, over a decade, Polly Teale's vision of Bertha Mason and her afterlives has dominated notions of *Jane Eyre* on the stage.[5]

Reader identification and *Jane Eyre*

Because of the narrators' use of the first person, readers have identified intensely with Charlotte Brontë's heroines. Here I want to provide a little more critical support to this assertion, and suggest the ways in which it leads to an overlap in feelings about Charlotte Brontë's heroines and Charlotte Brontë herself (and her sisters). As Cora Kaplan points out, it was Raymond Williams' 1970 account of *Jane Eyre* and *Villette* that established the essential idea of Charlotte Brontë's tactic of 'secret sharing', a narrative that creates an unremittingly close, one-to-one connection with the reader.[6] Williams found this idea disturbing, since its reliance on emotional subjectivity seemed to him to preclude the objective analysis of social relations, which he felt was the Victorian novel's great project. In the theatrical adaptations of *Jane Eyre* and *Villette*, this close identification can be figured as Charlotte Brontë writing disguised autobiography, and thus literally stepping into her stories to express a particular part of Jane Eyre or Lucy Snowe's experience. Many of these popular assumptions about disguised autobiography have their origins in Elizabeth Gaskell's 1857 biography *The Life of Charlotte Brontë*, as Lucasta Miller explores in her book *The Brontë Myth*: 'It was not designed to celebrate the work but to exonerate and iconize the authors. The legend it laid down – three lonely sisters playing out their tragic destiny on top of a windswept moor with a mad misanthrope father and doomed brother – was the result of the very particular mindset Gaskell brought to it...she was a novelist who had trouble disciplining her imagination.'[7] In short, *Jane Eyre* and, to a lesser extent, *Villette* are, in the twenty-first century, interpenetrated with a range of influences and discourses – Freudian, biographical/novelistic, critical, theoretical and educational – that tell us more about what we wish to see in Victorian female novelists than about the works themselves.

Thus, as Kaplan has written, *Jane Eyre* tends to generate a range of 'second-order' feelings, concerning not the novel but the intense critical debates surrounding it.[8] To concentrate on attitudes to Jane herself first, it is notable that Kaplan entitles her section on *Jane Eyre* in *Victoriana*, '*Jane Eyre* and Her Critics', suggesting grammatically, if not in the use of italics, that ideological objections to the character are closely linked to ideological objections to the book itself.[9] Micael M. Clarke has summarized one view of why Jane is not an exemplary character for modern readers, as she has 'narrowed the field of her efforts' to one man, Rochester, while her female friends are kept at arm's length, their needs counting as secondary to her husband's.[10] In a late twentieth/early twenty-first-century society that celebrates female friendship, if not the explicitly feminist notion of 'sisterhood', Jane's capitulation to patriarchal norms may be viewed as suspect. Laurie Stone, meanwhile, argues that Jane has nowhere left to go when the novel ends in marriage. Jane's wishes, Rochester's wishes and the limitations of Victorian society combine to create a situation in which Jane is a paralysed victim: 'On and on the two go, pushing and pulling, as the fabric of Victorian society comes unstitched.'[11]

Criticism of Jane's limitations and choices very soon spills over into criticism of Charlotte Brontë herself. Stone remarks of the novel's ending being a supposed 'marriage of equals' that 'Charlotte doesn't know what this looks like'.[12] Chris R. Vanden Bossche picks up on the tendency of an earlier essay by Cora Kaplan to regard *Jane Eyre's* feminism as ultimately middle class, an opinion 'based not on a reading of the text but on the "empirical" knowledge that Brontë was "bourgeois" ... this critical investigation opens up a textual regress, shifting our investigation from *Jane Eyre* to the texts – letters, memoirs, biographies, juvenilia – through which we constitute the "Brontë" who wrote the novel'.[13] As he goes on to note, the novel's popularity in the nineteenth century has led its author again to be regarded as suspect for creating a novel so conservative that it could become a mainstream success.[14] In contrast, the fact that Emily Brontë's *Wuthering Heights* was initially met with a degree of critical incomprehension seems to work in its favour, possibly an echo of the academic critic's reverence for the avant-garde, that which is felt to be 'before its time'. As Stone has suggested, 'Many readers prefer Emily to Charlotte, preferring enigma over unbosoming... [Emily] does seem the most postmodern of the two – at home with shifting versions of reality.'[15] This ascendancy of Emily over Charlotte, as Lucasta Miller points out, has its roots in the 1920s and 1930s, when Emily's apparent 'timeless spirituality' began to be preferred over Charlotte's 'too-Victorian' image of being 'prim, priggish, and a prude'.[16]

Brontë family biodramas

Still, British culture seems to be as obsessed with dramatizing the Brontës' life stories as their novels, if not more so. In 1974 the Brontë Parsonage Museum received its largest ever number of visitors – 221, 497[17] – as a result of Christopher Fry's television serial *The Brontës of Haworth*, a stark example of escaping into a version of the past (in the wake of the 1973 fuel crisis and its enforced reintroduction of candlelight) where people appeared to have it worse. Other adaptations of the Brontës' lives, centring on Haworth, during the 1970s and 1980s include Noel Robinson's play *Glasstown*, which ran in Cambridge then the West End in 1973; the play *Four from the Cauldron* (1987); a theatrical version of Fry's television serial, by Kerry Crabbe (1985); Beverley Cross's *Haworth* (1986),[18] Alfred Sangster's frequently revived 1930s play *The Brontës*; and André Techiné's French film *Les Soeurs Brontë* (1979).[19]

A comparison of three Brontë theatrical biodramas from the 1970s and 1980s – *Four from the Cauldron*, Crabbe's *The Brontës of Haworth* and *Haworth* – reveals certain features in common. First, the events covered are much the same: Charlotte's unauthorized reading of Emily's poems, Branwell's drinking, Charlotte and Anne's visit to London, the long sequence of deaths and Charlotte's eventual marriage. This prominence of particular 'set pieces' may well be due to the influence of Winifred Gérin's landmark biography, *Charlotte Brontë: The Evolution of Genius*, in

1967. As Lucasta Miller points out, this was the first biography to use the modern scholarly apparatus of footnotes and a bibliography, and it certainly influenced the writing of Fry's television serial.[20] Secondly, having been written during and after the second wave of feminism in Britain, the plays make reference to the Woolfian problem of having no room of one's own, a concern with women's work and women's status that is, as we have seen, echoed in the original television drama of the 1970s, such as *The Duchess of Duke Street*.[21] *Haworth* is the least concerned with the social status of women at the time, relying on situational detail, such as Charlotte having to write letters to Emily while working as a governess and also planning *Jane Eyre*.[22] In *The Brontës of Haworth*, however, the family friend Mary Taylor asks, 'When will civilisation be tolerable for women?', while Charlotte reflects, 'All sewing is a punishment to me' and 'The female must live the glorious life by proxy.'[23] In *Cauldron*, Branwell's reliance on drugs and drink is compounded by sexism: 'My whimsical sisters think they're to make their fortune publishing poetry! . . . You've met my sister Charlotte . . . the famous publisher? Ha ha ha ha!', while Emily, busy fighting with dogs and cauterizing her own wounds, as legend dictates, sneers, 'I don't need a man.'[24] In these latter two plays, Branwell represents something of a problem, in that he is the exciting element, the fourth Brontë, the forgotten influence on the sisters' writing, as Gérin's biography establishes; nevertheless, he must be made to look pathetic eventually, in order for the sisters to look strong.

Like the later Shared Experience *Brontë*, *Haworth* combines biography with staged scenes from the novels, and thus makes explicit what the other plays hinted at: that what started as the biography, tangential to the centre-point of the novels, has now become the focus of attention. The staged incidents from the novels help to elucidate the events of the sisters' lives, not vice versa. Taken together, the tendency of the Brontë biodramas is to suggest that the siblings were, first and foremost, three women and a man who lived together and were creative, but died young. What they created is not itself the subject of representation, and so feels incidental to this tragic bohemian family idyll.

In this context, it is perhaps inevitable that the personalities of Charlotte, Emily and Anne should be simplified, caricatured even, so that their differences resemble the contours of fiction, where each woman must be a specific 'type': the ambitious one, the wild genius and the mild and socially concerned one. Anecdotal incidents, such as the time when Charlotte found poems in Emily's private notebook and sent them off to be considered for publication alongside her sister's, are thus given great explanatory power, with Emily being assumed to be the unworldly genius and Charlotte the ambitious bourgeois, overly concerned with fame and the financial rewards of publishing. As Lucasta Miller argues, there is no evidence from this to suggest that Emily was against publishing *per se*.[25] Likewise, even the cherished myth that *Wuthering Heights* was so far ahead of its time that it was rejected by Victorian readers is shown to be untenable.[26] Despite the evidence that Miller reveals of Charlotte's propensity to edit and misrepresent her sister's work, there is still no real proof of her motives, and the lack of any evidence of what Emily thought of her own writing, and of her sister, has created a huge space for speculation: 'The absences surrounding her have made her all the more magnetic.'[27]

The supposed battle of wills between Charlotte and Emily, because of its reliance on a few apocryphal tales, blown up to offer enormous significance, can be seen as another form of anecdotalism. Charlotte, characterized as prim, priggish and prudish, stands in for all the qualities of 'Victorianism' that we choose to reject or configure as not us, not 'modern', as Foucault had it. Emily, the rebellious free spirit, can thus be configured as one of us, before her time, one of Steven Marcus/Foucault's 'other Victorians'.

Shared Experience's *Jane Eyre*

Shared Experience's stage adaptations of *Jane Eyre* also seem to allow feelings about Charlotte, and about her relative talent compared with Emily, and 'second-order' feelings about criticism of the novel, to spill into the telling of the story. I will argue that this is chiefly because *Jane Eyre* and the Brontë myth, like all treasured components of national identity, are the site of a number of cultural anxieties. The first worry is unease about the novel's generic status. As Catherine Belsey notes in her cultural history of desire, one of the recurring features of popular romances is that they feature 'governesses or nannies far from home, who fall in love with their dark, brooding, Byronic employers. Indeed, dark Byronic heroes with a secret are extraordinarily common in romantic fiction, as are heroines who do not consider themselves beautiful and who have to make a living...the canonical nineteenth-century novel returns to haunt twentieth-century popular fiction.'[28] As Belsey goes on to show, the structure of *Jane Eyre* (and indeed *Pride and Prejudice*) is frequently used in modern romance novels, soap opera plots and Hollywood films.[29] Anxiety about the source text also involves a certain unease that it is not adequate or a suitable source material, and that it thus requires a supplement to make it acceptable to twenty-first-century audiences. In a recent (critical) review of a different adaptation of *Jane Eyre* in Dublin, Karen Fricker remarked, 'playing Charlotte Brontë's 1847 novel as straight-up epic melodrama simply doesn't work any more', before praising, in contrast, Shared Experience's adaptation.[30] That company's fractured, expressionistic set, the presence of a cellist on the stage, its bursts of physical theatre-derived movement and uncanny juxtapositioning of Jane and Bertha on the same stage together assert *Jane Eyre*'s position as high art, helping to defuse the danger of its being taken for melodrama.[31]

Shared Experience also had an educational remit to fulfil as an Arts Council-funded body, which again tilts conceptions of *Jane Eyre* away from the providential certainties of melodrama, and emphasizes the novel/play as something to be analysed, the performance as a learning experience. *Jane Eyre* had an education pack made available online, and both the play text and the theatrical programme feature a five-page biographical supplement on Charlotte Brontë (so that we should be in no doubt about the autobiographical connections).

'Victorientalism'

The aspect that set Shared Experience's *Jane Eyre* apart from the other adaptations, however, was its playing on contemporary anxieties surrounding race and gender within the novel. Here I want to draw, for further consideration of the critical currents surrounding this *Jane Eyre* adaptation, on an article by Erin O'Connor, 'Preface for a Post-Postcolonial Criticism', which uses the term 'Victorientalism', an idea that, as the Introduction explained, has informed my own idea of 'anecdotalism'. In the article, O'Connor argues that Gayatri Chakravorty Spivak's 1985 postcolonial reading of *Jane Eyre*, 'Three Women's Texts and a Critique of Imperialism', 'has become the basic model for doing postcolonial readings of nineteenth-century fiction' where the collective project is 'to do literary history in such a way that it conforms to a predetermined sense of what literary history should say'.[32] This Spivakian approach, she continues, is 'relentlessly synecdochal' in that it is predicated on 'the fantastic reach of marginal details', such as the transportation of Magwitch in Dickens's *Great Expectations* and Bertha Mason's origins in *Jane Eyre*. Explaining her coinage 'Victorientalism' as an attempt to describe the reverse-colonization of Victorian fiction by postcolonial critics who only read the novels in order to find something to be offended by, she states, 'One might go so far as to say that the complexity of this branch of postcolonial thought depends on what it perceives to be the profound simplicity of the Victorian novel, which, for all its wordy variety, always seems to wind up telling the same old story... an interpretative mission whose enabling premises include an a priori assumption that the Victorian novel needs – like some recalcitrant – to be put definitively in its place.'[33]

While O'Connor, as Patrick Brantlinger has argued,[34] may well be overstating her case and homogenizing the nature of postcolonial criticism in order to defend what she considers her embattled territory, something of this 'Victorientalism' nevertheless applies to stage adaptations of *Jane Eyre*, notably Shared Experience's Brontë trilogy (and, before it, Debbie Sewell and Monstrous Regiment's 1990 *More Than One Antoinette*, which told the *Wide Sargasso Sea* version of Bertha in the first act and then the *Jane Eyre* story in the second). *Jane Eyre*, the Shared Experience adaptations imply, has fallen victim to its classic status and become a Mills-and-Boon cliché. It must be 'put definitively in its place' by a version that foregrounds the aspects of the story of which our narrator (and, by extension, Charlotte Brontë) was unconscious: her sexual self-repression, linked to her repression of the colonial 'other'.[35] The 'same old story' is reformulated and unsettled by Shared Experience, in that in the final moments it is shown that Bertha survives in Jane (a warning that the newly married and now blind and crippled Rochester must behave himself, and treat his new wife well – or suffer the consequences).[36] It is quite conceivable that, for Charlotte Brontë, Bertha symbolized the author's feelings of moral revulsion towards slavery. However, there has been no dramatic adaptation that presents the Bertha episodes in this way; it perhaps suits our ideas of the Victorians more to have them unconsciously repressed, or ignorant, than to entertain the idea that the author may have invested meaning in this 'marginal detail' all along.

Twinning *Jane Eyre* and *Wide Sargasso Sea*

As indicated above, I propose to read the Shared Experience/Polly Teale *Jane Eyre* not as a single adaptation but in the context of its sequel, *After Mrs Rochester* (2004), and its 'prequel', *Brontë* (2005). I hope to show how the 2006 revival of *Jane Eyre* at the Trafalgar Studios was fed by, and could be read differently in the light of, these supplementary texts.

Polly Teale, as previously mentioned, was not the first adaptor to incorporate *Wide Sargasso Sea* into what was nominally a *Jane Eyre* adaptation: *More Than One Antoinette*'s two-part structure had done that in

1990. Nor was Teale the first in theatre to draw explicit parallels between Charlotte Brontë's life and that of Jane Eyre; Fay Weldon's rewritten adaptation of the 1988 Leeds production of *Jane Eyre* had explored this territory earlier – not to mention the Brontë biodramas like *Four from the Cauldron*. Weldon's version, with its 'self-conscious textuality', had achieved 'major status', because of its popularity and numerous revivals, by the mid-nineties, according to Stoneman.[37] Nor should we forget that Shared Experience is not simply 'Polly Teale's company' but a complex balance of influences, with some traces still from the legacy of classic-novel work pioneered by Mike Alfreds, company founder; with Teale and Nancy Meckler the joint artistic directors; and with Helen Edmundson and Meckler also working together on productions.

It is also worth noting other factors that may have further prede-termined Teale's version. The yoking together of *Jane Eyre* and *Wide Sargasso Sea* has been, as Monstrous Regiment realized, an educational commonplace for some time. A-level syllabi, in a move that may have filtered down from university English departments' growing interest in postcolonial readings since the 1980s, now routinely twin the two for coursework. However, what I want to argue in this analysis of Shared Experience is that although the incorporation of Bertha Mason into the onstage action allows the production to seem to be taking a postcolonial interest in hearing the subaltern speak, in effect the *Jane Eyre* adaptation privileges Jane over Bertha in a decidedly domestic, interior analysis of femininity. In a similar way, it can be argued that the placing of *Wide Sargasso Sea* on educational reading lists has made *Jane Eyre* an even more essential component of the canon and the syllabus than it was before, since it is the essential springboard from which to launch com-parisons (and/or accusations of racism or colonialism). Both the school and theatre uses of *Wide Sargasso Sea* are thus a recuperation by the existing power structures and their tendencies. Teachers can continue to teach a text they know, and students can be encouraged to train their attention on that increasingly rare bird in schools, an entire Victorian novel, via the promise of some rather more explicit sex, racism and madness in Rhys's novella.

In looking more closely at Teale's published script, I hope also to provide an overview of the adaptation for those unfamiliar with its approach. In the introductory material, we are told that 'hidden inside the sensible, frozen Jane exists another self who is passionate and sen-sual . . . Bertha (trapped in the attic) embodies the fire and longing which Jane must lock away in order to survive in Victorian England'.[38] In the play script, whenever Jane, from childhood on, is thwarted or crushed,

Bertha emerges from the area of the set representing the burnt-out attic and writhes around next to Jane, caressing her and insinuating herself between Jane and Rochester. Even when the story ends in marriage and a supposed meeting of minds, Bertha remains curled up by Jane's side, an essential part of how the heroine achieved her heart's desire.[39]

The play's critical reception

The Shared Experience *Jane Eyre* was even more praised on its revival in 2006 than it was when it first opened in 1997. This is unusual in that one would expect adaptations to date quickly, particularly if they were considered innovative nine years earlier. In 1997, Aleks Sierz for the *Tribune* called it 'daring in its interpretation . . . the Brontë novel's passion is well mixed with a modern feminist message', and Charles Spencer called it a 'satisfyingly meaty experience' and 'a truly theatrical experience'.[40] Lyn Gardner's observation that the adaptation 'owes so much more to *Psycho* than to Mills & Boon' sums up the play's avoidance of romantic melodrama in favour of Freudian menace.[41] Nine years later, Spencer is still impressed by Teale's 'profound literary perception', and Benedict Nightingale opines that 'you will find nothing bolder or more imaginative' in the world of theatrical adaptation, a view echoed by Joyce McMillan in *The Scotsman*: 'as big, brave and challenging an adaptation as you are ever likely to see'.[42]

Other reviewers expressed reservations that are instructive to this chapter's analysis. Toby Young in the *Spectator* argued that 'there's something fundamentally misguided about this [method of interpretation] . . . Polly Teale doesn't leave the audience any room to come to this conclusion themselves. In effect, by decoding the book, she robs the story of its mystery and, as a result, it loses much of its power.'[43] The difficulty for Shared Experience must have been finding a balance between offering an adaptation that simply conveyed the novel's narrative (thus falling foul of the Arts Council's requirements for 'quality' and 'excellence') and offering one that was so open-ended in its interpretation that it risked alienating school and college-age theatre-goers. Hence it is understandable that the adaptation chose to enact or suggest feminist and postcolonial readings, the ones that had become critical orthodoxies, and would be recognized by audiences.

Nevertheless, it has to be said that Shared Experience's *Jane Eyre* appears to pay more attention to a postcolonial interpretation of the novel than it actually does. Cora Kaplan reminds us of the view that Jean Rhys, in *Wide Sargasso Sea*, 'as much as Brontë, privilege[s] the story

of European settlers over that of the non-white or indigenous population of the colonies. Anti-imperial Victoriana of this kind retroactively
counters some Victorian prejudices, but leaves others, if only by default,
in place.'[44] In other words, *Wide Sargasso Sea* focuses its sympathy on
the naturalized descendant of plantation owners, brought up to expect
privilege but living in trying circumstances, over the plight of the ex-
slaves and their descendants. In a similar way, in Teale's *Jane Eyre*, Bertha
amounts to an effect, a symbol of an educated white Englishwoman's
divided psyche, rather than a person with a history. As Lyn Gardner's
review puts it, 'if Bertha is merely part of Jane's imagination, it does
rather beg the question of who Grace Poole is and why she is feeding
soup to Jane Eyre's psyche'.[45]

After Mrs Rochester

It is in this context that we might see the first Shared Experience *Jane
Eyre* 'sequel', *After Mrs Rochester*, as an attempt to more thoroughly
explore the West Indian element that had been domesticized and psy-
chologized by the *Jane Eyre* adaptation. The play begins with a portrayal
of a stifling Edwardian colonial family in the West Indies, the mother
desperate for the family to hold on to their European identity. The
framing device is a biodrama of Jean Rhys, in the course of which,
from her upbringing on the island of Dominica onwards, she repeatedly encounters *Jane Eyre*. Her initial identification is with Jane, as
when she imaginatively re-enacts Jane's first interview with Rochester.[46]
Later, however – especially upon arriving in England, where Bertha is
shown crawling out of a chest as an extract from the novel about 'flow-
ers that open at night' is read aloud – Jean identifies with Rochester's
Jamaican Creole first wife.[47] Sometimes Bertha clings to her back, or
voices Jean's resentment of men who spurn her.[48] Occasionally, the theatrical construct is lightly mocked, as when Jean, reading bad reviews
of *Wide Sargasso Sea*, indicates Bertha saying 'That's her fault...why is
she here?', or when another review – 'there's too much self-pity...it's
relentless...the other characters, they have no life of their own' – is
recognized by the audience's laughter (in the videotaped performance
viewed at the V&A Theatre Archive) as an apt criticism of the play.[49]
    We are still no closer to a full engagement with the West Indian back-
story of *Jane Eyre*, however. Jean's childhood falling-out with her black
friend Tite is shown to be the direct source of corresponding incidents in
Antoinette/Bertha's life in her novel. Jean initially chooses Jane as her
alter ego, but on experiencing poverty and alienation in England she
sees herself as – is haunted by – Bertha. Yet Jean never returns to the West

Indies, and although there is a sub-plot about her reconciliation with her estranged daughter, Bertha is presented as the main figure in her life (and thus, implicitly, her writing life is overshadowed by *Wide Sargasso Sea*). As she does for Jane in the previous play, Bertha licenses aggression and needling resentment (Bertha's oft-repeated line is, 'If I were a dog, you wouldn't do this to me'),[50] but it could be argued that in doing this, Bertha is reduced by both plays to the all-purpose bogey(wo)man of pre-postcolonial readings of *Jane Eyre*, in that she only has a history in relation to another, European, woman's private experience: she is their permanent Edward Hyde.

Brontë: completing the cycle

After Mrs Rochester, then, does not offer an interpretation or adaptation of *Wide Sargasso Sea*; hardly anything from that novel, save the beginning and end scenes with Tite by the water, is dramatized. Instead, its content most purposefully comments on Charlotte Brontë's *Jane Eyre*; without *Jane Eyre* (the novel), *After Mrs Rochester* would certainly not exist (although *Sargasso*, in some form, conceivably might). Yet, in effect, it refers to the Shared Experience *Jane Eyre* rather more, taking scenes out of the context of the novel and presenting, like Jane and in a similar manner, the battle of another intelligent young woman without friends or money to make her way in a world of men. The play also problematically continues the process begun in Shared Experience's *Jane Eyre* of widening the applicability of 'Bertha Mason'; she becomes a floating signifier, effectively the Shared Experience trademark. *Brontë* completes this process, bringing it full circle, in that Jane is reintroduced, this time as Charlotte's alter ego. *Brontë*, as biodrama, also brings the stage life of the Brontës full circle in that its form revisits the 1970s and 1980s biodramas, with their extracts from the novels, that pre-date autobiographical or psychological treatments of *Jane Eyre* itself.

If, in *Brontë*, Jane is Charlotte Brontë's alter ego, then it follows, via the logic of the Brontë trilogy, that Bertha must also be Charlotte's alter (-alter?) ego, the rage and passion that she cannot express. This reading of Jane/Charlotte also has a history, of course. As Kaplan astutely notes, American feminist critics, with their psychic distance from the physical world of *Jane Eyre* and all the regional and class associations it holds for the British, incorporated Charlotte Brontë's works into a 1970s 'feminist aesthetics of anger'.[51] It is this view of Charlotte Brontë – creating *Jane Eyre* in order to live the passionate, outspoken life that she was unable to adopt for herself because she was female – that is the situation dramatized in *Brontë*. At one point her 'passionless' life becomes apparent to her and she snaps: 'How could you possibly know? You who have feasted on life...How could you know what it is to give everything? To look on from the shadows?'[52] In the same scene where Charlotte says these accusing words to Branwell, Bertha is also present, on all fours, repeating her *After Mrs Rochester* line, 'Me love you...If I was a dog you wouldn't do this to me.'[53] Bertha has gone from Jane's alter ego to Jean's, to Charlotte's. All have a Mr Hyde, an underside. Taken as a trilogy, there is a strong suggestion in these Shared Experience plays that a kind of festering female underbelly, mixing anger, a will to power, self-pity and self-loathing, has dogged professional and creative women from at least the mid-nineteenth to the mid-twentieth centuries, despite the nominal progress in female emancipation. The post-Victorian woman cannot escape the un-Victorian bogeywoman.

Initially in *Brontë*, all the signs are that Charlotte is the key creative figure. Charlotte's imagination dominates the set, since the flats carry blown-up, monochrome images from Paula Rego's series of pictures based on *Jane Eyre*. However, it emerges that the central struggle in *Brontë* is actually between Emily and Charlotte (the play's two recurring dream-figures, Bertha and the first (mad) Cathy from *Wuthering Heights*, are played by the same actress).[54] Emily and Charlotte, to Teale, writing in the introduction to the play text, represent different and seemingly incompatible forms of rebellion – withdrawing from society and nurturing literary ambitions, respectively.[55] The two sisters' views on how to help Branwell are sharply opposed throughout. In the course of the play, Cathy from *Wuthering Heights* intrudes on the biographical action nine times, while *Jane Eyre*'s Bertha intrudes eleven times (poor Anne only has one extract from *The Tenant of Wildfell Hall*).[56] This indicates a slight domination of the dream-action by Charlotte's creation, but on the other hand Cathy's is the closing image, long after her creator's death. Thus, the play can be seen as documenting the ascendancy of Emily and her work in the public's imagination. The cards are stacked against Charlotte in this sense, in that a mere five pages into the play we hear the first accusation from Emily to Charlotte (the actors are at this point part-way through transforming from 'actors' into their characters) that Charlotte burnt Emily's second novel.[57] This accusation, as well as Charlotte's actual burning of the novel enacted towards the end, produced audible gasps from the youthful audience in the performance that I saw at the Lyric, Hammersmith, in 2005.[58] At one point, Charlotte asks Emily, 'Why will you allow me to do nothing for you? Why must I always be pushed away? Why can I not love you?...What's wrong with me?', to which Emily replies, 'You want . . . Too much of me.'[59] Thus Emily is aligned with the mad Cathy figure who wants to be free as the birds whose feathers she endlessly sorts (which is the play's repeated, and final, image).

Charlotte, meanwhile, is presented as controlling, possessive, appropriating: she is shown rewriting her sisters' poems for a posthumous collection.[60] Moreover, it bespeaks of the strange cultural ambivalence towards Charlotte Brontë, discussed earlier, that her novel's images should be so thoroughly appropriated in the first two plays, but that in the final part she should be presented unequivocally as a book-burner, and upstaged by her sister's creation, even as Bertha is resurrected once more to explain and propel the narrative.

Even so, *Brontë* is considerably more subtle than its 1970s and 1980s Brontë family drama predecessors. Where those plays give the impression of having used one biography as source material (*Haworth* and Gaskell's *Life of Charlotte Brontë*, for instance), *Brontë* reflects the modern confusions of an overabundance of sources and commentary. The play takes *After Mrs Rochester's* slight theatrical self-consciousness a stage further, having the actors come onstage and dress themselves in Victorian stays and crinolines next to a table of Brontë books and biographies, emphasizing the constructed nature of their drama.[61] They tell us, not yet in character, that 'There have been endless films, documentaries, dramas.'[62] The sisters read the famous letter from Robert Southey aloud from a biography.[63] Both Charlotte and Emily are complex, difficult to like and yet vividly imagined in the play; there is an aversion to incorporating their stories into the genre of Victorian family melodrama, as *The Brontës of Haworth* and *Four from the Cauldron* seem at times to attempt to do. There is a question, though, as to whether this self-conscious, neo-Victorian framing device is still in the audience's consciousness by the climax of the play and the burning of Emily's novel. As Ellie O'Keeffe was quoted as saying in the previous chapter, live interpretation – and I believe the same to be true of this biodrama – cannot convey the idea of 'maybe'; an apocryphal or conjectured incident, once extracted from a printed biography and performed, is made to 'actually happen' in the world of the play.

Bertha Mason on film and television

It may be the case, too, that the somewhat contradictory critical orthodoxy that the Shared Experience *Jane Eyre* embodies (Bertha is the real victim, but she is also the wild side of Jane) is now beginning to be reflected in television adaptations of the novel. Most recent screen adaptations do not appear to have taken much interest in Bertha. The 1991 film by Franco Zeffirelli only has her onscreen for a few minutes in total; she is pale and unkempt (bearing an uncanny resemblance to Johnny Depp as Sweeney Todd in the Tim Burton film), says nothing intelligible apart from the occasional mild roar and the word 'No', as she sets fire to Thornfield, and, refusing Rochester's offer of help, throws herself from the balcony, rather than the roof, the day that Jane leaves. Similarly, Bertha's madness is taken as read in the 1999 Kay Mellor adaptation, directed by Robert Young and starring Samantha Morton as Jane. She is revealed, on the day of Jane's aborted wedding, in a room that has been made into a makeshift padded cell, with cushioned blankets attached to the walls. She appears lascivious, then violent, but this is not communicated in words.[64] The dynamic camera work roams queasily across the room, and combines with Bertha's moaning to create a nightmarish, disorientating effect.[65]

By contrast, the 2006 BBC version, as if in acknowledgement of the educational twinning of Brontë and Rhys's books mentioned earlier, screened an adaptation of *Wide Sargasso Sea* on terrestrial television the week after *Jane Eyre* finished, and in the same time slot. This version of *Jane Eyre*, scripted by Sandy Welch, takes a more psychological interest in the story, featuring flashback and nightmare sequences throughout (for instance, Jane's dream of Blanche Ingram, from which she awakes to find Bertha's candle in her face).[66] When Jane meets Bertha, she pursues the governess, still wearing the wedding dress, and calls out 'Puta! Puta!' (Spanish for 'whore'), revealing not only a quite rational reaction to Rochester's putative bigamous bride but also that her first language is Spanish, suggesting that Bertha may have been linguistically as well as culturally disenfranchised by the move to England. More attention is also paid to the Bertha back-story, with Rochester's recollection of the marriage in Jamaica being shown onscreen as well as explicit imagery of her infidelities.[67] When she is taken back to Thornfield, the camera zooms to extreme close-up on her bewildered, apprehensive face.[68] Finally, when Bertha throws herself from the battlements, she is shown to be imitating an owl seen a moment before, an echo of the recurring image of Cathy wanting to be free as a bird in Shared Experience's *Brontë*.[69]

Adapting *Villette*

Considerably more freedom seems to be available to adaptors who choose Victorian novels outside the most popular areas of the canon. Charlotte Brontë's *Villette*, for instance – hardly obscure itself, and considered by many her masterpiece – has been adapted four times in recent years, and each version has been quite different. Lisa Evans' adaptation, last revived by Frantic Assembly at the Stephen Joseph Theatre in Scarborough in 2005, is the most conventional version when read as a text, but in performance emphasized the atmosphere of paranoia and surveillance effectively through the use of carved gothic doorways enclosing the in-the-round space, and through some complex passages of movement, or movement and dialogue combined. Judith Adams' 1997 studio production at the Sheffield Crucible matched Teale's vision for its psychological horror in places (sample stage direction: 'THE GROUP PARTS AND THE NUN HAS BECOME THE CRETIN. SHE APPROACHES LUCY, LAUGHING'),[70] but also placed masks, dummies and puppets on the stage and had Lucy Snowe pursued by the allegorical figures of Common Sense, Drywood and Deadrock. In Julia Pascal's *Villette* adaptation, *Charlotte Brontë Goes to Europe* (2000), Lucy's narrative is interspersed with accounts of the modern Brussels' red-light district. Most strikingly, Patsy Rodenberg's 1990 version, written in collaboration with Graeae Theatre Company, draws out from the narrative Lucy Snowe's references to 'cripples' and 'cretins', and places it in dialogue with other scenes set in a modern-day disabled people's home. Granted, as well as being less famous than *Jane Eyre*, the *Villette* adaptations have all been written since the 1990s, when it might be argued that the success of Shared Experience's adaptation concept for *Jane Eyre* encouraged more vivid and daring approaches to classic novels. Nevertheless, *Jane Eyre*'s fame seems, up to the point of the Shared Experience production, to have discouraged theatrical innovation: the Jonathan Myerson, Ian Mullins, Joan Knight, and Hall and Smith adaptation scripts from the 1980s, available as typescripts in the British Library, all follow the narrative in linear fashion, transcribing substantial sections of the novel's dialogue and rarely threatening to break out of the naturalist frame.

The future of *Jane Eyre*

Such dutiful adaptations suggest the catch-22 of choosing such a canonical text to work with: that the name recognition encourages audiences but discourages radical experimentation. The adaptation has to 'tell the story', to, in a sense, attempt to render the theatrical form transparent, so that the production caters to casual and school-party audiences rather than Brontë scholars. Thus, for all its success since the 1990s with its Brontë plays, Shared Experience was always caught between the competing demands of popular recognition and experimentation. For an example of the kind of radical adaptation that appears not to have had to make these sorts of market concessions, from the days before Thatcherite economics required theatre to 'pay its way', we might consider John Spurling's 1975 oddity *Shades of Heathcliff*. The play features four characters – Ponden, Haworth, Keighley and Hebden – who are controlled by a writer, dictating as he drives across the moors. There are a series of references to the Brontës' Gondal juvenilia, Branwell's life, and Emily's novel in particular, woven into the claustrophobic storyline, which is reminiscent of Pinter's *The Homecoming* relocated to Yorkshire. In an absurdist series of interludes, the characters play God with foot-high figures, representing four utopian experiments: islands ruled by Samuel Beckett, Alexander Dubcek, the radical bishop Trevor Huddleston and Che Guevara. If these four do not succeed in solving the problems of humanity, we are told, 'the earth will be laid waste forever'.[71] Saturated in a spirit of post-1968 disillusionment, Spurling's play is far from an adaptation in the traditional sense but is rather a meditation on the contemporary resonances of *Wuthering Heights*, aimed at an audience familiar with the Brontës' work and lives.

Nevertheless, given the recent climate of the theatre industry, it can be argued that Shared Experience's Bertha reading of *Jane Eyre* took open-ended exploration of a canonical text as far as it could go, while foregrounding the potential of the theatre through its expressionist intensity and menace. Rather than going back to adapting *Jane Eyre* as naturalistic theatre, as if its adaptations were inevitably to be overshadowed by those of television and film, future stage versions of *Jane Eyre* might use more of the theatre itself. What I mean by this is that the theatrical analogue, the enabling framework that many successful adaptations of other Victorian novels have used, is frequently absent when the Brontës are adapted. Sometimes this framework is metatheatrical, as when Michael Fry uses a Greek chorus to narrate his version of *Tess of the D'Urbervilles*, or when David Edgar begins his adaptation of *The Strange Case of Dr Jekyll and Mr Hyde* as a performance by children in a country-house drawing room, or again, Fry's adaptation of Jane Austen's *Emma*, originally titled *Sarah's 'Emma', After Jane* and framed as a group of teenage girls performing the novel to each other in an attic. Lisa Evans' adaptation of Mrs Henry Wood's Victorian sensation novel, *East Lynne*, by contrast, features the protagonist, Lady Isabel Vane, as a ghost who introduces the story, acts her part in it and steps out occasionally to comment on the action (at one point she is seen with a copy of the novel on her lap, commenting on the author).[72] What these theatrical methods have in common is that they deliberately complicate the novel's narrative with questions of who is permitted to speak and how it is received by characters/actors on different levels of fictional awareness (without recourse to presenting the author, scribbling away in their study).

Jane, Bertha and claiming identities

As a final line of enquiry for this chapter, we might consider what it says about British views of themselves and their history, that Jane Eyre is no longer considered sufficiently sympathetic alone, without the presence of Bertha. The tendency to closely associate Jane with her creator means that we might be loath to fully take Jane's side because she is felt to represent those Victorian values – thrift, patience, hard work, a keenly felt consciousness of status and class distinction, Christianity and a consequent reverence for the obligations of marriage – that we tend to reject in our self-configuration as moderns. We may also feel uncomfortable with Jane because she does not question the idea of doing God's work in India, merely its advisability for her; imperialism and the conversion of indigenous peoples to Christianity are areas about which modern, multicultural Britain is somewhat embarrassed.[73] So perhaps we want to side with Bertha because we want to support the underdog, and in so doing we can project British imperialist attitudes safely onto Jane.

As the previous chapter indicated, solo biodrama of the 1980s, which was being produced at the same time as the Brontë family biographical plays, often favoured as its subject 'other Victorians' – those who broke social taboos and seemed in some way to anticipate the twentieth century: Oscar Wilde, Simeon Solomon, Marie Lloyd, Mary Seacole, James Barry. Perhaps this was a way of playwrights and actors contesting the monolithic view of the Victorians – as white, male, heterosexual and conservative – that Thatcher's 'Victorian values' seemed to imply. Nevertheless, in its staking out of separate identities – gay, female, black – and the reclaiming of those identities from a white, male, heteronormative view of history, these plays can also be seen as representative of the development of identity politics since the 1980s. It is the search for, and the making of, identities amid the rootlessness of modern Britain that will be a central concern of Chapter 6.

6
Staging Hauntings

As the previous chapters on Charles Dickens (Chapter 3) and Charlotte Brontë (Chapter 5) have demonstrated, literary adaptation has been one of the main means through which the Victorians have been represented on stage since the early 1980s. Nevertheless, there has been a steady stream of original drama since then, set wholly or in part in the Victorian period, from David Edgar's *Entertaining Strangers* (1985) to Sarah Daniels' *Gut Girls* (1988), and including Nigel Williams' *Country Dancing* in 1987 and Richard Nelson's *Two Shakespearean Actors* in 1990 (both first produced by the RSC), Royce Ryton's *The Royal Baccarat Scandal* (1988) and Frank McGuiness' *Mary and Lizzie* (1989). More recent examples include Nicholas Wright's *Vincent in Brixton* at the National Theatre and in the West End (2002–3), Peter Whelan's *The Earthly Paradise* at the Almeida (2004) and Michael Punter's *Darker Shores* at the Hampstead Theatre (2009).

However, the group of plays I want to examine in this final chapter have, in general, been smaller-scale productions that are connected by their use of a Victorian ghost in a predominantly contemporary setting. I begin by presenting an overview of this group of plays, and consider its near relations in the theatre. I then explain my use of the terms 'supernatural realism' and 'anecdotalism', and analyse in detail two of the most distinctive examples of the former, Mike Leigh's *It's a Great Big Shame!* and Kate Atkinson's *Abandonment*. I go on to explain the need these plays have to bring back the Victorians and their rigid social structures, through an analysis of recent conceptions of alienation and weightlessness in modern society, and through a discussion of other cultural manifestations of this need to render tangible our connection to the Victorians. Finally, the chapter interprets the current fascination for Victorian feats of engineering, and the way in which a quintessential

Victorian building (St Pancras Station in London) has been modernized, as a further indication that consumerism and postmodernity have made Britons feel like the ghosts in a country that still seems to 'belong' to the Victorians.

Victorian hauntings on stage

The plays considered here are all examples of the Victorians being used as ghosts in plays that are set in the modern era, in most cases between 1990 and 2001. In some of the plays, such as Alan Plater's on regional identity, the transport network and historical apology, *Only a Matter of Time* (2001), and *It's a Great Big Shame!* by Mike Leigh (1993), the first act has a Victorian setting and the second a contemporary setting, with the connection between the two left implicit. More often, however, the plays alternate between contemporary and Victorian events (the former receiving more detailed treatment), as in Shirley Gee's work about London sweatshop labour contrasted with 1840s Devon lace workers, *Ask for the Moon* (1986), and Emilia di Girolamo's *1000 Fine Lines* (1997), where the experiences of two women regarded as mentally ill are contrasted, one in the 1890s and one in the 1990s. Similarly, in Judith Cook's *Ill At Ease* (performed at the Barbican, Plymouth, in 1992), the scapegoating of people with HIV/AIDS in the 1990s is juxtaposed with the treatment of prostitutes in the 1860s.[1] In the two plays I want to examine in depth, *Abandonment* by Kate Atkinson (2000) and Leigh's *It's a Great Big Shame!*, feelings of unease and a sense of being haunted are explained by the discovery of the skeleton of a murdered Victorian woman, concealed somewhere in the house, creating the most explicit embodiment of such concerns.

There are a number of other plays from the 1990s and 2000s that deal, in a similar way, with our sociocultural inheritance from the Victorians, and also our sense of how particular locations, beyond the domestic, carry resonances of that era. Nick Stafford's *Luminosity* and Moira Buffini's *Loveplay* were first performed as part of the RSC's 'This England' season in 2001. *Loveplay* traces patterns of desire through the ages, imagining events on the same patch of ground over 2000 years. As one of the Saxon characters remarks, 'A place is never just a place. Everywhere you go, you have a crux... past events, future portents all crowding in, visible only to the mind.'[2] (The 'past event' that represents the Victorian period is the seduction of a clergyman by a painter.) *Luminosity* deals with the morally compromised history of the Mercer family, visiting the same spot in 1799, 1899 and 1999. Mike Margolis's biodrama about the music hall star Vesta Tilley, *Bertie* (1993), is set in the Theatre Royal, Gloucester, just prior to its demolition, where the nightwatchmen, Lemonjack and Tinker, notice temperature changes and moved items on the stage, which we discover is haunted by the ghosts of Dan Leno, Vesta Tilley, Marie Lloyd and Little Titch. In Sean Aita's darkly comic *Yallery Brown*, produced in association with Forkbeard Fantasy (2000), the use of a haunted projector by the Wellingborough and Kettering Film Appreciation Society leads to Tom Tyver, a nineteenth-century factory worker, bursting through the cinema screen to narrate the folk tale of Yallery Brown, announcing that he is 'a soul in torment: 'Tis my misfortune to wander the empty void, without rest, and no peace.'[3]

In a more tangential way, Lizzie Nunnery's *Intemperance*, performed at the Liverpool Everyman in 2007, is also about the way in which certain neighbourhoods carry the resonances of their Victorian past. It is set at the time of the grand opening of Liverpool's St George's Hall, and examines the lives of a family of slum-dwellers excluded from such grandeur, who dream of a house on Lime Street, built on the site of some cellars from which their neighbours had recently been evicted.[4] Similarly concerned with the resonances of place is Sarah Daniels' *Gut Girls* (1988), written for and first performed at the Albany Empire, which is about the decline of the nearby imported meat sheds at Deptford, where women would find employment and a degree of independence at the turn of the last century. Although written in a style that is far from social realism, April de Angelis's *Ironmistress* (1989) starts and ends with reference to the corpse of a soldier, killed in an ironworkers' riot, being discovered over a century later.[5]

Anthony Neilson's *God in Ruins*, which played at the Soho Theatre in 2007, might also be classified, in part, as a work of Victorian haunting. It takes the formula of Dickens's *A Christmas Carol* and inverts it, having the ghost of Ebenezer Scrooge visit a modern, alcoholic television producer, Brian, to try to help him mend his ways. Crispin Whittell's *Darwin in Malibu* has the ghosts of Charles Darwin, T.E. Huxley and Bishop Wilberforce meeting in a Malibu beach house to debate religion and evolution. The 18-year-old Californian girl, whom we – and the ghosts – assumed at the start was being haunted by Darwin, also turns out, by the end, to be dead, along with her serenading boyfriend.

This formula of the storyteller themselves turning out to be a ghost, though presented in an original way by Whittell, is reminiscent of the twist in Stephen Mallatratt's long-running adaptation of Susan Hill's *The Woman in Black*. It is worth, at this point, noting that in the context of these plays on Victorian hauntings, the latter has been running continuously in the West End since 1989, and also that Andrew Lloyd Webber, David Zippel and Charlotte Jones's *The Woman in White* ran at the Palace Theatre between 2001 and 2005, helping to keep in circulation the notion of the Victorian period as a locus for ghost stories. One major difference between the two is that in *The Woman in White*, adapted from Wilkie Collins's novel, the ghost apparently seen at the start turns out to be Anne Catherick, recently escaped from an asylum where she has been imprisoned. Collins was, of course, pioneering the detective novel form, and the appearance of the supernatural is supplanted by rational explanation under the intelligent scrutiny of Walter and Marian. *The Woman in Black*, however, uses the Victorian figure of Jennet as a variant on the banshee, presaging the death of a child, and, within the play-world, belief in the supernatural is reinforced. As the cast take their curtain calls at the end of the performance, Jennet's ghostly face appears behind the gauze, behind the two actors, elevated by several feet, the light lingering on her for a few seconds, suggesting, perhaps, that it is this Victorian demon that will continue to ruin families for generations to come.[6]

A stronger influence on the tendencies of the 'supernatural realist' genre, however, is Caryl Churchill's *Cloud Nine*. Although its presentation might best be described as absurdist (Clive's daughter in the first act is played by a dummy, his wife played by a man, his black servant by a white[7]), it can be said to be realist in its concerns, having originally been written for the Joint Stock Theatre Company in response to workshop work on sexual politics.[8] One prominent and much-imitated feature of the play is its setting of the first act in the Victorian period and the second act in modern times (in this case, 1978/9). Churchill's play, then, as with Sarah Woods' *Nervous Women* or Kate Atkinson's *Abandonment* many years later, has characters from the first act such as Edward, Ellen, Betty and Clive returning to 'haunt' and converse with the modern characters.[9]

Although it lies slightly outside the time period chosen for this study, with the historical scenes taking place in 1908, Charlotte Jones's *In Flame* (1999) is also a double-narrative work of 'supernatural realism', featuring the eccentric Clara, an Edwardian child with the gift of being able to hear the voices of the dead by listening to walls, and to see desire manifested as flame. The play has several plot points in common with *Abandonment*, premiered a year later, and there is the same use of parallel scenes where characters from both time periods share the stage space.[10]

Supernatural realism

Before covering two of these plays about Victorian hauntings in depth, I intend to introduce and define the term I will be using to classify them, 'supernatural realism'. Realism is, of course, a far from easy term to satisfactorily explain, not only because it can mean different things in different art forms but also because in theatre its definition so often overlaps with principles of naturalism. David Edgar explores this point in his essay 'Ten Years of Political Theatre, 1968–1978', arguing that because 'the dominant form of television drama is naturalism', realist drama tends to be interpreted through these 'individualist assumptions'.[11] By contrast, Edgar posits realism as that which presents people and their actions 'within a "total" context ... it relate[s] people's recognisable activities to the history that is going on around them'.[12] In other words, there is something didactic in this choice of action, and something typical or representative in the characters we see. David Hare seems to be supporting this notion of realism when discussing his translation of Gorky's *Enemies* for the Almeida Theatre in 2006: 'the portrayal not just of one section of society, but of its whole, all in the service of an idea ... that we are, every one of us, more or less condemned to believe what our class and social circumstances lead us to believe'.[13] Hare and Edgar are pointing to a notion of realism in the theatre where there is an objective reality, a truth, about social relations, which needs to be rendered visible through the drama and through a precise representation of people and their circumstances. The play's structure seems to promise us access to the real.[14] This bears some similarity to the Dickens novelistic technique, a point picked up by Peter Brooks in *Realist Vision*, where he discusses the famous passage in *Dombey and Son* where the narrator imagines lifting the roofs from the houses and seeing, from above, the lives that are lived there.[15] Nancy Armstrong, too, discusses the way in which nineteenth-century fiction equated seeing with knowing, making visual information the basis for the intelligibility of the narrative.[16] We might also relate this, in theatre, to some of the founding principles of Antoine and the Théâtre-Libre in late nineteenth-century Paris, in particular the idea of the stage presented as a room with the fourth wall removed, and the play as, in Jean Jullien's phrase, *une tranche de vie*.[17]

Hence, in the 'supernatural realist' plays under consideration, care is taken to include a representative spread of characters from the period's social context. In *Ask for the Moon*, Carlie is the socially conscious matriarch; Anwhela represents exploited immigrant labour; Eugene is the boss, his behaviour shown to be a result of financial pressure, the constant threat of being undercut by competitors; and Lil is the elderly seamstress, unable to accept that she is now too old to work. The Victorian characters with whom they are compared have parallel characteristics: like Lil, Annie struggles with physical incapacity (she is a young widow who is losing her sight); Fanny corresponds to Anwhela, the innocent, abandoned woman; and Mercy, like Carlie, is struggling to keep order on the shop floor. *Nervous Women* (1992), meanwhile, demonstrates its concern with the social pressures placed on women, which in turn lead to their classification as mentally ill, through the characters of Celia in the 1890s and Ali in the 1990s. The modern sequences contain a monologue on alienated, unemployed youth and a satirical sequence played out by Ali and her boyfriend Sam about the bureaucracy of the benefits system.[18]

There are, of course, differences between how a realist novel and a stage play habitually render this reality visible. Brooks writes of realism's 'desire to be maximally reproductive of that world it is modelling for play purposes'.[19] This may be the case for the novel, but as a staging technique it is something we tend to associate more with naturalism; a realist play, especially in modern studio productions, is perhaps more likely to have set and properties designed to highlight the significance, the representative quality, of certain objects, as with the characters it portrays. Nevertheless, Brook's concern, in his discussion of Balzac, Zola and Gissing, is that 'realism in the quest to know and to detail the environment in which ordinary experience unfolds discovers that vision alone is inadequate, that sight triggers the visionary': that realism has a tendency to undo itself and become hallucinatory or supernatural in its drive to render the workings of society visible through mimesis.[20]

It is confusing, then, that one of Brooks' concluding comments is that 'Whatever the particular rules of the game, it is important that there be no cheating, that the game board simulate conditions of the real, that it create a good model of its economies.'[21] How can a slippery concept like realism be said to have 'rules', and who decides when someone is cheating? Brooks's book, in its consideration of the 'realism' of painters as diverse as Courbet, Caillebotte and Manet, seems to be arguing against such rule-making, since he argues, for instance, that the illegibility of the barmaid's expression in Manet's *Un bar aux Folies-Bergère* indicates that the painting 'is, among other things, about the difficulty of interpretation from visual evidence'.[22] In the light of this, I argue that realism's promised access to the real – even assuming a pure, comprehensive and didactic purpose that, Brooks shows, is missing in those artists he writes of who use realist techniques – will always be compromised by the difficulties inherent in communicating this purported reality (given the instability of language and visual signs).

Theatrical realism is therefore a genre full of paradoxes: it promises a view of something more 'real' than everyday life, by inventing a fiction; it needs to present believable individuals, as they observably act in everyday life, but these individuals also need to be recognizable types; it needs to be panoramic enough to give the impression of a whole society, yet tends to focus on a small, related group of characters. With supernatural realism, these difficulties are heightened because the hidden reality that is being revealed is at one and the same time the subjective experience of haunting (we see a ghost that perhaps only one onstage character sees), and a metaphor promising an explanatory framework for our modern feelings of alienation or imprisonment.

Hence, as we shall see, *Abandonment* parallels the cynical exploitation of Victorian Agnes by the master of the house, Merric, with modern-day Elizabeth's ill-fated relationship with Alec, a modern-day 'abandoner'. *Nervous Women* and *1000 Fine Lines* tell contemporary and Victorian stories of women kept indoors and conditioned to be weak and helpless by domineering men (the latter featuring Charlotte Perkins Gilman, author of *The Yellow Wallpaper*, and a modern woman called Helen, who continues to grieve for the death of her child). *Only a Matter of Time* traces modern failures in the railway network, and the governmental preoccupation with apologizing for past injustices, back to a conversation, circa 1840, between a farmer on the Welsh borders, Meredith, and a railway official from London, Fanshawe.[23]

By presenting us with the subjective experiences of Celia and Ali, Charlotte and Helen, Elizabeth and Agnes, and linking them across time (in contrast with the conventional social realist strategy of attempting to represent a single social environment in its totality), these supernatural realist plays are using a single experience of the uncanny to make what seem to be broad assertions about modern life. Because we, as the audience, see the ghosts physically invading the performance, and because of the realist manner in which they are placed in social context by rank, education and occupation, we are encouraged to accept their objective existence in the world of the play. Once we do this, the 'objectivity' of the plays' analysis of the causal relationship between Victorian values (patriarchy in particular) and modern woes is easier to accept. Actually, it is a sleight of hand, and similar to those that we have come across before. The process by which events in supernatural realist drama are presented as fictional but also 'true', and as metonyms for the way we

live now, can be seen in terms of anecdotalism. The way in which supernatural realism uses experiences that might be described, if related in
everyday life, as anecdotal, offers a solution that could be taken as either
comforting, in its neatness, or alarming. If modern feelings of discomfort and alienation can be explained by the fact that our spaces, our
experiences, are 'ghosted' by the Victorians, then they are the root of
the problem, and we must understand how our modern predicaments
are Victorian inheritances. On the other hand, if we are haunted by the
Victorian past, then how can we ever be set free, given the millions of
Victorian stories and figures haunting buildings, their misery stretching
out into the future?

Anecdotalism in the ghost play

How might the idea of anecdotalism, explored in the Introduction, be
further refined as a critique of the explanatory project of the supernatural realist play? First, as stated in the Introduction, in Jacky Bratton's
definition, the anecdote is poised between fact and fiction, and stakes a
claim to a deeper truth, an 'ineffable "essence"' about the person.[24] The
anecdotalism in supernatural realism, meanwhile, makes no claim to be
literally true (in that it is presented on a stage in a theatre within conventions that we would recognize as social realism) but seeks to expand
its thesis from the imaginary individual to some ineffable essence about
society at large. Secondly, where Bratton remarked on the 'process of
identity formation'[25] carried by the anecdote, the play as anecdote
functions not to tell an individual's story (whom we know is fictional
anyway) but to form or propose group or community identity (the
British and how they relate to their Victorian past). This is, of course,
not far from the function of realist playwriting that Edgar delineated,
the process of taking representative figures in order to tell us a story
about who 'we' are now. Thirdly, if, following Schafer's thoughts on the
anecdote and containment, the supernatural realist play works to contain the Victorians as either villains or victims, then it is performing
the opposite of the Greenblattian idea of anecdote, also discussed in the
Introduction. Rather than making the familiar strange, as Greenblatt
declared his intention to be, supernatural realism introduces a sense of
the strange only to render it familiar. In this sense, supernatural realism
is aiming for what Greenblatt, later on in *Learning to Curse*, discusses in
terms of 'resonance'. Although he writes of resonance as being evoked
chiefly by museum displays and art exhibitions, the definition is one
that is implicitly applied to the play as object: 'the power of the object

displayed to reach out beyond its formal boundaries to a larger world, to evoke in the viewer the complex, dynamic cultural forces from which it has emerged and for which as metaphor or more simply as metonymy it may be taken by a viewer to stand' (and later 'The key [to resonance] is the intimation of a larger community of voices and skills, an imagined ethnographic thickness').[26] The key problem with this as an apt description for supernatural realism, however, is the self-conscious, constructed nature of this 'resonance'. Unlike a historical art object, the supernatural realist play is a set of fictional choices aiming for a metonymical effect, hinting at 'an imagined ethnographic thickness' that the particularity of its fictional frame cannot provide.

In taking further our consideration of the applicability of anecdotalism to supernatural realist plays, following Bruce Jackson's observations on our expectations of causality, we can remind ourselves that one of the paradoxes of fiction that asserts its realism is its conscious shaping of events to appear both credible and yet causal.[27] Lastly, as the Introduction noted, Jackson also discusses the stories that circulate within families, and argues that they function more as an index of how we regard the family now than 'a report of what happened then'.[28] Hence, as with Dickens and the 'lost child' motif, or the transition to modernity traced in Victorian biodrama, we might find that the prevalence of Victorian hauntings in contemporary theatre is a way for the English to tell themselves a national story (a 'family' story, as suggested in the Introduction), one in which they can feature as the victims of their Victorian predecessors. I will return to this suggestion later when discussing Paul Basu's insights into genealogy.

Nevertheless, useful as Jackson's book is in this respect, its catch-all use of the term 'stories' is worth challenging if we are to further refine the concept of the ghost story as an anecdote performed in the theatre. He considers stories in a wide variety of contexts, from current affairs broadcasting (the O.J. Simpson car chase) to popular culture (Bob Dylan at the Newport Folk Festival) and prose fiction. There is no explicit discussion of narratology in this latter section and his tendency is to draw connections between storytelling as a marshalling of factual events and explicitly fictional ones. It is notable, however, that he almost completely avoids the mention of dramatic literature, and when he does, it opens up a glaring problem. 'Works of art, whatever information is stacked up "outside", are perfectly self-contained,' he states, having earlier argued that no matter what else changes, *Hamlet* will always end the same way.[29] This is surely not a position that a cultural materialist or new historicist could accept, for are not works of art interpenetrated with the socially conditioned ways of seeing that are made most available within any given period? Given a completely stable semantic function of language and set of stage conventions (which is far from being the case with *Hamlet*) then, yes, the statements and actions of the characters may remain more or less consistent. But the story's meaning, perceived to be carried by the text, changes from age to age. In addition, of course, *Hamlet* in performance is subject to a huge range of potential variation in emphasis and, thus, perceived meaning.

An anecdote then – a self-contained narrative, referring to the real but in some measure apocryphal or unproven, carrying assumptions of shared knowledge or membership, carrying meaning (while closing down other topics or foci) and establishing some degree of causality – is a particularly pungent and slippery form of story. It is very different from a news report, a novel or, indeed, a contemporary myth about Bob Dylan.[30] This disruptive story form is hard enough to pin down in a consistent way in print, but when an anecdote – in this case a ghost story – is performed, it becomes even more unregulated, even more multivalent. First, this happens because performances are different every night, and theatrical performance is, in most cases, ephemeral; we only have our memories to tell us what took place and precisely when. Moreover, the audience is different every night, and may be predisposed, through region, class, contemporary events or their wider cultural context, to react in a certain way. Finally, the ghost-story-as-anecdote sets off two contradictory sets of generic expectations: that of the social-realist drama and that of the rattling, ghost-story yarn.

Mike Leigh's *It's a Great Big Shame!*

At this point I would like to consider two of these 'supernatural realist' plays in detail and, in so doing, I hope to justify my invention and application of the terms 'supernatural realism' and 'anecdotalism'. Both plays, *Abandonment* and *It's a Great Big Shame!*, continue the thematic concerns of *Cloud Nine*, having much to do with sexual politics and tensions within the family in the Victorian age and now. I have chosen to focus on them because, when performed, they were among the most high-profile productions within the genre, *Abandonment* having been performed on the main stage at the Traverse Theatre during the Edinburgh Festival in 2000, and *It's a Great Big Shame!* having been directed by the celebrated British realist film-maker, Mike Leigh, at the Theatre Royal, Stratford East, in 1993. They have also been chosen because they are the clearest possible illustration of my idea of the supernatural realist genre, both plays hinging on the discovery of a concealed Victorian skeleton within a Victorian house, whose spirit had been haunting the present-day family in some way. Because of this narrative pattern, they are also prime illustrations of anecdotalism, where the realist, representational function of the characters and the neat closure of the ghost story as anecdote come into conflict.

It's a Great Big Shame! is the story of two couples a century apart. Jim meets Ada in 1893 and, having married her and unable to tolerate her bullying manner, strangles her and hides her body in their new house. A hundred years later, Joy throttles her husband Randall, whom she deems a failure, at the very point where the Victorian Ada's corpse may be on the verge of being inadvertently uncovered during building work. *It's a Great Big Shame!* takes its title from a music hall song about a husband who is dominated by his wife, and thus it might be placed alongside the Marie Lloyd biodramas discussed in Chapter 4, as plays that use the everyday subject matter of music hall song to provide an insight into Victorian working-class life. In the case of *It's a Great Big Shame!*, the song acts as an indication that gender and domestic violence will be key themes. Other elements that help to locate the play in the social-realist tradition are the introduction of the new brewery manager, just down from Oxford, the interrogation of racism through the strange questions asked of the sailor Amos and the references to everyday life (the new omnibuses with leather seats that have just been introduced in 1893, the cooking and eating of sheep's head soup), which indicate that the company has been researching the area and period.[31]

The play bears the hallmarks of a devised work based on improvization, featuring certain conversations that appear to have been left in for local colour or comedic purposes, such as the exchange between Nellie and Fanny about a pool of vomit that had been left by a dwarf who was carried away by a huge bearded lady.[32] It also makes use of the repressive hypothesis about the Victorians for comic purposes, with the brewery manager's paramour, Augusta, becoming sexually excited when hearing about brewing processes, and wildly playing the cello[33] – a scene that might not seem out of place in a 1970s play like Snoo Wilson's *Vampire*. In fact, what is striking about the majority of the first act, set in Victorian times, is the apparent lack of anything happening: Nellie gets drunk, Jack smuggles some cheese, Jack and Jim play pitch and toss. It is only in the latter half of the act that a discernible narrative develops, featuring the taciturn brewery delivery man, Jim, and his romance with Ada, who works at the hardware shop. Ada is assertive, encouraging Jim to buy the most expensive items in the shop, and socially ambitious, refusing to mix successfully with Jim's friends in the pub. Nevertheless, having weighed up her options, Ada agrees to marry Jim, in a scene that asserts the casual, matter-of-fact approach to marriage at the time.[34] Once married, Ada expresses her resentment about having to keep house, having been independent before; she makes Jim scrub the floor and announces, 'your honeymoon days are over. You mark my words.'[35] Eventually, the frustrated, inarticulate Jim, prevented by Ada from going back to live with his mother, strangles his wife.[36] It is thus only in retrospect that we realize that certain scenes, such as Jim boxing a drunken Nellie unconscious, to the general approval of the pub crowd,[37] had been placed there to 'seed' the idea of the acceptability of violence against 'disorderly' women – indeed, the expectation that men should enforce physical control on them.

The second act is set in the same house where the murder took place, 13 Manbey Street, Stratford. Again, an insecure husband, Randall, is dominated by his wife, Joy. Contemporary social issues are presented in the form of Joy's bullying, and in the progress of her upwardly mobile sister Faith, who works in the Square Mile and is moving to an 'apartment' in the Barbican.[38] Husband and wife argue over whether their friend Barrington will be able to knock out the fireplace; Faith remarks that it is always cold in the house (temperature drops are reputed, of course, to be a sign of paranormal activity).[39] While Barrington is fetching his tools, Joy throttles Randall and drags the body into the garden; there follows an eerily calm scene where Barrington and Joy move the furniture in preparation for removing the brickwork around the fireplace, the implication perhaps being that they will discover Ada's skeleton there. In a short, final scene, Ada and Joy share the stage, Ada wailing, Joy justifying her actions to Ada: 'You understand, don't you, eh?'[40]

Taken as a whole, then, the very specific choice of period and location in *It's a Great Big Shame!* can be read as suggesting that explosions of domestic violence by bullied husbands or frustrated wives have their roots in the female emancipation movement that had become prominent by the 1890s. Such a reading might also bring in the emasculating effects of low socioeconomic status for men (Jim and Randall are both treated by their wives as though they have failed in their role as providers). Thus, the late Victorian period is shown as a point of emergence for modern gender relations; it is, to adapt Jackson's term, a 'family' story about the nation, explaining who 'we' are now by reference to what 'we' were like then. However, in telling such a story, as Jackson and Bratton pointed out, other stories are concealed or downgraded: was spousal murder never an issue in the eighteenth century, or the Middle Ages? As with anecdote, the story makes a series of claims for the real, referring to contemporary events and locating the murders in a particular type of house in a particular part of London (albeit with an ominous house number, 13); yet, of course, this address does not appear in a London A–Z map. Most importantly, the anecdotal aspects of the story undermine the class-based, socioeconomic analysis of why people behave so brutally. Anecdote tries to short-circuit this class-based causality, derived from Karl Marx, suggesting instead that this is an 'evil' house, haunted by an unquiet spirit that makes the place always feel cold and that urged on Joy's uncharacteristic murderous violence both as revenge against the male sex for Ada's own murder and because, if Randall gets his way, the fireplace will not be opened up and Ada's corpse will not be found. The final scene, with Joy talking to Ada, ends the play on a note of subjectivity, psychodrama even, that had not been present in the other scenes, and could even be taken as suggesting that Joy has made Ada's whole story up, after discovering the body, while the 'real' Ada, whom we can see, is simply a spirit forever in torment, with no reasoning capacity. Either way, we are clearly some distance from a materialist analysis of society.

Kate Atkinson's *Abandonment*

Abandonment has its focus even more strongly on the lives of women then and now. It is set in 'The living room of a flat in a converted Victorian mansion',[41] into which Elizabeth has just moved after the break-up of her marriage, and concerns the complex sexual and family relationships of Elizabeth, her mother, her sister Kitty and her friend Susie. Agnes, a Victorian governess who used to live in the house and was seduced by her employer, Merric, haunts the flat, having been murdered by Merric's wife. Although Elizabeth's relationship with a photographer called Alec does not last due to his failure to commit to the relationship, she does become pregnant by him, and the ghost is finally exorcized when Elizabeth decides to keep the baby and name her Agnes.

As we might expect with realist drama, each character has a career that is significant in representative terms: Elizabeth, an academic historian, is the one who discovers the remains of Agnes under the floorboards; her friend Susie is a lesbian geneticist who is struggling to have a baby with her partner. Minus the appearances of the ghost of Agnes, the play is a straightforward family drama, in which each female character is revealed to have been abandoned in some way: Elizabeth is told at an explosive dinner party with her mother and sister that she was adopted after being abandoned in a public lavatory; she is later seduced and abandoned by Alec; Susie is abandoned by her partner for a hospital porter; Callum, a carpenter who had first come to inspect the floorboards, sleeps with Elizabeth's sister Kitty and abandons his wife and young son. And, of course, in the Victorian parallel plot, Agnes the governess is seduced by Merric, falls pregnant, and is stabbed by his wife Laetitia.[42] By the end of the play, Elizabeth has met her birth mother and discovered that she, too, is pregnant; she will name the child Agnes. In the final moments, Agnes 'appears in the doorway carrying a candle. She blows the candle out./Darkness.'[43]

Throughout the play, Agnes walks across the set and hears the modern inhabitants' speech, and practises saying words from their conversations: Ikea, retriever, 'Dolly, Polly, Holly, Brolly, Jolly'.[44] 'Can no one help me?' she asks. 'This is not how I expected my life to turn out.'[45] The correspondences with Elizabeth's future abandonment by Alec are foreshadowed by a split scene that has Elizabeth and Alec, and Merric and Agnes, in bed together, having similar conversations.[46] It is hinted that the suitcase of old photographs, found when Elizabeth moved in,[47] includes the portraits of Agnes taken as part of the process of seduction by Merric (whose name, consciously or otherwise, echoes that of Joseph Merrick, the 'Elephant Man', hinting at the idea of Merric being morally monstrous or deformed, and perhaps of his photographing Agnes like a medical curiosity or specimen).

Where *It's a Great Big Shame!* uses comically pointless conversations and incidents to suggest the texture of everyday life, *Abandonment* is much more schematic, with the parallel plots alternating to communicate a much less equivocal view of gender relations than Leigh's. Atkinson's play seems to be arguing that women are abandoned now just as they were in the 1860s by feckless men, and implying that the difference now is that women are no longer murdered for objecting to their treatment. The play uses contemporary social issues connected with family life as a backdrop (same-sex parents and artificial insemination, adoption, the domestic violence that Elizabeth's mother Kitty recalls), yet the critique is mostly of Victorian attitudes: Merric's discomfort that his wife's money comes from trade; Laetitia's blind faith in the spiritualist, the Reverend Scobie; the limits placed on young women, even a well-travelled anthropologist's daughter like Agnes. The extremely neat sense of closure brought about by the ending, with Agnes laid to rest but about to be reborn in name as Elizabeth's daughter, confirms Elizabeth's remark near the beginning of the play: 'I think people's lives somehow imprint themselves on houses.'[48] It suggests that this is a personal connection, brought about by the parallels in these women's lives, as well as the undiscovered body, the unquiet spirit. Hence it is very difficult to read a sense of social critique, a diagnosis of what is wrong with modern society, into the play. The position seems to be that the benefits to women of 140 years of change are very much worthwhile, but that there is never any guarantee against being abandoned by a man. So, while *Abandonment* offers a social-realist picture of Victorian society in miniature, the modern plot is more like naturalism as conceived by Zola, exploring the consequences on his characters of their birth and background.[49] The play could even be read as ahistorical or evolutionary-determinist in tendency, arguing that men will always abandon women, regardless of the social constraints within a given historical period; it is only the forms of abandonment that are culturally determined.

Marxism and alienation

Why does contemporary theatre feature so many instances of being haunted by the Victorians, and is this a symptom of a wider fear or malaise in British culture? In this section, I will be arguing that Victorian hauntings are indeed a symptom of British, and particularly English, insecurity and alienation. I will begin by exploring alienation as a social and economic idea, then consider how such ideas have been developed by theorists of modern society and consumerism, and finally examine how modern movements, such as genealogy, might be seen as ways of seeking to address this state.

The notion of alienation that I wish to discuss here can be said to derive principally from Marx. In his 1844 paper 'Estranged Labour', he teases out the relationship between seemingly straightforward economic exploitation and the spiritual condition of man under capitalism:

Estranged labour not only (1) estranges nature from man and (2) estranges man from himself, from his own function, from his vital activity; because of this, it also estranges man from his species. It turns his species-life into a means for his individual life. Firstly, it estranges species-life and individual life, and, secondly, it turns the latter, in its abstract form, into the purpose of the former, also in its abstract and estranged form.[50]

Working in a factory, working merely in order to earn money and being 'abstracted' into a human machine, humans are isolated, unfulfilled

and reduced to the most basic attributes of the species. Furthermore, 'An immediate consequence of man's estrangement from the product of his labour . . . is the estrangement of man from man.' It is worth noting that the community spirit of the nineteenth century that is celebrated in, say, adaptations of Dickens is the very thing that Marx argued had already been lost in the move from cottage industry to huge manufactories. As mentioned in the chapter on Dickens (Chapter 3), for Raymond Williams, the prelapsarian age of harmony with the landscape is always retreating into the past, 'Just back, we can see, over the last hill' – however far back in history we go.[51]

Nevertheless, there was a fresh upsurge of Marx-derived discussion of alienation in the 1960s, at the beginning of the period on which this study is focused. Alienation was one of the founding assumptions of Guy Debord's theorization of the spectacle in *The Society of the Spectacle*, although his language is rather more mystificatory than Marx's: 'the spectacle is hence a technological version of the exiling of human powers in a "world beyond" – and the perfection of separation *within* human beings'.[52] Herbert Marcuse moved towards a critique of alienation in the 1970s. Where at the time of his 1967 'Essay on Liberation' he allows that corporate capitalism has some very 'comfortable and liberal realizations' that have to be resisted if one is to find new and more fulfilling values, by the time of *Counterrevolution and Revolt*, as Kellner points out, he is emphasizing the breakdown of advanced capitalism's stability and cohesion, due to the revolt against work, a decline in the real value of wages, unemployment and inflation, ecology and energy crises, all of which produced a new consciousness of the failures of capitalism.[53] There is also a sense that people are losing control over their economic and decision-making power and their own labour activity, becoming 'the direct servants of capital', which implies that alienation is once more taking on the stark contours of the nineteenth century after decades of mollifying progress.[54]

It was Erich Fromm, of this New Left generation, who was the most prescient in pinpointing the psychological and ontological dangers of consumerism. He warned in the mid-1970s that 'our goal should be to *be* much, not to *have* much' and that what many people are caught up in is a cycle of 'pathological consumption'.[55] Drawing explicitly on Marx ('the marketing character is the perfectly alienated human being'[56]), Fromm discusses the marketing of the self – as we shall see, one of Bauman's key motifs – stating that 'One can say that most people turn out as society wishes them so that they can be successful. Society fabricates types of people just as it fabricates styles of shoes or of clothes or of automobiles, that is, goods that are in demand. A person learns already as a child what type is in demand.'[57]

Alienation since the 1970s

Paul Basu, whose study of genealogy I shall be drawing on later, cites the classic work of sociology, *The Homeless Mind*, as one originator of the idea of modern man [*sic*] as dislocated and in search of a lost sense of home.[58] It is worth looking at the arguments of the authors of *The Homeless Mind* in a little more detail in order to differentiate the conditions that existed in the 1970s, according to their argument, from those which, I assert, pertain today. The authors envisage, as many did in the 1970s, a future in which affluence and leisure time will expand, hand in hand, so that 'more and more time is spent in private life'.[59] What *The Homeless Mind* does not anticipate is a future in which it is increasingly difficult to differentiate between a private and a public self, as evidenced by social networking sites, celebrity culture, confessional television and user-generated content on the web, not to mention the encroachment of work-related technologies into the home and into leisure time, making us contactable at any time. *The Homeless Mind* also conceives of 'modernization' as 'the growth and diffusion of a set of institutions rooted in the transformation of the economy by means of technology', a definition that seems rooted in an age before multinationals had the power to transform developing countries' economies without bringing to that nation the benefits of 'the modern state' to which they assume technological progress to be closely related.[60] *The Homeless Mind* also argues, after Weber, that in the late twentieth century, modernization was felt as a rationality that results in control, limitation and frustration;[61] by contrast, Bauman, as we shall see, points to the terrifying consequences of the 'emancipation' that consumerism offers us. And, where Berger, Berger and Kellner discuss the retreat into private life and private identities in response to frustration,[62] later theorists, such as Bauman and Barber, explore the ways in which consumerism usurps and homogenizes regional, generational and racial identities, another sense in which personal space is claimed as corporate space.

What *The Homeless Mind* certainly captures, however, is that sense, as the title suggests, of an individualistic retreat inwards in the modern consciousness as we adjust to our alienation from politics, now that '*All* the major public institutions of modern society have become "abstract"', and from our communities, now that 'the pluralistic structures of modern society have made the life of more and more individuals migratory, ever-changing, mobile'.[63]

The effects on culture and the individual psyche of alienation in late modernity, in the writings of a number of social theorists, have been described as a peculiar weightlessness, a sense of being cut adrift from social cohesion, solidarity and solidity. Frank Furedi noted this tendency in the 1990s in his book *Culture of Fear*, where he argued that the attempts by Margaret Thatcher in Britain and Ronald Reagan in the US to promote the individual actually had the effect of creating individuation, but at the same time undermining individuals.[64] What follows is a culture where there is no agreement over the most elementary forms of conduct, or what it means to be British.[65] This is a culture where 'The weakening of social cohesion means, ironically, the diminishing of the sense of individual autonomy. Individuals are unlikely to transcend the mood of caution that afflicts a society that is uneasy with itself.'[66] Furedi discusses, as examples of this crippling fear and uncertainty, the need for sexual harassment codes at work, health and safety legislation, and the counselling and helplines offered to schoolchildren.[67]

These ideas are taken up and developed by two other recent thinkers on society and consumerism: Benjamin R. Barber and Zygmunt Bauman. For Barber, writing from a North American perspective, consumerism essentially infantilizes the subject, paradoxically promising 'age without dignity ... sex without reproduction ... life without responsibility ... In the epoch in which we now live, civilization is not an ideal or an aspiration, it is a video game.'[68] Barber here highlights consumerism's tendency to cut the subject adrift from traditional patterns of the human life cycle, from growth and maturity, and to substitute instead something virtual and weightless, a simulacrum of reality, the video-game *Civilization*.[69] The ageing adults who are encouraged to continue as youth consumers by the marketing of global brands are 'frozen in time', and retain the impatience of children, though often for 'retro' clothes, films and other commodities that again seem to confuse the traditional process of ageing.[70] Furthermore, for Barber, consumerism erodes 'race, religion, and other forms of ascriptive identity along with voluntary political and civic identity', replacing them with consumer branding, which 'comes to define who we are'.[71] 'Liberated' from older forms of identity, infantilized consumers freed from the constraints of parental control, we consume without thinking of the social or environmental consequences, with no truly adult sense of cause and effect.[72] And yet, as in Furedi's formulation, this individuation does not make us happy, or more free: 'the dynamics of consumption actually render the individual more rather than less vulnerable to control, much in the same way that the infant, for all its sense of power, is actually powerless in a world from which it cannot distinguish itself'.[73]

In Bauman's *Consuming Life*, published, like Barber's book, in 2007, the idea of the subject cut adrift is given additional dimensions. Bauman discusses the trend towards flexibility of labour, picking up on Arlie Russell Hochschild's use of the term 'zero drag' – the ideal employee, who is 'free-floating, unattached, flexible, 'generalist' and ultimately 'disposable'.[74] Bauman notes the 'thriving waste-disposal industry' that is needed by the modern consumer to separate themselves from the material consequences of their ever-intensifying patterns of consumption.[75] Similarly, relationships become virtualized via online dating, and rendered discretely disposable.[76] Like Barber, Bauman notes modern consumerism's *'renegotiation'* of the meaning of time, describing it in terms of Michel Maffesoli's *'pointillist* time', Thomas Hylland Eriksen's 'tyranny of the moment' and Elżbieta Tarkowska's 'presentist culture'.[77] He notes the growing tendency in consumer societies towards the 'blasé attitude' first noted by Georg Simmel in the nineteenth century, and links this detachment to a prevalent sense of political disengagement, encouraged by the power of markets to override state sovereignty.[78] Like Furedi, Bauman discusses the way in which consumer societies tend to create artificial states of emergency, where, in Bauman's formulation, individuals are panicked into further seemingly urgent, conformist patterns of consumption.[79] The consumer is never permitted to rest; the consumer life is not about acquiring and possessing, Bauman posits, but about being *'on the move'* and being continually unsatisfied.[80] In common with Barber again, Bauman is suspicious of consumerism's assault on personal identity, by the 'constant pressure' it exerts 'to be *someone else'*, and notes consumerism's promises of emancipation 'from the constraints on choice imposed by the past'.[81] Finally, as with Furedi's and Barber's analysis, this individuation – and in Bauman's analysis, the pressure to consume in order to define oneself as not a member of the underclass – does not lead to a new, exhilarating sense of freedom but incomprehension, impotence, fear: 'a society convulsed by anxieties too numerous for it to be able to say with any degree of confidence what there is to be afraid of, and what is to be done to assuage the fear'.[82]

Summarizing the common ground of these three commentaries, then, we can discern certain patterns of imagery: the offer of 'emancipation' that actually results in being cut adrift from history, identity, communal and national sense of self; the consequent replacement of teleological interpretations of national or individual life with notions of 'nowness' and immediacy, which make us restless and fearful of the next emergency; the replacement of manufacturing with service industries, staffed by employees with 'zero drag'; and the replacement of face-to-face personal and civic encounters with online equivalents and video-game simulations of such.

'How could it have come to this?'

I argue that it is the feelings, institutions and identities that are felt to be missing from late modernity, as expressed by these writers, that are projected onto our idea of the Victorians in supernatural realist drama. The plays mentioned are far from being simply nostalgic about life in Victorian Britain, but *It's a Great Big Shame!* presents us with a picture of a local, working community that cannot be represented by the isolated office spaces referred to in the 1990s sequence. *Abandonment*, meanwhile, as I have shown, focuses on the personal-as-political, which can be taken as arguing that it is institutions and systems of thought, such as domestic service, class snobbery and spiritualist religion – a dogmatic, too-secure sense of each person's place in this world and the next – that tarnished Victorian optimism. Both plays take us back to the Victorians, seemingly asking, with reference to the modern characters, 'how did it come to this?': how could female emancipation have led to such 'shame' that the wife now kills the husband; how could the social freedoms gained by the 1990s have led to a widespread sense of being abandoned? Hence, while there is no suggestion of a 'national decline' feeling like the one that circulated in the 1960s and 1970s, these supernatural realist stories are much less optimistic than the found child/return of the dead motif described in the chapter on Dickens (Chapter 3). They might be viewed as taking the 'body of evidence' idea suggested in the biodrama chapter (Chapter 4) and turning it into a corpse in order to construct an anecdotalist explanation of the emergence of modernity, the loss of illusory certainties, from fictional materials.

Victorians and contemporary art

Perhaps the appeal of the Victorian more generally in our culture is that where we feel cut adrift and weightless, the Victorians appear to have the certainty of a nationalistic 'island story', jingoism, communities centred on agriculture, trades or industries. Where we provide services and are alienated by technology and being constantly on the move,

the Victorians had slow, more tangible emergent technologies like photography, led the world in heavy industry, and work, for most people,
was heavy manual labour. Most pertinently for the sense of haunting
to be discussed in my final section on St Pancras, their buildings, their
bridges, their sewers, their infrastructure, has lasted, and at times seems
to surround and overwhelm us in the urban environment.

Where else might we go to find expression of this notion that modernity has encouraged a powerful need to identify with, or to inhabit,
the Victorian past? Two celebrated contemporary artists seem to have
picked up on this national preoccupation. In 1996, Rachel Whiteread
made a concrete cast of a room in a Victorian house scheduled for
demolition, called the cast *Room*, and exhibited it. In 1999, she repeated
this process with an entire Victorian house, calling the work *House*.
As with a plaster cast of a face, what we are invited to contemplate is a
model with its recesses turned inside out, the absences made presences,
emptiness enclosed, as Catherine Belsey describes it in her discussion
of Whiteread's work.[83] Belsey sees *House* as an illustration of our lack of
direct access to the real, an idea made manifest by the filling in of pure
space, dis-placing it and putting it once more beyond our reach. *House*
could also be interpreted as a commentary on estate agents' fetishizing
of the 'period property', and the premium that buyers are willing to
pay for a particular façade (which has been rendered redundant, a mere
shell, by Whiteread's creation). Or it could, like the plays under discussion here, be pointing out that when we move into a 'period property'
and have fantasies of creating a pure or minimalist 'space' (the interior
design holy grail of the late 1990s), the space is in fact anything but
pure; rather, it is thick with marks, gaps, alcoves, smells, objects, echoes;
the births and deaths that have taken place in that building. We covet
the cachet that accompanies 'owning' that piece of history, but idealize
it as empty space, 'neutral décor throughout', as the estate agent pat-
ter has it. The supernatural realist plays I have discussed would seem to
indicate that such neutrality is a vain hope.

My second contemporary artist who has engaged with the resonances
of the past is Cornelia Parker, whose collection of photographs of the
Brontë sisters' possessions, taken using an electron microscope, went
on display at the Haworth Parsonage Museum in 2006; they then
became part of a larger exhibition, *Never Endings*, which was shown at
Birmingham's Ikon Gallery in 2007. Alongside what Parker has named
Brontëan Abstracts, the later exhibition shows us clods of earth from
the Leaning Tower of Pisa, a doll dressed in Dickensian costume, and
called Oliver, chopped in half by the guillotine that beheaded Marie

Antoinette, and, with 'Stolen Thunder', a collection of handkerchiefs that have the tarnish on them from the silverware of historical figures such as Lord Nelson. The Brontë material is expanded, with recordings of psychics in the Haworth Parsonage, a video interview with an elderly couple who claim to be related to Branwell Brontë, and a copy of *Wuthering Heights* autographed by Gabriel Garcia Marquez. As Sadie Plant remarks in the exhibition catalogue, Parker's work has 'The ability to miss the point, escape the thing, and attend to the connections and the in-betweens... Off-cuts, scraps and residues are rendered more important than their origins.'[84] Particularly in the cases of the works I have just mentioned, there seems to be an ongoing meditation on the futility of attempting to touch the past, of trying to make visible or tangible some tenuous link to history, and yet our need to collect and claim 'off-cuts, scraps and residues'. Does the Oliver Twist-like doll look any different because it was sliced in two by a historic guillotine (how do we even know that it was?)? There is something of the conversation piece, begging for an explanatory anecdote, about such an item (how was the doll-mutilation arranged – whom does one contact to acquire use of the guillotine?), and also a need to validate the violence inflicted on a pretty doll by reference to the real. It also makes, perhaps intentionally, spurious 'connections and... in-betweens' in order to link Dickens with the French Revolution, presumably by connecting elements of *Oliver Twist* and *A Tale of Two Cities*.

The supernatural realist dramas that this chapter has been investigating can be seen in the light of a similar attempt, in the theatre, to 'attend to the connections' between the Victorian age and our own, and to make visible this historical residue. The difference is that Parker's exhibition is presented in such a way that the authenticity of the pieces (or exhibits, as it is tempting to regard them) may be called into question, and the value of collecting such residues is opened up to debate. Supernatural realism, as I have argued, takes for granted that the residue, the connection, is real, explicable and susceptible to the closure of anecdote.

Genealogy and imaginary homelands

The huge upsurge in interest in genealogy over the last two decades can also be seen as a response to this need to find spiritual succour or understanding in an imagined past. In this section, I would like to draw some parallels between the anecdotalism of supernatural realism and the narratives that family-history researchers uncover/recreate. The available literature on genealogy is almost all written from the 'how-to' perspective (Amazon lists *Ancestral Trails: The Complete Guide to British Genealogy and Family History, Early Modern Genealogy: Researching Your Family History 1600–1838,* and *Writing Up Your Family History: A Do-it-yourself Guide* among its search results for 'genealogy'). Hence, Paul Basu's book *Highland Homecomings* (2007), a study of genealogy as a social phenomenon that focuses on notions of British heritage, is an especially significant and timely contribution. I shall be using his book to help make sense of the popularity of genealogy in an age of global travel and communication (while acknowledging that only one of the 'supernatural realism' plays that I have discussed, Kate Atkinson's *Abandonment,* is set in Scotland). Basu does explore, however, the tensions between the frequently romantic idea of Scotland entertained by members of the 'Scottish diaspora' across the world, and the more quotidian attitude towards the country held by its residents and other UK residents, as represented in websites aimed at these different groups and the differentiation in online communities between 'real Scots' and 'heritage Scots'.[85] In the light of this, it is worth considering the idea that where contemporary Scottish writers or theatres do represent nineteenth-century Scotland, the plays go quite deliberately against the 'heritage' grain of Balmoral, clanship and kilts: Ann Coburn's *Get Up and Tie Your Fingers* from 1995 is about the Clythe fishing disaster; Rona Munro's *The Maiden Stone* concerns a family of impoverished travelling players and is unsettling in its use of folklore and storytelling; Sue Glover's *Bondagers* (1995, revived 2001) deals with a group of female land labourers; and Riccardo Galgani's *The Found Man* (2005) presents a dystopic island community where outsiders are murdered on a misunderstanding. *Abandonment,* meanwhile, might be characterized as lowland Scottish, bound to the educated, middle-class world of Edinburgh (and aimed at an international, Edinburgh Festival audience), rather than the more working-class Glaswegian identity, or the romantic myths of highland clans.

Basu argues that the condition of the 'homeless mind' and the pluralization and protean evolution of identity leads to contemporary individuals wishing to '[have it] both ways', to be at home in a world of movement but also to feel that home is a permanent, physical place.[86] This contradictory pairing of needs leads to some peculiar habits of thought within the roots-tracing, amateur-genealogist community. One might first of all note that the desire to discover one's true, spiritual nature, to reject the discontents of twenty-first-century materialism, inevitably involves more consumption, of holidays, magazines and souvenirs. Roots tourists tend to keep copies of significant documents or pieces of wood or stones from ancestral sites as relics that they invest with spiritual significance.[87] This latter, and the chasing of traces of a long-extinct human life, are themes, as we have seen, of Cornelia Parker's recent work.

A second inconsistency, as Basu points out, drawing on Peter Novick's idea of the culture of victimization,[88] is that this nostalgia – the mourning for a lost home – often manifests itself in an identification with particular ethnicities. It seems there is a menu of 'ethnic options' from which individuals choose to identify, and it is far more popular to claim Scottish and Irish ancestry than English.[89] Basu quotes one correspondent who had mixed Scottish, Irish, English and Swedish ancestry but declared, 'I feel absolutely no affinity for England at this time', and so would not be visiting to trace her roots, as she had done with the other three countries.[90] This need, even in the face of the results of one's family research, to identify with the ethnic group that might be considered victims, outcasts or refugees is, as Basu notes, particularly strong among white Caucasian residents of the US, Canada and Australia. They rationalize their sense of being cut adrift in a modern world of affluence – but also deep dissatisfaction and anxiety – by telling themselves that they have been exiled from their ancestral homeland, lost the innocence of their Eden. Such a rationalization also neatly sidesteps the idea that Scottish or Irish emigrants often themselves dispossessed native peoples of their land and gained advantage from their whiteness.[91] With regard to notions of origin, alienation and the Victorian past, it is worth noting that the present-day English (and possibly, by extension, middle-class, lowland Scots) have no such story to tell themselves, and perhaps the plays I have named are an attempt to fill that absence of a victimological narrative by presenting the English as having been victims of their own Victorian ideologies. In this sense, then, supernatural realist plays are creating the opposite perspective to that of Shared Experience's *Brontë* and the *Jane Eyre* criticism quoted in the previous chapter. Instead of looking back from the perspective of the supposedly liberated present and finding fault with Charlotte Brontë for being the middle-class, ambitious woman who was able to write her novels, supernatural realism makes us all poor Jane, or even Bertha, still the victims of pernicious and persistent Victorian values.

In the light of these assumptions about Scottish and Irish exile and persecution, it follows that family history research involves, as Basu claims, a narrativization of the past, which acquires a coherence and meaning that is not intrinsic to the events.[92] Rather, this 'self-narration' is a generative act through which the self emerges.[93] Paradoxically, the narrating self may then choose to reject the notion of choice, and instead to see the process as a recovery of what was already there, waiting to be found.[94] As Basu notes, there is a correspondence here with False Memory Syndrome, the condition where, during psychoanalysis, episodes of sexual abuse in a patient's past are 'recovered', despite having never taken place. The link is that in both cases there is an assumption that if the pieces fit together as a story, then that story must be true. One invents a trauma to account for the symptoms of trauma.[95] Again, in my consideration of the misleading neatness of anecdote, I referred to the seductiveness of such pseudo-explanatory narratives, the 'perfect causality' that Jackson described in his student's work.

Part of the motivation for claiming a history of minority persecution and lost home is that one can find others with similar claims, and form face-to-face or online communities. In doing so, one also absorbs wider sets of values and assumptions about racial identity, characteristics, and places and dates of significance. Basu notes the profound sense of 'resonance' found by roots tourists on certain sites, which is variously rationalized as race memory, ancestral memory or genetic memory.[96] Rather than singling out a focus for ancestral feeling, the plays I have mentioned that explore resonances of place – *Intemperance*, *Gut Girls*, *Only a Matter of Time*, *Loveplay* – seem to be, as a group, doing the opposite. Collectively, they imply that Britain has Victorian resonances everywhere, in a remote field or beneath a uniform row of houses. Like Whiteread's house, the nation seems to be crammed solid with Victorian memory and history.

Remaking the Victorians

This final section aims to further the proposition that the residues of the Victorian – in terms of people, institutions and the built environment – can at times threaten to overwhelm the modern British sense of identity. Such an exploration might best begin, once more, with Raphael Samuel's *Theatres of Memory*, where he coins the term 'retrochic' to describe everything from faux-Victorian streetlights and cobbles to heritage centres and country kitchens. For our purposes, his astute comment that 'Beneath the period dress, a great deal of what passes for restoration is modernization in disguise, a continuation and extension of the 1950s ideals of open-plan living, rather than a reversal of them' is worth bearing in mind.[97] We evoke the Victorians, in architecture and design, on our own terms, taking only what is in some sense useful. Again, we might recall Parker's exhibits, with their claims to authenticity: it is the postmodern evocation of the Victorian, the claiming of connection (again, we think of Basu's family history hobbyists), that excites rather than the genuine, prosaic, undifferentiated remnants.

St Pancras Station

A further example is the contemporary interest in the Victorians as visionary engineers, as exemplified by the increased profile of Isambard Kingdom Brunel. Jeremy Clarkson presented a television programme about him in 2002, and – possibly in part as a result of this celebrity endorsement – he finished second (to Winston Churchill) in that year's BBC poll of 'greatest Britons'.[98] Brunel has also been kept in the public eye by lottery-funded plans to renovate the SS *Great Britain* in Bristol Docks.[99] The notion of the Victorians as creators of the shape and structure of our built environment is perhaps best exemplified by the recent restoration and modernization of London's St Pancras Station. Work started on this project in 2001, and it cost £800m; the transport system for which it is intended to act as a hub, 'High Speed 1', is expected to cost £5.8 billion, making it the UK's largest construction project in history and the first major railway project for 100 years.[100] Therefore, there is a sense that the British are harking back to their Victorian past as a touchstone for contemporary success.

The renovated station is, as one might expect, a striking mixture of old architecture and new technology. Care has been taken to leave the brickwork of the station building exposed; as a consequence, the coffee shops and snack bars that line the ground floor have their corporate territory marked by huge sheets of reinforced glass reaching to the top of the arches. The result lends a sense of the impermanence of modern retail, almost an attempt to dematerialize commerce. The glass, of course, also lets in the maximum amount of light, but one might conjecture that it has a further figurative meaning in that it suggests (appropriately for the Eurostar terminus) a sense of 'travel without barriers', of free-ranging, wireless modernity where one is plugged in but floating free. It is interesting to note, for instance, the difference between the original first floor ticket hall, with its wooden door frames, carefully restored brass fittings and frosted glass, and the new one, directly below it, with its bilingual signage, clear glass walls and sliding entrance doors (Figure 2). Similarly, the much-publicized champagne bar on the first floor has no enclosure (Figure 3), allowing patrons to see and be seen – to slide off a stool and onto a high-speed train to the Continent in minutes. And the self-styled 'bar and kitchen', the Baby Betjeman, is far from the dinginess of,

Figure 2 Original first-floor ticket hall with new Eurostar ticket hall beneath it, St. Pancras Station, London

Figure 3 The champagne bar with Eurostar platforms in the distance, St. Pancras Station, London

say, the William Shakespeare pub on the concourse at Birmingham New Street station: the former has no walls, not even glass ones, and provides a resting place from which to view Paul Day's huge bronze sculpture, 'The Meeting Place'.

The lionization of John Betjeman, who campaigned to save St Pancras in the middle years of the twentieth century when the anti-Victorian modernizing impulse was at its height, is a distinctive feature in the new station; he is materialized as a statue, and lines from his poems are embedded in the ground. There is a sense of gratitude in these tributes, of history having vindicated the lone voice against the tyranny of modernist brutalism, that is almost Churchillian in its profundity. Nevertheless, the quotations chosen do seem to suggest the sense of being overwhelmed by Britain's past that this book has been exploring: one refers to the feeling of being 'exultant, neutral, free' that can only be gained by going where 'the cliffs alone prevail'. The lines 'Beyond the throb of the engines is the throbbing heart of all', meanwhile, seem all the more poignant when set in stone, and used to welcome visitors to a state that palpably no longer contains the workshop of the world.

St Pancras was officially reopened in November 2007, precisely 40 years after it was declared a Grade I listed building, saved for the nation by figures like Nikolaus Pevsner and Betjeman. One of the station's most imposing features is the rebuilt station clock by Dent (Figure 4), the original having been sold to an American collector and accidentally smashed, the pieces kept by a retired railwayman in his garden since the 1970s.[101] It makes for a striking symbol of the cultural wish to, in a sense, arrest time's decay by making anew times past.

By way of contrast, we might think back to that heady atmosphere of 1967, and the concluding comments of David Cooper at the Congress on the Dialectics of Liberation, mentioned in Chapter 1. Cooper recalls

a story that Herbert Marcuse told us [at the congress]. During the Paris Commune, before they started shooting at people, the Communards shot at the clocks, at all the clocks in Paris, and they broke them. And they did this because they were putting an end to the time of the Others, the time of their rulers, and they were going to invent their own time.[102]

He claimed to see 'a vista beyond your sea of faces, going way out there. I see a vista of broken clocks. And now, I think, it is our time!'[103] Cooper and his fellow radicals can surely not have envisaged a twenty-first century vista of lovingly rebuilt replica clocks, but as we have

Figure 4   The new station clock, St. Pancras Station, London

seen, nostalgia altered the direction of British culture decisively in the intervening years.

Thus, in conclusion, the Victorians haunt our sense of ourselves as modern Britons, their walls and oak doors and brass fittings (even in replica) serving as reminders of past glories, optimism, expansiveness, and that the restorers hope a little of this spirit will rub off on the new project. However, I argue the opposite: that it is the Victorian, in a building like St Pancras Station, that has kept its solidity, renewed its sense of permanence, while we twenty-first-century travellers are the ephemeral, ghostly ones, drifting from glass enclosure to glass enclosure, from the kitchen area to the champagne area, with our cashless accounts, e-tickets and wireless devices, reaching the end of William Henry Barlow's shed structure and passing through what used to be the wall, into the new extension where the train awaits. We have made ourselves ghostly in order to make the Victorians solid again.

Conclusion: Restaging the Victorians

In most cases, in keeping with the 'thick description' principle, the previous chapters have concentrated on a 'snapshot' of how a series of theatrical manifestations of the Victorians functioned in their immediate cultural and political context. However, several styles from the 1970s and 1980s persist today as ways of representing the Victorians in performance, such as classic novel adaptation, while others survive in an altered form, as with live interpretation and biodrama. This conclusion also sets out some possibilities for how the Victorians, and their relationship with modernity, might change as the twenty-first century wears on. Picking up on themes from the final chapter, I consider the idea of Victorian solidity and modern ghostliness in site-specific performance, and argue for the continuing importance of the public forum of theatre using the Victorians as a way of articulating the relationship between private and public life.

Popular revivals

The plays that began this study, *Early Morning* and *The Ruling Class*, are rarely revived today, and as the first chapter suggested, this may well be because they are so strongly linked to that mid-twentieth-century impulse to reject the Victorians and all they were perceived to stand for, a cultural tide that was soon to turn. It may also be because, as the chapter noted, they date from a period of experimentation in British theatre, where the play and the happening seemed to overlap, and were playing with then-fashionable motifs like the anti-psychiatry movement, *Alice in Wonderland* and references to the censorship of Bond's previous play. Hence, difficult as they were to interpret then, they place an even greater burden of meaning-making on audiences now, and perhaps that effort is not felt to be worthwhile in terms of contemporary relevance by theatre producers and programmers at present.

Another aspect of the countercultural 1960s is worthy of comment here, however; the brief period of 'cool Britannia' in the mid-1990s, which helped propel a handful of so-called Britpop bands to national (and, at times, international) fame, was highly self-conscious about its Britishness (or, more precisely, its Englishness) being taken from late 1960s reference points. Blur paid musical homage to the Kinks and the Small Faces, while Oasis trumpeted their devotion to the Beatles.[1] Journalistic comment predictably attempted to map Tony Blair's rise as prime-minister-in-waiting to the 'feelgood factors' of the mid-1960s. What is striking, so many years on, is first the brevity of the cultural moment (all the major bands associated with Britpop were disowning the connection with 'cool Britannia' well before the end of that decade), and secondly the way in which it consolidated the status of the 1960s as a key decade in the formation of a modern national identity, certainly for the English. Victorian-inflected Swinging London offered an already-ironic, relatively shame-free rallying point for national pride.

Agit-prop revisited

In terms of agit-prop's use of the Victorians, discussed in Chapter 4, one recent major production appears to have revived the form, bringing many of the aspects of the neo-Victorian theatre of the late 1960s and 1970s to a contemporary audience. *Holding Fire*, performed at Shakespeare's Globe in July 2007, is a history of the early Victorian Chartist movement, intertwined with a love story between Lizzie, a flower-seller, and Will, a boot-boy. It also manages to weave in appearances by Friedrich Engels and Ira Aldridge. The production seemed very much like an immersive or promenade performance, such as *Lark Rise to Candleford* might have felt, with the audience made part of the action as a Punch and Judy show in the pit opens the play; or as a trio of folk-singers, with squeeze-box, fiddle and bagpipes, narrate the connecting sequences; or as a bare-knuckle prize-fight is held among the groundlings as government spies discuss their plans; or as the actors re-enact Chartist meetings among the audience in the balcony. The playwright, Jack Shepherd, had been a member of the Royal Court's English Stage Company during the Gaskill years, and even played Gladstone in the original production of *Early Morning*.[2] There is even a comic sequence where Queen Victoria and the soon-to-be Prince Albert perform a clog-dance and sing a duet, very much in the vein of Monty

Python or a late 1960s Bond play (this is, a moment later, revealed to be two servants in the Harrington household rehearsing the Christmas concert).[3]

Although *Holding Fire!* made full use of the performance possibilities of Shakespeare's Globe, it did feel as though a site-specific performance, which might have worked very well in a Victorian free-trade hall or corn exchange, had been oddly transplanted into a reconstructed Elizabethan space. The play featured so many recreations of speeches and meetings that, at times, it seemed like a historical re-enactment that might be performed at a heritage site, and the production invited audience response and involvement, as live interpretation often does. However, as playgoers, there seemed to be an expectation that they sit or stand in specified places, while as tourists many of them wished to move around, change their seating position, talk and take photographs as they would at a heritage site. Where a local, politically committed audience in the 1970s would have followed and responded to the play's political narrative, this international, more individuated audience of a generation later sought out the experience of heritage tourism, in whose patterns of behaviour they seemed quite at home.

Adaptation

Adaptations, too, could be said to have shifted ground since the 1980s/1990s peak of Dickens and Brontë novels. Kneehigh Theatre's recent productions of *A Matter of Life and Death* at the National Theatre and *Brief Encounter* at the Haymarket have explored the possibilities of adapting twentieth-century film classics for the stage, and Katie Mitchell's *Waves* at the National offered radical possibilities for adapting the twentieth-century modernist novel. Patrick Barlow's adaptation of John Buchan's *The Thirty-Nine Steps* at the Criterion Theatre is a further instance of the novels and films of the period up to 1950 now forming a productively distanced imaginative landscape.

Television has certainly moved away from the cycle of Dickens and Austen adaptations that defined the previous decade and more, an initiative that has been blamed on diminishing audiences for recent productions, such as *Little Dorrit*.[4] Indeed, the 2009 comedy-drama series about the Pre-Raphaelite Brotherhood, *Desperate Romantics*, actually featured a characterization of Dickens (by Mark Heap) that rendered him pompous and not a little smug: a far cry from being the BBC's Sunday night 'bread and butter'. There is now a well-worn path from neo-Victorian novel to television serialization, including the Sarah Waters novels and Michel Faber's *The Crimson Petal and the White*.[5] The retelling of the twentieth century (as well as the old BBC–ITV rivalry) has been revived by the popular and critical success of ITV's *Downton Abbey* and BBC1's *Upstairs Downstairs*, which picks up the family saga in the 1930s.

Site-specific Victorians

In terms of the guiding themes of Chapter 6, our consciousness of the landscape as haunted by Victorian enterprises and institutions might be said to have filtered into the practice of site-specific performance. In 1995, Deborah Warner directed a site-specific work in St Pancras Chambers as St Pancras Station in London was about to begin its renovation project,[6] and Dreamthinkspeak theatre company performed its adaptation of Dostoevsky's *Crime and Punishment, Underground*, at The Old Abattoir in Clerkenwell, London, using the large underground brick spaces, and variations in level and perspective, to create an absorbing and immersive experience. Perhaps the most acclaimed recent production in this vein was Punchdrunk's *The Masque of the Red Death* at the Battersea Arts Centre, which used the centre's Victorian building to create a detailed and menacing adaptation of Edgar Allan Poe's short stories. David Leddy's *Sub Rosa*, set in an Edinburgh townhouse and dealing with a Victorian actress and her doomed relationship with an employer, was also a critical success at the Edinburgh Festival in 2010.

Another variation on this theme of using Victorian spaces for their resonance is *Hysteria*, by the Brazilian Grupo XIX de Teatro, performed in June 2008 at the Great Hall of St Bartholomew's Hospital in London. The production, although an occasionally moving one that incorporated many of the female audience members into the performance, nevertheless raises questions about how distinctively Victorian spaces are used. The Great Hall's walls are covered with the names of philanthropists of the eighteenth and nineteenth centuries whose donations allowed that wing of the hospital to be built. Prominent among the names is Prince Albert, and a portrait hangs next to the plaque commemorating his gift of £50; there is also a bust of Queen Victoria in the room, as well as another large portrait of Edward VII. In the performance, however, we are told several times that we are in a mental institution in Brazil in the 1890s. The actual interactions with the space mainly consisted of the use of the balcony outside and the window ledges. The production could thus be seen as a form of reverse-colonization, where a theatre group brings a performance to another continent, and behaves as if the local Brazilian references still pertain, 'writing over' the history of the indigenous space in which they perform. Clearly, a balance must be struck between a building's general, atmospheric potential as a performance site, and its own specific history and resonance only to be used as settings for plays set in Victorian abattoirs. However, on the evidence of the productions mentioned, it seems unusual for Victorian spaces to actually be used to explore some aspect of Victorian life, rather than to be a backdrop, the assumed semiotics of which are 'haunting', 'industrial', 'decaying', 'decadent' or 'institutional'.

Invisible worlds

In the Introduction, I referred to an article by Martin Hewitt asserting that, contrary to recent historiographical dissent, the Victorian period does indeed exist as a cohesive historical category. I would like to refer further to some of his points in the article in order to draw together some concluding comments. First, Hewitt asserts that, to us, the Victorians seem to be a people with 'history' when contrasted with the post-modern, de-narrativized civilization of the twenty-first century, although, of course, the Victorians had their own anxieties about their place in history;[7] hence, as I have argued in this study, our eagerness to tell simple stories – anecdotes – about the Victorians in order to create a contrast with ourselves. Secondly, as Hewitt argues, modern notions of 'invisible worlds' – those that exist beyond human perception but that can be scientifically demonstrated to have rules of operation and tangible effects – arise in the Victorian period, destabilizing assumptions about what constitutes reality. As he states, 'Developments at the turn of the century' – x-rays, radioactivity, the discovery of the structure of the atom – 'called into question the meaningfulness of the visible.'[8] In this sense, as Hewitt suggests, H.G. Wells stands as one prophet of this 'post-visible' world,[9] and we might consider his short stories dating from the turn of the twentieth century, such as 'The Remarkable Case of Davidson's Eyes', 'The New Accelerator' and 'The Door in the Wall' – along with the novel *The Invisible Man* – as cases in point. This idea of a post-visible world and the limits of seeing is an important one, as the previous chapter explained, for stage realism, where something invisible – the 'real' forces of society under capitalism – must be rendered visible. As such, in its 'scientific' approach to the problems of humanity, the 'realist perspective which must stretch outside realism to make itself seen' is a child of the late Victorian age.

Shifting mental geographies

Thirdly, Hewitt argues that it was the 1830s and 1840s that produced the 'key mental geographies' of Victorian Britain – the domestic, the family, the opposition between public and private and the 'separate spheres' ideology.[10] It could be argued that only in the last 40 years have these 'mental geographies' come under strain and begun to reshape themselves. The parliamentary reforms on divorce, abortion and homosexuality in the late 1960s challenged the cultural dominance of the Victorian ideal of the 'nuclear family'. The growing 'individuation' of society since the 1980s, as discussed in Chapters 3 and 6, placed further strain on group ties, such as those to family and neighbourhood. And, as Chapter 6 then suggested, the advent of mobile working has made 'travel without borders' an attractive notion. This means that the technology of modern life increasingly involves a bringing of the private self into the public sphere, whether it be private telephone conversations conducted on a packed train, closed-circuit television monitoring our movements, social networking websites or participation in reality television shows. Yet the encouragement to make public our private lives comes at the same time as political party membership and voter turnout are at historically low levels. This is why the visual iconography of the Victorian is still a useful political tool in theatre. To take two fairly recent examples, Elizabeth Kuti's play *The Sugar Wife*, about a prosperous Dublin sugar and coffee merchant using American slave labour (performed at the Soho Theatre in 2005), and Jimmy McGovern's *King Cotton*, about the Manchester cotton trade's involvement in the American Civil War (performed at Salford Quays in 2007), are both dramas about the Victorians that are able to make connections between public and private life visible and explicit. This is because they evoke the pre-digital world of factories, slave ships and cash crops, where status is embodied in dress rather than concealed or homogenized as twenty-first-century fashion tends to make it, and where the connection between the international and the local is made relevant.

Hewitt's essay creates a coherent picture, as all history does, of how the late Victorians became 'modern' from our own, twenty-first-century perspective. Later generations will no doubt create other 'decisive decades', and one of these might well be the 1990s, when analogue methods of recording, communicating and storing information came to be surpassed by digital ones. As Matthew Sweet asks in his concluding part of *Inventing the Victorians*, 'Is there any way to liberate the Victorians from ... the approval of reactionaries and the hindsighted moralism of the progressives? Only perhaps to say that, one day, when the Victorians are no longer needed to fulfil this role, it will happen to us. In the next few decades of the twenty-first century, the stereotypes about the twentieth will begin to accrue and ossify ... What stereotypes will our grandchildren and great-grandchildren use to punish us for our shortcomings?'[11] These 'ossifying stereotypes' of the twentieth century might be beginning to be seen in the plays *The 39 Steps* and *A Matter of Life and Death*, mentioned above.

Feats of loneliness

Final consideration is due to one of the most interesting recent works of theatre making use of the Victorians, *Edward Gant's Amazing Feats of Loneliness* by Anthony Neilson, first staged at the Theatre Royal, Plymouth, and revived for a tour by Headlong Theatre in 2009. It can be read as a meditation on the place of theatre, and the place of Britain, in the world, both conceived in a twisted version of their Victorian pomp. The play revives a number of trends that had begun to peter out in stagings of the Victorians, not least the attraction of important contemporary playwrights for the period's tropes, as was so often the case in the 1960s and 1970s. The script presents itself, in knowing neo-Victorian fashion, as a rediscovered travelling show from 1881, transcribed by Neilson, and it features vivid character sketches in pseudo-Victorian prose. Taking us through a series of acts and stories, the play is provocatively scabrous and scatological, accommodating some deliberately ham-fisted political commentary, and flirting, in its post-PC way, with imperial stereotypes in the form of an Indian fakir, Ranjeev the Uncomplicated. The play ends with Gant's death, and with Neilson leaving it up to the actors to decide whether to take the curtain call in character (that crucial question of biodrama), and leaving it up to the audience to decide whether the performance should be taken 'as truth' or as an artifice created by Gant (and, indeed, Neilson), 'ever the showman'. The piece's meta-theatricality is all the richer, I would suggest, when read through a history of the Victorians on the British stage, to which this book has made an opening contribution.

There are, of course, many other lines of enquiry in considering the connections between theatre, heritage and nostalgia. Indeed, there are plenty of other approaches to writing the history of staging the Victorians, which might include the revival history of Victorian stalwarts like *Charley's Aunt* in the twentieth and twenty-first centuries, or the success and impact of Victorian revivals (of Wilde or W.S. Gilbert, for instance) in Australia, the US and Canada. Nevertheless, this book has offered a framework for debate and development, and a network of explanations for why we continue to write, direct, perform and listen to the imagined voices of more than a century ago.

Notes

Introduction: Staging the Victorians – 'Angry Ghosts'?

1. There were productions at the Lowry, Salford, and at least three theatres in London; see theatre listings in *The Guardian* Guide, 11 December 2010, p. 33.
2. *Dracula* by Liz Lochhead (1985) was revived by Sell a Door Theatre Company at the Greenwich Playhouse in November 2010; Ken Hill's version of *The Invisible Man* (1991) was revived at Menier Chocolate Factory in February 2011.
3. See *Sherlock Holmes: The Death and Life* starring Roger Llewellyn (Yvonne Arnaud Theatre, Guildford), and the spoofs *Ha Ha Holmes* (Warehouse Theatre, Croydon) and *Move Over Moriarty* by Lip Service (UK tour, spring 2010).
4. *Andersen's English* by Sebastian Barry. Both plays then toured the UK.
5. See Ruth Little and Emily McLaughlin, *The Royal Court Theatre Inside Out*, p. 112.
6. Shellard, Dominic, Steven Nicholson and Miriam Handley, *The Lord Chamberlain Regrets*, pp. 134, 143.
7. Little and McLaughlin, *The Royal Court Theatre Inside Out*, p. 112.
8. See Michael Billington, p. 296, for a discussion of the way in which anti-Thatcherism has been retrospectively attached to the production's outlook.
9. Martin Hewitt, 'Why the Notion of Victorian Britain *Does* Make Sense', p. 396.
10. See Louisa Hadley, *Neo-Victorian Fiction and Historical Narrative*, pp. 25–6 for an overview of this debate. See also Raphael Samuel's 'The Return of History' in *Island Stories*, pp. 214–23, for a perspective on these issues from the Thatcher–Major years.
11. See, for instance, Ian Hislop's television series *Ian Hislop's Age of the Do-Gooders* (BBC2, 2010), an attempt to reclaim the period for its reforming and philanthropic heroes.
12. Hart-Davis, Adam, *What the Victorians Did For Us*, p. 9.
13. Hadley, *Neo-Victorian Fiction and Historical Narrative*, p. 7; Mike Leigh, 'Topsy-Turvy: A Personal Journey', p. 158.
14. I take the scope of my idea of the 'neo-Victorian' from the scholarly journal *Neo-Victorian Studies*, which states that while it is 'most evident in the proliferation of so-called neo-Victorian novels, the trend is also discernible in a recent abundance of nineteenth century biographies, the continuing allure of art movements such as the pre-Raphaelites, popular cinema productions and TV adaptations, and historical re-evaluations in such fields as medicine, psychology, sexology, and studies in cultural memory' (see 'Aims and Scope').
15. Cora Kaplan, *Victoriana: Histories, Fictions, Criticism*, p. 3.

16. Ann Heilmann and Mark Llewellyn, *Neo-Victorianism: The Victorians in the Twenty-First Century, 1999–2009*, p. 4.
17. Ibid., p. 5.
18. Ibid., p. 231.
19. Hadley, *Neo-Victorian Fiction and Historical Narrative*, p. 29.
20. Ibid.
21. Also, of course, early television drama based its claims to cultural significance on theatrical models, with works taken directly from the theatre and such series as *The Wednesday Play* and *Armchair Theatre*.
22. Hadley, *Neo-Victorian Fiction and Historical Narrative*, p. 159.
23. Matthew Rowlinson, 'Theory of Victorian Studies: Anachronism and Self-Reflexivity', p. 245.
24. Kate Flint, 'Why "Victorian"?: Response', p. 231.
25. Michel Foucault, *The Will to Knowledge: The History of Sexuality: 1*, p. 5.
26. Ibid., p. 57.
27. Michel Foucault, 'Questions of Method', p. 76.
28. John M. Ellis, 'Is Theory to Blame?', p. 99; Mark Bauerlein, 'Social Constructionism: Philosophy for the Academic Workplace', p. 343; Thomas Nagel, 'The Sleep of Reason', pp. 551–2.
29. Jonathan Gill Harris, 'Materialist Criticisms', *Shakespeare: An Oxford Guide*, p. 478.
30. Ibid.
31. Stephen J. Greenblatt, *Learning to Curse*, p. 170.
32. Ibid.
33. Quoted in Hugh Grady, 'Shakespeare Studies, 2005: A Situated Overview', p. 110; Harris, 'Materialist Criticisms', p. 482.
34. Harris, 'Materialist Criticisms', p. 481.
35. Grady, 'Shakespeare Studies, 2005: A Situated Overview', p. 114.
36. Ibid.
37. Ibid.
38. Hadley, *Neo-Victorian Fiction and Historical Narrative*, p. 18.
39. See, most controversially, the Private Finance Initiative begun in the New Labour years.
40. Although in Britain, in the wake of the ongoing credit crisis of September and October 2008 and the collapse of Northern Rock a year earlier, there was much talk of the British government temporarily nationalizing more banks, this 'nationalization' rescue scheme is, as indicated above, a long way from the post-war, welfare-state government model of, for example, steeply progressive income tax, permanently nationalized heavy industry and transport, a cradle-to-grave health service and means-tested, full maintenance grants for university students.
41. Erin O'Connor, 'Preface for a Post-Postcolonial Criticism', p. 305.
42. Matthew Sweet, *Inventing the Victorians*, pp. xiv, xii.
43. Ibid., p. xv.
44. Greenblatt, *Learning to Curse*, p. 5.
45. Ibid.
46. Ibid.
47. Ibid., p. 8.
48. Bratton, *New Readings in Theatre History*, p. 103.

49. Ibid., p. 102.
50. Ibid., pp. 102–3.
51. Schafer, *Lilian Baylis: A Biography*, p. 2.
52. Jackson, *The Story is True*, p. 110.
53. Ibid.
54. Ibid., p. 36.
55. Ibid., p. 34.
56. Ibid., p. 36; Bratton, *New Readings in Theatre History*, pp. 104, 105.
57. George Orwell, 'The Lion and the Unicorn', pp. 155–6.
58. Jackson, *The Story is True*, p. 113.
59. Hadley also uses the metaphor of the family to characterize our relationship to the Victorians now: 'the Victorians... seem to have moved from the position of oppressive parent-figures to benign grandparents' (p. 1).
60. Shelton Waldrep, 'The Uses and Misuses of Oscar Wilde', pp. 52, 50–52, 62. See also Richard A. Kaye, 'The Wilde Moment', for another consideration of Wilde's popularity as a dramatic subject.
61. Joyce McMillan, *The Traverse Theatre Story 1963–1988*, p. 41.
62. Ian Brown, *Scottish Theatre Since the Seventies*, p. 88.
63. Ibid., pp. 91, 97.
64. Ibid., p. 95.
65. Ibid., p. 97.
66. Nic Ros, 'Leaving the Twentieth Century: New Writing on the Welsh-Language Mainstage 1979–1995', p. 22; Charmian C. Savill, 'Brith Gof', p. 102; Anne-Marie Taylor, 'Welsh Theatre and the World', p. 115.
67. Heike Roms, 'Performing *Polis*: Theatre, Nationness and Civic Identity in Post-Devolution Wales', pp. 179–82; Lisa Lewis, 'Welsh-Language Production/Welsh-Language Performance: The Resistant Body'.
68. Edward Bond, 'Author's Preface', p. 8.

1   Staging the Bad Old Days

1. Robert Hewison, *The Heritage Industry*, p. 47.
2. Raphael Samuel, *Theatres of Memory*, pp. 91, 95, 114, 77–8, 73, 182.
3. Ibid., p. 8.
4. Miles Taylor, 'Introduction', p. 8.
5. Nicholas de Jongh, *Politics, Prudery and Perversions*, p. 231.
6. Ruth Little and Emily McLaughlin, *The Royal Court Inside and Out*, p. 112.
7. Although the script for *Narrow Road* says it is set in Japan in the 'seventeenth, eighteenth or nineteenth centuries' (Bond, *Narrow Road to the Deep North*, p. 172), the characters of the Commodore and his evangelical wife/sister Georgiana appear Victorian. It is of Gilbert and Sullivan that we tend to think when picturing pompous sea-captains and first lords of the Admiralty, and indeed, in the revised edition of Bond's play, after Shogo's execution, the stage directions suggest a Sullivan medley, played out of tune (p. 222). Although W.S. Gilbert steered clear of explicit discussion of religion among his characters, Georgiana in *Narrow Road* might easily be related to the ultra-severe and 'respectable' Lady Sophy from the

lesser-known work *Utopia, Limited* (1893). And, of course, Shogo's rule exercises power far more savagely, but just as autocratically, as the Mikado, who expresses his intention to 'let the punishment fit the crime' (William Schwenck Gilbert and Arthur Seymour Sullivan, *Complete Plays*, p. 331). Georgiana is also dressed, according to a picture illustrating a review in *The Best of Plays and Players* ('The Director in Rep', pp. 22–6), in Victorian style, wearing floor-length black.

8. Edward Bond, *Early Morning*, pp. 223, 217.
9. Ibid., p. 223.
10. Quoted in Dominic Shellard et al., *The Lord Chamberlain Regrets*, p. 156.
11. De Jongh, *Politics, Prudery and Perversions*, p. 25.
12. Ibid., p. 31.
13. Shellard et al., *The Lord Chamberlain Regrets*, p. 134. The four plays in question were *The Querulous Queens* by Madge Pemberton, 1945; *Birthday Bouquet* by Ginsbury and Maschwitz, 1950; *My Good Brown* by Kemp, 1952; and *Old Ladies Meet*, author and date unrecorded.
14. Ibid., p. 137, 138.
15. De Jongh, *Politics, Prudery and Perversions*, p. 137.
16. See 'John Bird may play "lesbian" Victoria'.
17. Shellard et al., *The Lord Chamberlain Regrets*, p. 173; de Jongh, *Politics, Prudery and Perversions*, p. 236.
18. De Jongh, pp. 234–5.
19. Ibid., p. 235.
20. Quoted in Niloufer Harben, *Twentieth Century English History Plays*, p. 223.
21. See 'Review of *Early Morning*'.
22. Quoted in Harben, p. 241; 'Overwhelmed by Hypocrisy' (interview with Edward Bond).
23. See Gerard Garrett, 'Censored playwright wins £1000 award'.
24. Bond, *Selections from the Notebooks of Edward Bond*. Vol. 1, pp. 89–90.
25. Bond, *Early Morning*, p. 144.
26. Ibid., p. 175.
27. Ibid., p. 141.
28. Ibid., p. 185.
29. Ibid., pp. 159, 204.
30. Ibid., p. 206.
31. Ibid., p. 215.
32. Ibid., p. 219.
33. Ibid., p. 223.
34. Michael Patterson, 'Early Morning', pp. 129–30.
35. Catherine Itzin, *Stages in the Revolution*, p. 79.
36. Sigmund Freud, *Introductory Lectures*, p. 180.
37. Bond, *Early Morning*, p. 155.
38. Ibid., p. 201.
39. Freud, quoted in Josh Cohen, *How to Read Freud*, p. 22.
40. Bond, *Early Morning*, pp. 184–7, 194; Freud, *Introductory Lectures*, p. 182.
41. Ibid., p. 187.
42. Ian MacDonald, *Revolution in the Head*, pp. 18–22; Robert Hewison, *Too Much*, p. 140; Little and McLaughlin, p. 139.
43. Dominic Sandbrook, *White Heat*, p. 414.

44. The same year, Cook and Sellers also starred alongside Dudley Moore, John Mills and Ralph Richardson in *The Wrong Box*, a farcical chase movie making further comic capital out of popular notions of Victorian eccentricity, sexual repression, hypocrisy and greed. Completing a trio of Peter Sellers-related projects lampooning the Victorians, it has recently been revealed that 'The Phantom Raspberry Blower of Old London Town', a Jack the Ripper-inspired spoof serial featured on the sketch show *The Two Ronnies* in 1976, was originally written by Spike Milligan as a comeback project for the stars of *The Goon Show*. Sellers apparently turned down the reunion, but the draft manuscript, offered for sale by Sotheby's, was 'probably created between 1967 and 1969', according to the firm's specialist Gabriel Heaton (Jack Malvern, 'Pthpthpthpthp!', p. 17).

45. Humphrey Carpenter, *That Was Satire That Was*, p. 167. *Monty Python's Flying Circus* also frequently featured, in Terry Gilliam's animations, 'colourised' versions of Victorian and Edwardian sepia photographs, which are made to chase, eat or fondle each other – another instance of the 1960s and 1970s determination to 'unmask' Victorian sexuality.

46. John McGrath, *The Cheviot, the Stag and the Black, Black Oil*, p. 37.

47. See Ian Herbert, Christine Baxter and Robert E. Finlay, eds., *Who's Who in the Theatre: Playbills* 1976–9. See 'A thin line between farce and horror'.

48. See Herbert et al. (eds.), *Who's Who in the Theatre: Playbills* 1976–9.

49. Ibid., see 'The Director in Rep', pp. 20–2.

50. Peter Barnes, *The Ruling Class*, p. 113. In the film, they are corpses in various stages of decomposition.

51. R.D. Laing, quoted in Robert Hewison, *Too Much*, p. 134; Laing, 'The Obvious', p. 13.

52. Ibid., p. 19.

53. See David Cooper, 'Introduction', p. 7.

54. Ibid., p. 11.

55. Barnes, p. 83.

56. Ibid., pp. 36, 74.

57. Ibid., p. 107.

58. Ibid., pp. 103, 46.

59. Ibid., p. 115.

60. Ibid., p. 114.

61. Ibid., p. 31.

62. Brian Woolland, *Dark Attractions*, p. 34.

63. Barnes, p. 102.

64. Jonathon Green, *All Dressed Up*, p. 85.

65. Ibid., p. 74.

66. Barnes, pp. 42, 51, 75, 88, 111, 113. In the film, Jack goes hunting in a top hat and cape, and he surrounds himself with 'Victorian bric-a-brac'.

67. Michael Billington, *State of the* Nation, p. 186.

68. Bond, 'Author's Preface', p. 8.

69. Jeffrey Richards, 'Dickens – Our Contemporary', p. 346.

70. Ibid.

71. Samuel, *Theatres of Memory*, pp. 421, 422.

72. Similarly, 'Who Will Buy?' can be interpreted along these lines, where there is a conflation in meaning of buying (from the street traders) this morning

and buying the morning: 'Who will tie it up with a ribbon/And put it in a box for me?'. It can be read as a commentary on the nascent consumer society of Victorian London, and the logical extension of this: the wish to commodify and privatize experience: the only thing that cannot be bought in this middle-class mercantile world is the morning itself.

73. This image was used as a front drop for the original Broadway production of Sondheim and Wheeler's *Sweeney Todd* (Stephen Sondheim and Hugh Wheeler, *Sweeney Todd*, p. 113).
74. Asa Briggs, *A Social History of England*, pp. 313–5.
75. Hewison, *The Heritage Industry*, p. 37.
76. Quoted in Sandbrook, *White Heat*, pp. 566, 568.
77. Ibid., pp. 589, 591.
78. Ibid., p. 586.
79. Ibid., p. 583.
80. Ibid., p. 580.
81. Samuel, *Theatres of Memory*, p. 68.
82. Paul Addison, *No Turning Back*, p. 142.
83. Quoted in Hewison, *The Heritage Industry*, p. 45. See also Paul Addison, who notes, 'Rarely were council tenants or the general public invited to express their own preferences... [the high-rise blocks] seem to have had a psychologically damaging effect, as though they were felt to be prisons or workhouses rather than homes' (Addison, p. 165). Addison's language here points to a paternalistic Victorian authoritarianism cloaked in the guise of progress.
84. Ibid., p. 39.
85. Hewison, *The Heritage Industry*, p. 38. Addison quotes Anthony Sampson's startlingly cavalier claim that the railways 'are the most embarrassing of all Britain's Victorian leftovers' as indicative of the climate of thought that led to the 'Beeching axe' (Addison, pp. 143–4).
86. Hewison, *The Heritage Industry*, p. 36; Sandbrook, *White Heat*, p. 599.
87. Ibid., p. 598.
88. Samuel, *Theatres of Memory*, p. 68.
89. Raymond Williams, *The Country and the City*, pp. 194, 202.
90. Samuel, *Theatres of Memory*, pp. 51–2.
91. Addison, pp. 184–5.
92. John Gardiner, 'Theme-Park Victoriana', pp. 175–6.
93. Samuel, *Theatres of Memory*, p. 91.
94. Sandbrook, *White Heat*, p. 425.
95. Ibid., pp. 424–5.
96. Ibid., pp. 410, 249, 250.
97. Ibid., pp. 428, 430.
98. Samuel, *Theatres of Memory*, p. 96. Green, *All Dressed Up*, p. 79.
99. John Gardiner, 'Theme-Park Victoriana', p. 169.
100. Ibid., p. 175.
101. Ian MacDonald, *Revolution in the Head*, p. 184. The album, of course, features a song, 'Being for the Benefit of Mr Kite!', based around the wording of a Victorian circus poster (Ibid., p. 188).
102. This ambivalence is captured very well on the Kinks' 1968 album, *The Kinks Are the Village Green Preservation Society*, the title of which echoes

such august Victorian institutions as the Commons, Footpaths and Open Spaces Preservation Society (founded 1865), the Society for the Protection of Ancient Buildings (1877) and the National Trust (1895) (Hewison, *The Heritage* Industry, p. 26). In the title song's arch, riddling lyrics, songwriter Davies seems to wish to save, in particular, the most egregious villains of Victorian adventure fiction rather than the heroes. Other lines in the song resonate more clearly with the concerns of this chapter, not only declaring the Society 'the office block persecution affinity', but 'the skyscraper condemnation affiliates'. In the song 'Village Green', meanwhile, Davies seems to present Englishness as threatened by Americanization. Such British cultural consciousness, even while playing American-derived rock music, can also be heard in Cream's album *Disraeli Gears* (1967), which, along with its Victorian prime minister title pun, contains a very English novelty pub-piano song, 'Mother's Lament', after ten tracks of blues-rock.

The Kinks are also an example of rock music's interest in the pastoral, folk music and returning to nature in the period – another strain of the turning away from modernity – in such songs as 'Animal Farm', 'Village Green' and 'Apeman'. As Ian MacDonald observes, it was the Beatles' single 'Strawberry Fields Forever' in 1967 that 'effectively inaugurated the English pastoral mood explored in the late sixties by groups like Pink Floyd, Traffic, Family and Fairport Convention' (MacDonald, pp. 173–3). Many of these artists' songs, like 'Strawberry Fields', have a 'child's-eye view' (Ibid., p. 173), another element of nostalgia to be found in late 1960s songs, like David Bowie's 'When I'm Five', 'Uncle Arthur' and 'There Is A Happy Land', and one of the best-selling albums of 1968, the Incredible String Band's *The Hangman's Beautiful Daughter*.

103. Clare Lockhart (dir.), *The 1970s Edwardian Resurrection*.
104. Billington, *State of the* Nation, p. 229; Addison, *No Turning Back*, p. 136; Sandbrook, *White Heat*, p. 572.
105. Sandbrook, *White Heat*, pp. 614, 616.
106. Ibid., p. 573.
107. Ibid., pp. 574–5.
108. Quoted in Sandbrook, *White Heat*, p. 640. See also Addison, *No Turning Back*, pp. 250–3.
109. Sandbrook, *White Heat*, pp. 644, 738.
110. Once again, there is a parallel in The Kinks' recorded output: *Arthur, or the Decline and Fall of the British Empire* (1969) opens with the profoundly ambivalent 'Victoria' and proceeds through the two world wars ('Some Mother's Son', 'Mr Churchill Said') and into the post-rationing age of consumerism ('Shangri-La').
111. See Bill Bain (dir.), *The Duchess of Duke Street*, series 1, episode 1.
112. Claude Whatham (dir.), *Disraeli: Portrait of a Romantic*, episode 1.
113. Peter Graham Scott (dir.), *The Onedin Line*, episode 1.
114. Noel Greig, *The Dear Love of Comrades*, pp. 83–90.
115. Ibid., p. 134.
116. Samuel, *Theatres of Memory*, p. 163.
117. As if to emphasize the dizzying fluidity of roles in Carpenter's South Yorkshire farmhouse, his three lovers all happen to be called George; two of them are married, and the silence around Fanny and, in particular, Lucy's

misery over her miscarriage and her husband's neglect of her (p.138, p.113) is one of the most striking aspects of the play.

118. John Downie, *Mary Ann: An Elegy*, pp. 84–7, 96–9, 101–2, 108–17.
119. Ibid., pp. 32, 81.
120. Keith Dewhurst, *Lark Rise to Candleford*, p. 52. The criticism is made in Richard H. Palmer, *The Contemporary British History Play*, p. 68.
121. Dewhurst, *Lark Rise to Candleford*, pp. ix.
122. Ibid., pp. 116–18.
123. Ibid, p. 115.
124. Ibid., pp. 38, 67.
125. Ibid., pp. 10, 16.
126. Samuel, *Theatres of Memory*, p. 193.
127. MacDonald, *Revolution in the Head*, p. 29.
128. Cora Kaplan, *Victoriana*, p. 5.

2   Staging the Empire

1. See Little and McLaughlin, *The Royal Court Theatre Inside Out*, p. 112.
2. See 'Historical Archive'.
3. See Dominic Shellard, et al., *The Lord Chamberlain Regrets*, pp. 170–1, 134, 171, 137.
4. Quoted in Little and McLaughlin, *The Royal Court Theatre Inside Out*, p. 112.
5. De Jongh, *Politics*, p. 251.
6. Michael Billington, *State of the Nation*, pp. 305–6.
7. Samuel, *Theatres of Memory, Vol. II*, p. 91.
8. Michel Foucault, *The History of Sexuality: 1*, p. 3.
9. Ibid., p. 6.
10. Ibid., p. 7.
11. See Hewison, *Too Much*, p. 126; Sandbrook, *White Heat*, p. 319.
12. See Jonathon Green, *All Dressed Up*, pp. 132, 150; Sandbrook, *White Heat*, pp. 511–2. The 'School Kids Issue' was the subject of a much-debated obscenity trail in 1971, where the magazine's editors, Richard Neville, Felix Dennis and Jim Anderson, were defended by John Mortimer.
13. Herbert Marcuse, 'Essay on Liberation' p. 23; 'Affluent Society' p. 178.
14. Ibid., p. 185.
15. Erich Fromm, *The Essential Fromm*, p. 31.
16. Ibid., pp. 34, 27.
17. Benjamin Barber, *Consumed*, pp. 96, 22.
18. However, there is still debate as to how situationist in nature the majority of the occupations, strikes, marches and 'happenings' were (see Richard Lane, *Jean Baudrillard*, pp. 19–22).
19. Guy Debord, *The Society of the Spectacle*, p. 33.
20. Ibid., pp. 34, 126.
21. See Paul Addison, *No Turning Back*, pp. 196–7, for a discussion of the use of the term.
22. By the 1970s, Bond's drama did come to reflect a more consistent Marxist position, as demonstrated in other historical dramas, like *Bingo* and *The Fool*,

and Bond's prefaces to these works, where he writes of art, like the land, being taken away from the masses (*Plays 3*, p. 76), creating 'a scientific barbarism' (ibid., p. 71) where a worker has to 'reduce[e] himself to a tool for two-thirds of his awake life' (ibid., p. 69).

23. See Karl Marx, *Capital*, p. 274.
24. Marx, 'Future Results', p. 16.
25. Charles Wood, *'H'; being Monologues at Front of Burning Cities*, pp. 61, 82, 162.
26. Ibid., p. 121.
27. Ibid., p. 127.
28. Ibid.
29. Ibid., pp. 129–31.
30. Ibid., pp. 92–3.
31. Ibid., p. 83.
32. Ibid., p. 156.
33. Ibid., p. 179.
34. Tony Harrison, *Phaedra Britannica*, pp. 181, 192.
35. See Cohen, *How to Read Freud*, p. 84.
36. David Pownall, *Livingstone and Sechele*, p. 129.
37. The programme shows a cartoon Livingstone and Sechele on bright yellow paper, looking a little like a colonial Punch and Judy show ('Livingstone and Sechele').
38. Cohen, *How to Read Freud*, pp. 83, 84.
39. Caryl Churchill, *Cloud Nine*, p. 288.
40. Gray, p. 67; Wood, *'H'*, p. 102.
41. Marx, *Capital*, pp. 166, 174, 322.
42. Sondheim and Wheeler, *Sweeney Todd*, p. 105.
43. Foucault, *The History of Sexuality: 1*, p. 59.
44. Ibid., p. 67.
45. Foucault, *The History of Sexuality: 2*, p. 4.
46. Foucault, *The History of Sexuality: 1*, p. 152.
47. Ibid., pp. 152–3.
48. Ibid., p. 157.
49. Ibid., p. 154.
50. Ibid., p. 158.
51. Ibid., p. 157.
52. Wood, *'H'*, pp. 145–6.
53. Bond, *Narrow* Road, p. 223. Interpretation is made more problematic here by the fact that Georgiana is mad at this point, but her pronouncements while mad do relate to her experiences in the play; they are not gibberish, nor do they appear to be the opposite of what she thinks or wants; instead she closes her eyes and prays again, offering to 'lead a cleaner life' (ibid.).
54. Bond, *Early Morning*, pp. 153–4.
55. We might also add, as a co-text illustrating the supposedly humorous use of rape at time, the *Oz* 'School Kids Issue', which depicted 'a rampant Rupert Bear ... violently raping an American comic character, Gipsy Granny' (Billington, *State of the Nation*, p. 229).
56. Little and McLaughlin, *The Royal Court Theatre Inside Out*, p. 196.
57. *Cloud Nine* was far from being an instant classic on its first production; *Punch* worried that it supported 'every sexual movement at once, suggesting

that incest, homosexuality and feminism are equal' (review of *Cloud Nine*), and Robert Cushman thought that the 'author and company do not seem to have made up their minds'. What Cushman and Billington's comments in their reviews, as found in the V&A file on *Cloud* Nine, are implying is that it was fashionable by the late 1970s to laugh at Victorian 'hang-ups', and that this had become the new orthodoxy. Indeed, Cushman seems to have been nostalgically reminded in this instance of plays like *'H'* and *Narrow Road*.

58. Churchill, *Cloud Nine*, p. 270.
59. Ibid, p. 262.
60. Review of *The Rear Column*.
61. Review of *Ipi Tombi*; 'We are a happy people'; Hope-Wallace. The opening minutes of the film *Zulu* depict a mass Zulu wedding that seems to have something in common with the kind of prurience to which *Ipi Tombi* appealed. The film sequence features slow pans of bare-breasted tribeswomen and cutaways to the concerned faces of the missionary, Mr Witt, and his daughter, Margareta.
62. Linda Christmas, 'Rhapsody in Black'.
63. '"Ipi Tombi" Rebels in Own Show'.
64. Dominic Hingorani, p. 175.
65. Ibid.
66. Macmillan, p. 50; Roland Rees, p. 101; Macmillan, p. 50.
67. Caryl Philips,'I Could Have Been a Playwright', pp. 40–3.
68. Chesney in *The Victorian Underworld*, quoted in Hall et al., *Policing the Crisis: Mugging, the State, and Law and Order*, p. 4.
69. Quoted in Hall et al., *Policing the Crisis: Mugging, the State, and Law and Order*, p. 16.
70. Ibid, p. 34.
71. Ibid., p. 50.
72. Sandbrook, *White Heat*, pp. 627, 470.
73. *Hudson Report*, 1974, quoted in James Walvin, *Victorian Values*, p. 5.
74. Hall et al., *Policing the Crisis: Mugging, the State, and Law and Order*, p. 140–7.
75. Ibid., pp. 149, 147.
76. Ibid., p. 158.
77. Ibid., p. 161.
78. For instance, decolonized states of the former British Empire during the 1960s included Nigeria in 1960, Sierra Leone in 1961, Jamaica, Trinidad and Tobago and Uganda in 1962; Kenya and Malaysia in 1963, Malta, Malawi and Tanzania (united with Zanzibar) in 1964; Gambia in 1965; and Lesotho, Guyana and Botswana in 1966.
79. Jon Savage, *England's Dreaming*, pp. 364–5, 266–7.
80. Hall et al., *Policing the Crisis: Mugging, the State, and Law and Order*, pp. 164, 165.
81. See Sandbrook, *White Heat*, pp. 647.
82. Hall et al., *Policing the Crisis: Mugging, the State, and Law and Order*, pp. 163–4.
83. Sandbrook, *White Heat*, p. 547. See also Addison, pp. 201–2.
84. Sandbrook, *White Heat*, pp. 647, 559.
85. Michael Billington, *State of the Nation*, p. 322.

3 Staging Dickens

1. James Thompson, 'The BBC and the Victorians', John Gardiner, *The Victorians*, p. 161.
2. As the literary scholar Andrew Sanders notes, Dickensian as a term 'has achieved a unique and unrivalled breadth of application', from Christmases to schools to hospitals (Sanders, *Charles Dickens*, p. 177).
3. Peter Ackroyd, *The Mystery of Charles Dickens* [DVD].
4. See David Hare, *Obedience, Struggle and Revolt*, pp. 145–71.
5. Ricks quoted in Fred Inglis, *Raymond Williams*, p. 237.
6. Quoted in John Higgins, *The Raymond Williams Reader*, p. 33.
7. Quoted in ibid., p. 40.
8. Fred Inglis, pp. 220, 221, 238.
9. As Inglis demonstrates: ibid., p. 247.
10. Raymond Williams, *The Country and the City*, p. 191.
11. Ibid., p. 192. There is an implicit suggestion in the use of the term 'developed fiction' that only Dickens's later, more realist novels, as opposed to the earlier, more picaresque works, are 'developed', as if Dickens was slowly evolving into a higher form of novelist, rather more like George Eliot.
12. Ibid., pp. 194, 198.
13. Ibid., pp. 192–3.
14. Quoted in Higgins, *The Raymond Williams Reader*, pp. 121, 123.
15. Jennifer Hayward, *Consuming Pleasures*, p. 51.
16. Ibid., pp. 45–6.
17. Williams, *The Country and the City*, pp. 202–20.
18. Raymond Williams, *Keywords*, p. 76.
19. The journalist Stephen Poole has detailed this rhetorical generalization of the word 'community' in his book *Unspeak*, pp. 25–40.
20. D.G. Meyers, 'Bad Writing', p. 357.
21. Catherine Itzin, *Stages in the Revolution*, p. 339. Robert Hewison also lists a series of moves in the 1980s that collectively sent out the same message: Richard Hoggart effectively being dismissed as vice-chairman of the Arts Council in 1982, the departure of Sir Roy Shaw the following year, and their replacement with more conservatively inclined figures; the abolition of the Greater London Council in 1986; rate-capping, which encouraged local authorities to reduce spending on 'non-essentials' (Hewison, *The Heritage Industry*, pp. 113, 116, 120.
22. Michael Billington, *State of the Nation*, p. 297.
23. *Theatre Record*, 1986, 6, p. 23.
24. David Edgar, 'Adapting Nickleby', p. 150.
25. James Procter, *Stuart Hall*, p. 97.
26. 'New times' features in Hall's conception of Thatcherism as 'regressive modernisation' in *The Hard Road to Renewal: Thatcherism and the Crisis of the Left*.
27. See Janine Gibson, 'Style Bible of the 80s Defined Ripping Era'.
28. See Suzy Feay, 'Suzi Feay: At the Sharp End'.
29. Stephen Jeffreys, *Charles Dickens's Hard Times*, p. 1.
30. Ibid., pp. 4, 68.

31. Ibid., p. vi.
32. See 'Tebbit, Norman' in *The Oxford Dictionary of Quotations*.
33. Samuel, 'Mrs Thatcher's Victorian Values', pp. 24, 26.
34. Adrian Jarvis, *Samuel Smiles and the Construction of Victorian Values*. London: Sutton, 1997, pp. 129–48, 136. Allen McLaurin has pointed out that Thatcher's former education secretary, Sir Keith Joseph, wrote the introduction for a Penguin Business Library edition of *Self-Help*, where he de-emphasized the philanthropy and peer-support that had been so important to Smiles in order to magnify the potential of the individual (McLaurin, 'Reworking "Work" in some Victorian Writing and Visual Art', p. 33).
35. See Margaret Thatcher, 'Speech to Zurich Economic Society'; 'Speech to Greater London Young Conservatives'.
36. Billington, *State of the Nation*, p. 297.
37. See Margaret Thatcher, 'Speech on Women in a Changing World (1st Dame Margery Corbett-Ashby Memorial Lecture)' *Margaret Thatcher Foundation*, 2005, Access date: 22 Aug 2006 <http://www.margaretthatcher.org/speeches/displaydocument.asp?docid=105007>; Margaret Thatcher and Brian Walden, 'TV Interview for London Weekend Television's *Weekend World* ("Victorian Values")' Transcript, *Margaret Thatcher Foundation*, 2005, Access date: 22 Aug 2006 <http://www.margaretthatcher.org/speeches/displaydocument.asp?docid=105087>.
38. Shirley Robin Letwin, *The Anatomy of Thatcherism*, pp. 32–3.
39. Ibid., p. 35.
40. Samuel, *Theatres of Memory*, p. 417.
41. David Edgar, 'Adapting Nickleby', p. 152.
42. Performance of *The Life and Adventures of Nicholas Nickleby* at Chichester Festival Theatre, Jonathan Church (dir.), 8 July 2006.
43. It has also not generally been noted that Smike gains much of his audience appeal from characteristics that had already been tried and tested in Bernard Pomerance's *The Elephant Man*, first produced three years earlier. Like Smike, Joseph Merrick labours under physical disabilities that draw attention to the actor's skill; both characters' speech is also laboured, and peppered with remarks of wisdom or simplicity that draw audience laughter (as experience brought home viewing the two plays close to one another: the Chichester Festival Theatre's revival of *Nicholas Nickleby* playing in London during early 2008 while Sheffield Theatres' revived *The Elephant Man* was touring). Finally, both Merrick and Smike dwell verbally on the concepts of being an 'outcast' and of having a 'home'.
44. In addition to the totemic significance that Smike was to take on in 'Hard Times' Britain, it seems likely that the patriotic song, 'England Arise!', which closes the first part of Edgar's play, and is part of the Crummles' faintly ridiculous performance, would come to be read in the early 1980s context as a comparison between the jingoism of the nineteenth century and its late twentieth-century variant in the wake of the Falklands conflict (even though the production's first few years, of course, pre-date the 'Falklands effect').
45. Edgar, 'Adapting Nickleby', p. 147.
46. Ibid., pp. 148, 147–8.

47. Ibid., p. 148. Ian Herbert, Christine Baxter and Robert E. Finlay, eds., *Who's Who in the Theatre: Playbills*. 1976–9.
48. David Edgar, 'Festivals of the Oppressed', p. 231. Alfreds, by contrast, even trained his actors to mime the presence of desks, spectacles and pianos. See Mike Alfreds, 'A Shared Experience: The Actor as Story-Teller', p. 19.
49. Jim Goddard (dir.), *The Life and Adventures of Nicholas Nickleby* (DVD).
50. Samuel, *Theatres of Memory*, p. 418.
51. Edgar, 'Adapting Nickleby', pp. 157–8.
52. 'Transformation was a key element of Mike Alfreds's doctrine: 'The actor, by transforming himself and therefore transcending himself, confirms that untapped potential within us all to understand and express ourselves beyond our apparent abilities' (Alfreds, 'A Shared Experience', p. 5).
53. Billington, *State of the Nation*, pp. 301, 299.
54. Of course, one did not have to go far at all to support the idea of Dickens, the man and his work, as 'theatrical'. Perhaps most importantly, there were Dickens's reading tours, in which his impersonation of his characters while narrating their actions bears a remarkable similarity to the Alfreds/Edgar narration technique. See, for instance, Philip Collins quoting a witness on how sharply Dickens 'isolated his parts' from the narrative, as Alfreds instructed his actors to do; and another reviewer's perception that the readings were 'running critical commentaries upon his own works' (Collins, *The Public Readings*, p. lxiii). Moreover, the reading tours, in an age of cuts, provided inspiration for another aspect of theatre's appropriation of Dickens: the one- and two-person show based on the readings. Miriam Margoyles' *Dickens' Women*, first performed at the Hampstead Theatre in 1991, and Simon Callow in Peter Ackroyd's *The Mystery of Charles Dickens* (2001) are two of the most famous, the latter having much in common with the 'biodrama' movement discussed in Chapter 4.
55. Edgar, 'Adapting Nickleby', p. 150.
56. Jeffreys, *Hard Times*, p. 1.
57. Declan Donnellan, *Great Expectations*, pp. 7, 26, 95, 96, 97. John Clifford, *Great Expectations*, pp. 234, 236, 237.
58. Neil Bartlett, *Charles Dickens' Oliver Twist*, p. 9.
59. Ibid., p. 7.
60. See *Theatre Record*, 1984, 4, p. 1000.
61. See *Theatre Record*, 1985, 5, pp. 6–7.
62. In the scene when Estella was introduced to society, she danced on a table to what sounded like an eastern European folk tune, while Miss Havisham held a 1950-style microphone and stand and commanded 'Love her!' (Alan Lyddiard, *Great Expectations*).
63. See *Theatre Record*, 1984, 4, p. 1001.
64. Robert Hewison, *The Heritage Industry*, p. 51.
65. R. Giddings, K. Selby and C. Wensley, *Screening the Novel*, p. 92.
66. John Caughie, *Television Drama: Realism, Modernism and British Culture*, p. 209.
67. Ibid., p. 204.
68. Giddings et al., *Screening the Novel* , p. 139.
69. Ibid., p. 139.
70. Graeme Burton, *Talking Television*, p. 284.

71. See 'Dame Judi Dench to star in BBC One drama Cranford Chronicles'.
72. See Justin Chadwick, *Bleak House*, episode 1, 0.41 min, 0.6 min; episode 1, 0.42 min.
73. Ross Devenish, *Bleak House*, episode 1, 0.35–8 min.
74. Justin Chadwick, *Bleak House*, episode 1, 0.15 min.
75. See, for instance, the description on the DVD sleeve of the Chadwick/Davies 2005 *Bleak House*.
76. Jonathan Bignell, *An Introduction to Television Studies*, p. 90.
77. Again, the DVD packaging features a review quotation from the *Times*, opining that 'this glorious adaptation transforms soap opera into art'. The BBC's own publicity highlighted this angle, as in 'Bleak House to Become BBC "Soap"'.
78. Giddings, Selby and Wensley, *Screening the Novel*, p. 45.
79. Ibid., p. 81.
80. John Caughie, *Television Drama*, p. 216.
81. See Charles Dickens, *Bleak House*, pp. 5–45.
82. See 'BBC Consumer: TV and Radio'.
83. Other casting choices invite comparisons between an actor's film and television work, as when Robert Lindsay, having taken the role of Fagin in a 1997 Palladium revival of *Oliver!*, played the character very differently in Alan Bleasdale's adaptation in 1999. Simon Callow, who played Count Fosco in the BBC's *The Woman in White*, took over the role (in a very different interpretation) in Andrew Lloyd-Webber's musical version at the Palace Theatre in 2005.
84. Ann Heilmann and Mark Llewellyn, *Neo-Victoriansim*, p. 229.
85. Sarah Cardwell, *Adaptation Revisited*, p. 87.
86. Ibid., p. 88.
87. Ibid., pp. 89, 68. This is especially likely when a film has produced a 'classic' version at an earlier point. The 1999 television serialization of *Oliver Twist* featured several visual quotations from the David Lean film of 1946, such as the opening shot of Oliver's mother running through the rain to a cliff-edge, and the panning to the right during Brownlow's meeting with Nancy at London Bridge, to reveal a spying Dodger hidden in an alcove.
88. Raymond Williams, *Television: Technology and Cultural Form*, pp. 84–5.
89. Ibid., pp. 86, 87, 111.
90. Marshall McLuhan, *Understanding Media*, p. 29.
91. Renny Rye, *Oliver Twist*, 0.47 min.
92. Colin Counsell, *Signs of Performance*, p. 56.
93. Ibid., p. 69.
94. John Gardiner, *The Victorians: An Age in Retrospect*, pp. 172–3.
95. Renny Rye, *Oliver Twist*, 1.04 min; 1.14 min.
96. Quoted in Samuel, 'Mrs Thatcher's Return', p. 13.
97. Williams, *Television: Technology and Cultural Form*, p. 39.
98. The focus in studio psychodrama on the individual's experience, it could also be argued, fits with the persistent use in GCSE literature courses of such coursework assignments as the character study, the retelling of the story from another character's perspective and the character diary.
99. Williams, *The Country and the City*, p. 18.

100. Edgar, 'Adapting Nickleby', p. 158.
101. Ibid., p. 159.
102. Ronald R. Thomas, 'Detection in the Victorian Novel', pp. 169, 176, 181.
103. Maryanne C. Ward, 'Romancing the Ending: Adaptations in Nineteenth-Century Closure', p. 18.
104. Ibid., p. 21.
105. Ibid., p. 22.
106. Paul Basu, *Highland Homecomings*, p. 157.
107. Samuel, *Theatres of Memory*, p. 385; for an indication of the penetration of the criminal underworld, see Cruikshank's famous illustration, 'Monks and the Jew' (Dickens, *Oliver Twist*, p. 257).
108. Conversely, Edgar's ending to *Nicholas Nickleby* challenges this anecdotalism, since, while Dickens's novel requires the extraordinary coincidence of Smike being Nicholas's cousin for his identity to be recuperable, Edgar suggests, through Nicholas's picking up of the boy in the snow, that each waif should be scrupulously saved, one at a time, despite the unlikelihood of that child being a blood relative.

4   Staging Life Stories

1. Heilmann and Llewellyn, *Neo-Victorianism: The Victorians in the Twenty-First Century, 1999–2009*, pp. 174–210.
2. Ibid., p. 210.
3. The phrase is again suggested by Heilmann and Llewellyn, p. 210.
4. Nigel Morris, 'Gothic (post)modernism and *The Prestige*'.
5. Christopher Nolan (dir., *The Prestige*, 1.59 min; 0.18 min.
6. This idea of the emergence of modernity is also a popular trope in other neo-Victorian films. *From Hell*, for instance, a retelling of the Jack the Ripper story based on the Alan Moore graphic novel, tells us twice that Jack the Ripper claims to have given birth to the twentieth century, and the story's portrayal of anti-Semitism and Masonic ritual seems to suggest a connection between the Ripper and the Nazi death camps. The more light-hearted action film *The League of Extraordinary Gentlemen* (Stephen Norrington, 2003), meanwhile, represents Captain Nemo's submarine as a piece of twentieth-century technology before its time, and the league conducts a high-speed car chase through Venice; in effect, part of their 'superhero' power comes from their having access to late twentieth-century technology in an 1899 world.
7. Nicholas Ridout, *Stage Fright, Animals, and Other Theatrical Problems*, p. 162.
8. Ibid., p. 167.
9. See Ian Herbert, Christine Baxter and Robert E. Finlay (eds.), *Who's Who in the Theatre: Playbills*, 1976–9.
10. Source: *Theatre Record*, 6–9.
11. Specifically, these were Michael Bath's *Black Nightingale* (Oval House, 1989), Linsay Kemp and David Haughton's *Alice*, 'a dream play for Lewis Carroll' (Sadler's Wells, 1989), Katrina Hendrey's *An Evening with Queen Victoria* (Greenwich Theatre, 1989), Jean Binnie's *Colours* (Leeds Playhouse, 1988),

Neil Bartlett's *A Vision of Love Revealed in Sleep* (Drill Hall, 1989), Richard Osborne's *Our Ellen* (Battersea Arts Centre, 1989) and Laurier Lister's *Fanny Kemble at Home* (Waterman's, Brentford, 1986).

12. David Edgar, 'Adapting Nickleby', p. 153.
13. Edgar, 'Provocative Acts', pp. 18, 19.
14. Roland Rees, *Fringe First: Pioneers of Fringe Theatre on Record*, pp. 78, 81, 63.
15. Edgar, 'Provocative Acts', p. 19.
16. *Theatre Record* 1981, 1, p. 166.
17. See *Theatre Record*, 1990, 10.
18. Edgar, 'Provocative Acts', p. 14.
19. Robert Hewison, *The Heritage Industry: Britain in a Climate of Decline*, p. 122.
20. Ibid., p. 126.
21. Edgar, 'Provocative Acts', p. 5.
22. Ibid., p. 7.
23. *My Dearest Kate* by Ellie Dickens (Edinburgh Fringe, 1983), a one-man version of *Heart of Darkness* by Philip Cade and John Tordoff (Edinburgh and The Gate, London, 1983) and Peter Gale's *Hopkins!* (New End Theatre, 1983, revived in 1984 at Regent's Park).
24. Brian Clark and Rudyard Kipling, *Kipling – East and West*, p. 2.
25. Ibid., p. 14.
26. Ibid., pp. 18, 27.
27. Ibid., p. 35.
28. Ibid., p. 3, 12.
29. Ibid., p. 3.
30. Ibid., p. 3.
31. Rudyard Kipling, *Rudyard Kipling's Verse*, p. 642.
32. Clark and Kipling, *Kipling – East and West*, pp. 17, 40, 36, 3.
33. *Theatre Record*, 1984, 4, p. 467.
34. Ibid., p. 468.
35. Ibid.
36. David Trotter, 'Something of Himself', p. 667.
37. *Theatre Record*, 1984, 4, p. 468; ibid., p. 1782.
38. John Peter, 'Prophet of Empire'; Clark and Kipling, *Kipling – East and West*, p. 50; David Trotter, 'Something of Himself', p. 667.
39. See 'Kipling Set For India', and Rosemary Say, *Theatre Record*, 1984, 4, p. 468.
40. Victoria Radin, 'St Mark's Gospel'.
41. See Roy Perrott, 'The Kipling Burden', and Gordon Gow, 'One Man and His Script', *Plays and Players*, June 1984, p. 10.
42. Christopher Robinson, 'A Singular Calling'.
43. See 'Ian McKellen Stage'.
44. Rosie Millard, 'Notebook', p. 42. Simon Callow, *Being an Actor*, p. 188.
45. Ibid., pp. 99–105, pp. 50–52. In 2010–11, Callow also toured in a one-man Shakespeare biodrama, *The Man from Stratford*, co-written with Shakespeare scholar Professor Jonathan Bate.
46. By 1989, the young actor writing and talking about himself had become such a cliché that it was parodied in Christopher Douglas and Nigel Planer's book and television series *I, an Actor*. The central figure of this spoof autobiography is Nicholas Craig, a composite figure bringing together Olivier's competitiveness with Kenneth Branagh's precociousness and what

it appears to view as McKellen's preciousness about Shakespeare (p. 101). Other incidents in the book may be reflecting a perception of actors like Sher as neurotic (compare the bookshop incident in *Year of the King* (p. 40) and *I, an Actor* (pp. 20–22)) and Callow as self-important and pretentious ('A Good Performance' in *Being an Actor* is mercilessly parodied in *I, an Actor* (pp. 45–6)). Perhaps another indication of the media's awareness of and irritation with actors talking about themselves, their struggles and their pet projects, is that the *Oxford English Dictionary* records the first printed use of the term 'luvvy' to describe an actor who is 'considered particularly effusive or affected' in 1990.

47. See 'Alec McCowen '.
48. Michael Owen, 'How Alec Hit the Road to Mandalay', p. 26.
49. Gordon Gow, 'One Man and His Script', p. 10.
50. See Roy Perrott, 'The Kipling Burden'.
51. Ibid.
52. George Orwell, 'Rudyard Kipling', p. 211.
53. For a succinct discussion of the contradictions in Thatcher's contention that Victorian values are 'timeless', see Hadley, pp. 9–10.
54. Margaret Thatcher, 'Speech to Conservative Party Conference'.
55. Quoted in Eric Hobsbawm, 'Falklands Fallout', p. 260.
56. Clark, p. 36.
57. As the *Guardian* reported it, 'Someone in the audience shouted that Mrs. Thatcher had "showed guts". Mr Kinnock replied: "It's a pity others had to leave theirs on the ground at Goose Green to prove it." ' (see Anne McHardy and Richard Norton-Taylor, 'Kinnock's Gibe Reopens Row over Falklands').
58. Andrew Rutherford, 'Select Bibliography'.
59. See Leigh Spencer, 'Pat Kirkwood: "Britain's Betty Grable" ', and 'Marie Lloyd Fails to Draw the Audience'.
60. Daniel Farson, *Marie Lloyd and Music Hall*, p. 167.
61. Geoffrey Moorhouse, 'No Laughing Matter', p. 5. Helen Dawson, 'Honeymoon Leftovers', p. 24.
62. See 'Memorial Plaque'.
63. Michael Parkin, 'Music Hall Hath Charms', p. 13.
64. Neville Cardus, 'A Little of What we Fancied', p. 9.
65. Joyce McMillan, *The Traverse Theatre Story 1963–88*, p. 144.
66. Robyn Archer and Rodney Fisher, *A Star is Torn*, no page numbers.
67. See Mike Margolis, *Bertie*.
68. This may go some way to explaining why neither the film's credits nor the BBC's online publicity listed a screenwriter.
69. Steve Trafford, *Marie: The Story of Marie Lloyd*, p. 9.
70. Peter Cheeseman, *The Knotty: A Musical Documentary*, introduction, pp. xi, v, vi–viii.
71. Nicholas de Jongh, 'The Human Jungle', p. 6.
72. Cheeseman, *The Knotty: A Musical Documentary*, p. vii.
73. The play also, perhaps rather incongruously, was included in the Royal Court's 'Come Together' festival of 1972 (see Chapter 1).
74. Cheeseman, *The Knotty: A Musical Documentary*, p. xii.
75. Catherine Itzin, *Stages in the Revolution*, p. 123.

76. John McGrath, *The Cheviot, the Stag and the Black, Black Oil*, pp. 37, 43.
77. See Lindsay Mackie, 'Scot's Gist'.
78. Itzin, *Stages in the Revolution*, p. 41.
79. Ibid., p. 42.
80. Ibid., pp. 141–2.
81. Red Ladder, *Taking our Time*, pp. vii, 51–2.
82. Itzin, *Stages in the Revolution*, pp. 48–50; Red Ladder, *Taking our Time*, p. 11.
83. Steve Trafford, *Marie: The Story of Marie Lloyd*, p. 13.
84. Ibid., pp. 28–9.
85. Ibid., pp. 22–4, 36.
86. Ibid., p. 45.
87. Christopher Nolan (dir.), *The Prestige*, 1 min.
88. Ridout, *Stage Fright, Animals, and Other Theatrical Problems*, p. 162.
89. Robin Davis, *Up in the Gallery*, p. 98.
90. Ridout, *Stage Fright, Animals, and Other Theatrical Problems*, pp. 161, 167.
91. Ibid., p. 164.
92. Ibid., p. 166.
93. Christopher Godwin, *The Guv'nor*, p. 1.
94. The magician, whose real name was William Robinson, died as the result of a 'bullet-catch' trick that went wrong. The trick became necessary, our narrator explains, because in 1918 men needed to believe that bullets do not kill (Raymond Yiu and Lee Warren, *The Original Chinese Conjuror*). The bullet-catch trick gone wrong, and Chung Ling Soo, both feature briefly in *The Prestige*.
95. Trafford, *Marie: The Story of Marie Lloyd*, pp. 40–1.
96. At the end of *Sing a Rude Song*, for instance, an ageing and ill Marie returns for an encore, announcing to the audience: 'All right then, girls and boys. I'll sing you a song. I sang it the first time I appeared in this house and that was a long time ago. I'll sing you that song; and it isn't a rude song! (*she sings unaccompanied*)' (Ned Sherrin and Caryl Brahms, *Sing a Rude Song*, p. 34).
97. Peter Brooks, *Realist Vision*, p. 24.
98. Ibid., p. 25.
99. Raphael Samuel, *Theatres of Memory*, p. 193.
100. These observations are based on two performances seen at the Performing Heritage conference at the University of Manchester, 3–5 April 2008. The performances were John Gregor's *The Gunner's Tale*, based on the experience of an English gunner at the Battle of Trafalgar, and *This Accursed Thing*, a performance on the history of slavery, which took place in the Manchester Museum and featured writer/performers Andrew Ashmore and Paul Etuka taking on a number of roles to explain British complicity in the slave trade during and after its abolition.
101. Catherine Hughes, 'Mirror Neurons and Simulation'.
102. Ridout, *Stage Fright, Animals, and Other Theatrical Problems*, p. 167.
103. Ellie O'Keeffe, 'From Pen and Ink to Flesh and Blood'. NB: *Kipling* toured to India, and Trafford's *Marie* had a run on Broadway.
104. For instance, Elizabeth Mansfield stated in a *Sunday Times Magazine* article that *Marie Lloyd: Queen of the Halls* was conceived in order to give her career a boost, and it has certainly been an effective vehicle for her; Mansfield still

regularly appears as Marie 20 years later (Anne Karpf, 'Dilly-Dallying with the Lusty Queen of the Halls', p. 52).

5 Staging the Brontës

1. See Daisy Bowie-Sell, 'Arts Cuts: Winners and Losers'.
2. See 'Shared Experience'. See Olivia Turnbull, *Bringing Down the House* (for instance, pp. 64–9, 210–11) for an account of the Arts Council's history of vacillating between the encouragement (and punishment) of innovation and experimentation, access and social programmes, and commercial success.
3. Spoofs and parodies are another means by which these supposedly defining characteristics circulate (albeit probably themselves influenced by adaptation practice). One might compare the world of Dickens, as represented through Adam Long's 2007/8 comedy *Dickens Unplugged* (which played on the Edinburgh Fringe and later at the Comedy Theatre, London) and Mark Evans' 2007 Radio 4 spoof serial *Bleak Expectations* with the Lip Service stage show *Withering Looks* (Fox and Ryding) and the National Theatre of Brent's radio programme *The Brontës and How They Done Their Novels* (Barlow and Ramm).
4. These figures were correct as of 2008.
5. For this reason, I have not felt it necessary to dwell in depth on adaptations of *Jane Eyre* in the 1970s and 1980s. The period before Shared Experience's work on the Brontës is documented and discussed in detail in Patsy Stoneman's book *Brontë Transformations* (pp. 186–205). What is more, having read all the adaptations held by the British Library's manuscripts collection, it appears there was little to set the lesser-known adaptations apart from the ones that Stoneman considers.
6. Cora Kaplan, *Victoriana: Histories, Fictions, Criticism*, p. 22.
7. Lucasta Miller, *The Brontë Myth*, p. 57.
8. Kaplan, *Victoriana: Histories, Fictions, Criticism*, p. 31.
9. Ibid., pp. 15–36.
10. Micael M. Clarke, 'Brontë's 'Jane Eyre' and the Grimms' Cinderella', pp. 695–6.
11. Laurie Stone, 'Why Charlotte Dissed Emily', p. 69.
12. Ibid.
13. Chris R. Vanden Bossche, 'What Did *Jane Eyre* Do?', p. 53.
14. Ibid., p. 54.
15. Stone, p. 67.
16. Miller, p. 135.
17. Ibid., p. 106.
18. The manuscript in the British Library is adapted from a 1978 version.
19. For reference to *Glasstown*, see *Who's Who in the Theatre*; the Crabbe and Cross plays are reviewed in *Theatre Record*. For Sangster and *les Soeurs Brontë*, see Miller, pp. 143, , p. 151.
20. Miller, pp. 150–1.
21. Interestingly, Gemma Jones, who played the lead in *The Duchess of Duke Street*, is cast as the housekeeper Mrs Fairfax in Kay Mellor's 1999 LWT/A&E adaptation of *Jane Eyre*, a version that, like *The Duchess of Duke Street* is

notable for its focus on the domestic servants' work (see, for instance, the scene where Mrs Fairfax instructs the servants on Mr Rochester's unexpected news of guests (0.42)).

22. Beverley Cross, *Haworth*, p. 24.
23. Kerry Crabbe, *The Brontës of Haworth*, Act 1 pp. 57, 19.
24. Sam Dowling and Andrea Kealy, *Four from the Cauldron*, pp. 21, 6, 17.
25. Miller, pp. 172–3.
26. Ibid., pp. 187–8.
27. Ibid., p. 171.
28. Catherine Belsey, *Desire*, p. 12.
29. Ibid., p. 31.
30. Karen Fricker, 'Jane Eyre'.
31. This does not appear to have succeeded entirely: Kieron Quirke reports in a 2006 review for the *Evening Standard* that 'James Clyde's heartthrob act as Mr Rochester is a little laughable, but my lady companion assured me he did the business' (*Theatre Record*, 26, p. 571).
32. Erin O'Connor, 'Preface for a Post-Postcolonial Criticism', p. 305.
33. Ibid., p. 308.
34. Patrick Brantlinger, 'Let's Post-Post-Post "Victorientalism"', p. 101.
35. The connection, in theatre about the Victorians, between repressed sexuality at home and its 'going naked in the colonies' (after Marx), has, of course, been explored in Chapter 2.
36. Polly Teale, *Jane Eyre*, p. 85.
37. Stoneman, p. 203.
38. Teale, p. 3.
39. Ibid., p. 85.
40. See *Theatre Record*, 17, pp. 1327, 1326.
41. Ibid., p. 1325.
42. See *Theatre Record*, 26, pp. 570–1.
43. Ibid., p. 572.
44. Kaplan, p. 155.
45. See *Theatre Record*, 17, p. 1325.
46. Shared Experience, *After Mrs Rochester*, 0.19. Numbers refer to timings in the videotaped version viewed at the V&A Theatre Archive.
47. Ibid., 0.47.
48. Ibid., pp. 1.10, 1.16.
49. Ibid, pp. 1.51, 1.27.
50. Ibid., p. 1.26.
51. Kaplan, pp. 23–4.
52. Polly Teale, *Brontë*, pp. 63–4.
53. Ibid., p. 63.
54. Ibid., p. 12.
55. Ibid., p. 7.
56. Ibid., p. 70.
57. Ibid., p. 17.
58. Ibid., p. 90.
59. Ibid., p. 88.
60. Ibid., p. 91.
61. Ibid., p. 13.

62. Ibid.
63. Ibid., p. 33.
64. See Robert Young (dir.), *Jane Eyre*, 1.21.
65. Ibid., 1.23.
66. See Susanna White (dir.), *Jane Eyre*, episode 2, 0.41.
67. Ibid., 0.50, 0.51.
68. Ibid., 0.53.
69. The DVD extras provide further evidence that postcolonial and psychological readings are now becoming the norm for screen adaptations of *Jane Eyre*. In the 'Deleted Scenes' section, there is a brief passage where reference is made to a caged boy, a 'savage' that one of the ladies had seen in France, and who is thought to have 'bad blood' (0.6). In the 'Interviews' section, Toby Stephens observes that Jane and Rochester are both 'sexual people' and that this adaptation wanted to reject the dominant image of Jane being 'rather prim' (0.10). He also, in a break with the predominant image of feminist criticism of the novel, proposes that Bertha, chained up in the attic, is a metaphor for Rochester's own repressed sexuality (0.11).
70. Judith Adams, *Villette*, p. 88.
71. John Spurling, *Shades of Heathcliff*, p. 29.
72. Lisa Evans, *East Lynne*, p. 80.
73. See the Introduction, and also Kaplan's comments in *Victoriana*, p. 7.

6   Staging Hauntings

1. See *Theatre Record*, 12, p. 482.
2. Moira Buffini, *Loveplay*, p. 20.
3. Sean Aita, *Yallery Brown*, unpaginated typescript.
4. Lizzie Nunnery, *Intemperance*, p. 49.
5. There are several more plays featuring visitations from Victorians the manuscripts of which were not available in the British Library but that have reviews in *Theatre Record*;. These are *The Sharing of Bright Matter* by James Stock (Contact Theatre, Manchester, 1991), which features a nineteenth-century lunatic in a contemporary setting (11, p. 665); *Three Tides Turning* by Louise Ware (1995), which features a Victorian washerwoman among other characters from different periods (15, p. 988); and Molly Fogarty's *Pork Bellies* (1998), where a Chicago trader is visited by her Irish great-great grandfather (18, p. 698). *Theatre Record* also reported in 2004 on a play called *Seed* (Finborough Theatre), an Anglo-Indian variant on supernatural realism by Souad Faress, where the protagonist, Andrea, has a grandfather who communes in the attic with the spirit of their Anglo-Indian ancestor (24, p. 1417).
6. These observations are based on the performance of the play seen at the Fortune Theatre, London, on 22 July 2007, directed by Robin Herford.
7. See Caryl Churchill, *Cloud Nine*, p. 248.
8. Ibid., p. 12.
9. Ibid., pp. 311, 316.
10. See, for instance, Charlotte Jones, *In Flame*, pp. 158–9.
11. Edgar, 'Ten Years of Political Theatre, 1968–1978', p. 29.

12. Ibid., p. 28.
13. See David Hare, 'David Hare on Enemies'. Similarly, Nancy Armstrong, in her discussion of how photography and the novel informed each other during the Victorian period, defines realism as 'any representation that establishes and maintains the priority of the same social categories that an individual could or could not occupy' (Armstrong, *Fiction in the Age of Photography* , p. 168).
14. It is likely that Hare and Edgar's ideas of realism in turn derive from Brecht, who made a very similar point in the essay, 'The Popular and the Realistic', that there are many types of realism, but that 'We must not abstract the only realism from certain given works, but shall make a lively use of all means, old and new, tried and untried, deriving from art and deriving from other sources, in order to put living reality in the hands of living people in such a way as it can be mastered' (p. 109), or as he puts it later, so that the workers can 'get a more exact representation of the real social forces operating under the immediately visible surface' (p. 111).
15. Peter Brooks, *Realist Vision*, p. 3.
16. Armstrong, *Fiction in the Age of Photography*, 7.
17. See J.L. Styan, *Modern Drama in Theory and Practice*, pp. 35–6.
18. Sarah Woods, *Nervous Women*, pp. 55–6, 71–2.
19. Brooks, *Realist Vision*, p. 2.
20. Ibid., p. 147.
21. Ibid., p. 229.
22. Ibid., p. 179. Brooks makes a similar point about Tissot's painting *Reading the Illustré*, earlier, claiming that 'The very sketchiness of his brushwork seems a kind of defensive maneuver, saying: you can only go so far in your approach to what I have captured here, it won't yield a more detailed meaning' (p. 176).
23. See Alan Plater, *Only a Matter of Time*, p. 1.
24. Jacky Bratton, *New Readings in Theatre History*, p. 103.
25. Ibid., p. 102.
26. Greenblatt, *Learning to Curse*, pp. 170, 176.
27. Bruce Jackson, *The Story Is True*, p. 110.
28. Ibid., p. 36.
29. Ibid., pp. 125, 15.
30. See Ibid., pp. 139–50.
31. Mike Leigh, *It's a Great Big Shame!*, Act 1, pp. 14–15, 52–3, 115.
32. Ibid., Act 1, p. 27.
33. Ibid., Act 1, pp. 16–20.
34. Ibid., Act 1, pp. 101–4.
35. Ibid., Act 1, p. 120.
36. Ibid., Act 1, p. 132.
37. Ibid., Act 1, p. 58.
38. Ibid., Act 2, p. 28.
39. Ibid., Act 2, pp. 29–30.
40. Ibid., Act 2, p. 63.
41. Kate Atkinson, *Abandonment*, p. 5.
42. Ibid., p. 102.
43. Ibid., p. 107.

44. Ibid., p. 39.
45. Ibid.
46. Ibid., pp. 76–7.
47. Ibid., p. 7.
48. Ibid., p. 17.
49. Styan, *Modern Drama in Theory and Practice*, p. 6.
50. See Karl Marx, 'Estranged Labour'.
51. Williams, *The Country and the City*, p. 18.
52. Guy Debord, *The Society of the Spectacle*, p. 18.
53. Herbert Marcuse, 'Essay on Liberation', p. vii; Douglas Kellner, *Herbert Marcuse and the Crisis of Marxism*, pp. 294–5.
54. Marcuse, *Counterrevolution and Revolt*, p.9.
55. Erich Fromm, *The Essential Fromm*, pp. 51, 116.
56. Ibid., p. 24.
57. Ibid., p. 25.
58. Paul Basu, *Highland Homecomings*, p. 7.
59. Berger et al., *The Homeless Mind*, p. 171.
60. Ibid., pp. 15, 16.
61. Ibid., p. 163.
62. Ibid., pp. 166–7.
63. Ibid., p. 165.
64. Frank Furedi, *Culture of Fear*, p. 141.
65. Ibid., p. 148.
66. Ibid., p. 162.
67. Ibid., pp. 145, 165.
68. Benjamin R. Barber, *Consumed*, p. 7.
69. Ibid.
70. Ibid., pp. 18, 21.
71. Ibid., p. 15.
72. Ibid., pp. 30, 35.
73. Ibid., p. 36.
74. Zygmunt Bauman, *Consuming Life*, p.9.
75. Ibid., p. 21.
76. Ibid., pp. 21–2.
77. Ibid., pp. 104–6.
78. Ibid., pp. 41, 66.
79. Ibid., pp. 93–6.
80. Ibid., p. 98.
81. Ibid., p. 100.
82. Ibid., p. 125.
83. See Catherine Belsey, *Culture and the Real*, p. 150.
84. Sadie Plant, 'Introduction', p. 12.
85. Basu, *Highland Homecomings*, pp. 81, 110–12.
86. Ibid., pp. 159, 10.
87. Ibid., p. 60.
88. Ibid., pp. 22–3.
89. Ibid., p. 198.
90. Ibid., p. 41.
91. Ibid., pp. 16–17.

92. Ibid., p. 61.
93. Ibid., p. 160.
94. Ibid., p. 162.
95. Ibid., p. 199.
96. Ibid., p. 161.
97. Samuel, *Theatres of Memory*, Vol. 1, p. 75.
98. See 'Clarkson backs Brunel as top Briton' and 'Great Response to Great Britons'.
99. See '£7m Rescues Brunel's Rusting Ship'.
100. See 'Not Just Another Rail Station...'.
101. See 'St Pancras Case Study'.
102. David Cooper, 'Beyond Words', p. 202.
103. Ibid.

Conclusion: Restaging the Victorians

1. See John Harris, *The Last Party*, p. 202. Blur also paid homage, via these 1960s bands, to the music-hall tradition; their *The Sunday Sunday Popular Community Song CD* featured renditions of 'Let's All Go Down The Strand' and 'Daisy Bell' (see John Harris, p. 97).
2. See Edward Bond, *Plays 1*, p. 137.
3. Jack Shepherd, *Holding Fire!*, pp. 54–8.
4. See Ann Heilmann and Mark Llewellyn, *Neo-Victorianism*, p. 238.
5. As Louisa Hadley notes, these books' neo-Victorian-ness tends to 'write white' on the television screen, however, where, bar the sexually explicit scenes, they could easily be taken as adaptations of actual Victorian novels (Hadley, *Neo-Victorian Fiction and Historical Narrative*, pp. 142–3).
6. See *Theatre Record*, 25, p. 883.
7. Martin Hewitt, *Victorian Studies*, pp. 430–2.
8. Ibid., p. 419.
9. Ibid., p. 420
10. Ibid., p. 408.
11. Matthew Sweet, *Inventing the Victorians*, p. 229.

Works Cited

N.B: All play scripts are listed under the name of the playwright, and novels under the author's name. Unsigned articles are listed in alphabetical order by either title or, if untitled, by the title of the work under review. Recordings of live performances are listed under the surname of the director of the performance, and films and television programmes are also listed under the director's surname (where possible), including adaptations.

I have used the abbreviations 'n.p.' where no page number is available, and 'n.d.' where a source is not dated.

Archive articles (unless otherwise stated, available in the V&A Theatres Collection, London)

'A thin line between farce and horror', review of *Jack the Ripper* by Ron Pember and Denis DeMarne, *Jack the Ripper* press file.

Billington, Michael, review of *Cloud Nine*, *Guardian*, 30 Mar 1979, n.p., *Cloud Nine* press file.

Christmas, Linda, 'Rhapsody in Black', *Guardian*, 10 Dec 1975, n.p., *Ipi Tombi* press file.

Churchill, Caryl, interview, *Sunday Telegraph*, 25 Mar 1979, *Sunday* magazine, 9, *Cloud Nine* file.

Review of *Cloud Nine*, *Punch*, 11 Apr 1979, n.p., *Cloud Nine* file.

Review of *Cloud Nine*, *Sunday Telegraph*, 1 Apr 1979, n.p., *Cloud Nine* file.

Cushman, Robert, review of *Cloud Nine*, *Observer*, 1 Apr 1979. n.p., *Cloud Nine* file.

Review of *Early Morning* by Edward Bond, *Evening Standard*, 1 Apr 1968, n.p., *Early Morning* press file.

Garrett, Gerard, 'Censored Playwright Wins £1000 Award', *Evening Standard*, 30 May 1968, n.p., *Early Morning* press file.

Hope-Wallace, Philip, review of *Ipi Tombi*, *Guardian*, 20 Nov 1975, n. p., *Ipi Tombi* press file.

Review of *Ipi Tombi*, *Over 21*, Feb 1976, n. p., *Ipi Tombi* press file.

'Ipi Tombi Rebels in Own Show', *Guardian*, 14 Jan 1977, *Ipi Tombi* press file.

'John Bird may Play "Lesbian" Victoria', *Daily Mail*, 4 Aug 1967, n.p., *Early Morning* press file.

Karpf, Anne, 'Dilly-Dallying with the Lusty Queen of the Halls', *Observer*, 17 Mar 1991, *Living*, 52.

'Kipling Set for India', *Evening Standard*, 1 Jun 1984, n.p., Alec McCowen personal file.

'Marie Lloyd Fails to Draw the Audience: Little Sentiment at Auction', *Guardian*, 31 Aug 1961, 14.

Memorial plaque, untitled photograph, 1972, Marie Lloyd personal file.

'Overwhelmed by Hypocrisy', interview with Edward Bond, *The Times*, n.d., n.p., *Early Morning* press file.

Perrott, Roy, 'The Kipling Burden', *Sunday Times*, 13 May 1984, n. p., Alec McCowen personal file.

Peter, John, 'Prophet of Empire', *Sunday Times*, 3 Jun 1984, n.p., Alec McCowen personal file.

Radin, Victoria, 'St Mark's Gospel', *Observer*, 5 Feb 1984, *Sunday Plus*, n.p., Alec McCowen personal file.

Review of *The Rear Column, Sunday Times*, 26 February 1978, n.p., *The Rear Column* file.

Robinson, Christopher, 'A Singular Calling', *Shakespeare, Cole and Co.* Theatre programme, 1998, Alec McCowen personal file.

'St Mark's Gemini', *Evening Standard*, 28 Dec 1978, n.p., Alec McCowen personal file.

'Second Coming', *Telegraph*, 28 July 1978, n.p., Alec McCowen personal file.

Shulman, Milton, review of *Cloud Nine, Evening Standard*, 30 Mar 1979, n.p., Theatre Museum press file on *Cloud Nine*.

'We Are a Happy People', review of *Ipi Tombi, Sunday Telegraph*, 23 Nov 1975, n.p., *Ipi Tombi* press file.

'Why the Smart Money's Now on Alec', *Guardian*, 12 Feb 1982, n.p., Alec McCowen personal file.

Young, B.A., review of *Cloud Nine, Financial Times*, 30 Mar 1979, n.p., *Cloud Nine* file.

Unpublished play scripts (unless otherwise indicated, from the British Library Manuscripts Room, London). Listed with modern play manuscript number

Adams, Judith, *Villette*, 7543.

Aita, Sean, *Yallery Brown*, 9325.

Archer, Robyn and Rodney Fisher, *A Star is Torn*, 1633.

Barrie, Frank, *Macready!, A Celebration of the Actor*, 1387.

Brock, Jeremy, *Oliver Twist: Adapted for the Stage by Jeremy Brock*, 4328.

Clark, Brian and Rudyard Kipling, *Kipling – East and West*, 5266.

Coe, Peter, *Great Expectations*, 2478.

Cross, Beverley, *Haworth*, 1325.

Davis, Robin, *Up in the Gallery: The Story of Marie Lloyd*, 4121.

di Girolamo, Emilia, *1000 Fine Lines*, 7676.

Dowling, Sam and Andrea Kealy, *Brontës: Four from the Cauldron*, 3743.

Farson, Daniel, *'Marie': The Story of Marie Lloyd*, 89.

Fox, Maggie and Sue Ryding, *Withering Looks: An 'Authentic' Evening with the Brontë Sisters*, 5305.

Fry, Christopher, *The Brontës of Haworth*, adapted by Kerry Gardner, 2774.

Gale, Peter, *Hopkins!*, 1896.

Gearing, Nigel, *Snap!*, unpublished typescript, 1981, kindly loaned by the author.

Godwin, Christopher, *The Guv'nor*, 4449.

Hall, Judith and Jenny Smith, *Jane Eyre: A Classic Tale by Charlotte Brontë*, 3013.

Hendrey, Katrina, *An Evening with Queen Victoria: A Portrait in her Own Words*, 2984.

Hill, Roger, *Great Expectations*, 2032.

Horlock, David, *Crocodiles in Cream*, 5208.

Knight, Joan, *Jane Eyre*, 244.

Kohler, Estelle, *Shakespeare Lady: The Life and Times of Fanny Kemble – Passionate Victorian*, 910.

Leigh, Mike, *It's A Great Big Shame!*, 5952.

Mackintosh, Iain, Tobey Robertson and Timothy West, *The Undisputed Monarch of the English Stage*, 873.

Margolis, Mike, *Bertie*, music composed by Kenny Clayton, 5987.

May, Val, *Tribute to the Lady: An Impression of the Life and Work of Lilian Baylis for Her Centenary*, 873.

Morrow, Melvyn, *A Song to Sing, O!*, 1235.

Mullins, Ian, *Jane Eyre*, 3472.

Myerson, Jonathan, *Jane Eyre*, 2434.

Osbourne, Richard, *Our Ellen*, 4212.

Pascal, Julia, *Charlotte Brontë Goes to Europe*, 5494.

Plater, Alan, *Only a Matter of Time*, 9844.

Rodenberg, Patsy, *Not Much to Ask*, 2141.

Royal Exchange Theatre, Manchester, *Great Expectations*, 2554.

Sewell, Debbie, *More than One Antoinette*, 4482.

Sherrin, Ned and Caryl Brahms, *Sing a Rude Song*, 234.

Trafford, Steve, *Marie: The Story of Marie Lloyd*, 3477.

Woods, Sarah, *Nervous Women*, 5548.

Live events and performances

Church, Jonathan (dir.), *The Life and Adventures of Nicholas Nickleby, Parts I & II*, performance, Festival Theatre, Chichester, 8 Jul 2006.

Gill, Peter (dir.), *Gaslight* by Patrick Hamilton, performance, Old Vic Theatre, London, 6 Jul 2006.

Havergal, Giles (adapt. and dir.), *David Copperfield*, performance, West Yorkshire Playhouse, Leeds, 14 May 2005.

Herford, Robin (dir.), *The Woman in Black* by Stephen Mallatratt, performance, Fortune Theatre, London, 22 Jul 2007.

Hughes, Catherine, 'Mirror Neurons and Simulation', keynote speech, Performing Heritage Conference, University of Manchester, 3 Apr 2008.

'Hysteria: Grupo XIX de Teatro', theatre programme, Barbican Bite Festival 08, 26 Jun 2008.

King Cotton by Jimmy McGovern, performance, The Lowry, Salford, 22 Sep 2007.

Long, Adam (writer and dir.), *Dickens Unplugged*, performance, Comedy Theatre, London, 22 Jun 2008.

Lyddiard, Alan (dir.), *Great Expectations*, adaptation by Neil Bartlett, performance, Taliesin Arts Centre, Swansea, 24 Mar 2007.

Morris, Nigel, 'Gothic (post)modernism and *The Prestige*', 'Attend the Tale: New Contexts for Sweeney Todd' Symposium, University of Lincoln, 31 May 2008.

Neilson, Anthony (writer and dir.), *God in Ruins*, performance, Soho Theatre, London, 29 Nov 2007.

O'Keeffe, Ellie, 'From Pen and Ink to Flesh and Blood', Performing Heritage Conference, University of Manchester, 4 Apr 2008.

Sharrock, Thea (dir.), *Cloud Nine* by Caryl Churchill, performance, Almeida Theatre, London, 22 Nov 2007.

Teale, Polly (dir.), *After Mrs Rochester*, performance, Diana Quick, James Clyde, video recording, Theatre Museum, 10 Oct 2003.

——*Brontë*, performance, Lyric Theatre, Hammersmith, London, 29 Oct 2005.

Yiu, Raymond and Lee Warren, *The Original Chinese Conjuror: A Musical Diversion Suggested by the Lives of Chung Ling Soo*, performance, Almeida Theatre, London, 7 Jul 2006.

Reviews

Review of *Alice* by Linsay Kemp and David Haughton, *Theatre Record*, 1989, 19, 826.

Review of *Black Nightingale*, *Theatre Record*, 1989, 466.

Review of *Brel*, *Theatre Record*, 1990, 10, 1340.

Review of *The Brontës of Hades*, *Theatre Record*, 1995, 15, 1157.

Review of *Colours* by Jean Binnie, *Theatre Record*, 1988, 8, 1480.

Review of *Fanny Kemble at Home*, *Theatre Record*, 1986, 6, 627.

Fricker, Karen, 'Jane Eyre', review of *Jane Eyre* by Polly Teale, *Guardian*, 9 Dec 2003, access date 26 Feb 2007, http://arts.guardian.co.uk/reviews/story/0,1102769,00.html.

Review of *Heart of Darkness*, *Theatre Record*, 1983, 3, 925.

Hickling, Alfred, '*Great Expectations*', review of Northern Stage production of *Great Expectations*, *Guardian*, 27 Jan 2006, accessed 18 Dec 2006, http://www.guardian.co.uk/stage/2006/jan/27/theatre1.

Review of *Ill at Ease*, *Theatre Record*, 1992, 12, 482.

Review of *Jane Eyre*, *Theatre Record*, 1997, 17, 1325–7.

Review of *Judas Worm*, *Theatre Record*, 1998, 18, 956.

Review of *Kipling – East and West*, *Theatre Record*, 1984, 4, 467–8.

Review of *My Dear Emily*, *Theatre Record*, 1996, 16, 1197.

Review of *My Dearest Kate*, *Theatre Record*, 1983, 3, 767.

Review of *Our Marie* by Alfred Shaughnessy and Christopher Barry, *Guardian*, 11 Feb 1953, 3.

Review of *Plague Wind*, *Theatre Record*, 1983, 3, 276.

Review of *Pork Bellies*, *Theatre Record*, 1998, 18, 698.

Ratcliffe, Michael, review of *Great Expectations* by the Royal Exchange Theatre, Manchester, *Theatre Record*, 1984, 4, 1000.

Review of *The Sharing of Bright Matter*, *Theatre Record*, 1991, 11, 665.

Review of *Three Tides Turning*, *Theatre Record*, 1995, 15, 988.

Review of *Vivian*, *Theatre Record*, 1990, 10, 1465.

Thorncroft, Antony, '*A Song to Sing, O!*' review of *A Song to Sing, O!*, *Theatre Record*, 1981, 1, 166.

Trotter, David, 'Something of Himself', review of *Kipling – East and West*, *Times Literary Supplement*, 15 Jun 1984, 667.

Young, B.A., review of *Great Expectations* by the Royal Exchange Theatre, Manchester, *Theatre Record*, 1984, 4, 1001.

Television, radio and film

Bain, Bill (dir.), *The Duchess of Duke Street* by John Hawkesworth, 1976, DVD, *The Duchess of Duke Street: Series 1 Volume 1*, playback, 2003.

———and Derek Bennett (dirs), *Upstairs, Downstairs* by Alfred Shaughnessy and Jeremy Paul, 1971–5, DVD, *Upstairs, Downstairs: The Complete First Series*, Network, 2005.

Barlow, Patrick and John Ramm, *The Arts and How They was Done 4: The Brontë Sisters and How They Done Their Novels*, radio programme, BBC Radio 4, 25 Apr 2007.

Bierman, Robert (dir.), *The Moonstone* by Wilkie Collins, DVD, WGBH Boston, 2005.

Chadwick, Justin (dir.), *Bleak House* by Charles Dickens, screenplay by Andrew Davies, 2005, DVD, BBC/2 Entertain, 2006.

Curtis, Simon (dir.), *David Copperfield*, screenplay by Adrian Hodges, DVD, BBC, 2001.

Devenish, Ross (dir.), *Bleak House* by Charles Dickens, screenplay by Arthur Hopcraft, 1985, DVD, Acorn Video, 2006.

Evans, Mark, *Bleak Expectations*, BBC Radio 4, 4 Sep 2008.

Farino, Julian (dir.), *Our Mutual Friend* by Charles Dickens, screenplay by Sandy Welch, 1998, DVD, BBC, 2001.

Garland, Patrick (dir.), *The Mystery of Charles Dickens* by Peter Ackroyd, performed by Simon Callow, 2002, DVD, Heritage Theatre, 2002.

Goddard, Jim (dir.), *The Life and Adventures of Nicholas Nickleby*, adapted by David Edgar, 1982, DVD, Metrodome, 2003.

Gorrie, John and Christopher Hodson (dirs), *Lillie*, screenplay by David Butler, 1978, DVD, Network, 2007.

Hughes Brothers (dirs), *From Hell*, feature, Johnny Depp, Heather Graham, DVD, Fox, 2008.

Laughland, Nick (dir.), *Under the Greenwood Tree* by Thomas Hardy, DVD, 2 Entertain, 2006.

Lean, David (dir.), *Oliver Twist*, screenplay by David Lean and Stanley Haynes, 1948, DVD, Carlton, 2003.

Lockhart, Clare (dir.), *The 1970s' Edwardian Resurrection*, narrated by Peter York, BBC4, 28 Jan 2007.

MacNaughton, Ian (prod.), *Monty Python's Flying Circus: The Complete First Series* by Graham Chapman, John Cleese, Terry Gilliam, Eric Idle, Terry Jones and Michael Palin, BBC, 1969, DVD, BBC Worldwide, 2007.

Maher, John (dir.), *Wide Sargasso Sea* by Jean Rhys, DVD, Acorn, 2008.

Medak, Peter (dir.), *The Ruling Class*, performed by Peter O'Toole, Alastair Sim, 1972, DVD, Momentum Pictures, 2001.

Miller, Jonathan (dir.), *Alice in Wonderland* by Lewis Carroll, BBC, 1966, DVD, BFI, 2003.

Miller, Marc and Michael Ferguson (dirs), *Dickens of London*, screenplay by Wolf Mankowitz, 1976, DVD, Network, 2007.

Nolan, Christopher (dir.), *The Prestige*, DVD, Warner Home Video, 2007.

Norrington, Stephen (dir.), *The League of Extraordinary Gentlemen*, 2003, DVD, Twentieth Century Fox Home Entertainment, 2004.

Polanski, Roman (dir.), *Oliver Twist*, screenplay by Ronald Harwood, 2005, DVD, Pathe, 2006.

Reed, Carol (dir.), *Oliver!* by Lionel Bart, Columbia, 1968, DVD, Sony Pictures Home Entertainment, 2006.

Renton, Nicholas (dir.), *Wives and Daughters* by Elizabeth Gaskell, DVD, 2 Entertain, 2001.

Rye, Renny (dir.), *Oliver Twist*, screenplay by Alan Bleasdale, 1999, DVD, ITV, 2006.

Sax, Geoffrey (dir.), *Tipping the Velvet*, screenplay by Andrew Davies, 2002, DVD, Contender, 2002.

Scott, Peter Graham (dir.), *The Onedin Line* by Cyril Abraham, featuring Peter Gilmore, Anne Stallybrass, 1971, DVD, *The Onedin Line: The Complete First Series*, BBC Worldwide, 2007.

Sharp, Ian (dir.), *Tess of the D'Urbervilles* by Thomas Hardy, DVD, ITV, 2007.

Whatham, Claude (dir.), *Disraeli: Portrait of a Romantic*, screenplay by David Butler, 1978, DVD, Network, 2007.

White, Susanna (dir.), *Jane Eyre*, performed by Ruth Wilson, Toby Stephens, DVD, BBC, 2006.

Wilson, Ronald (dir.), *The Pallisers* by Anthony Trollope, 1974, DVD, Acorn Media, 2005.

Young, Robert (dir.), *Charlotte Brontë's Jane Eyre*, DVD, A&E Home Video, 1999.

Zeffirelli, Franco (dir.), *Charlotte Brontë's Jane Eyre*, DVD, Pathé, 2003.

Music

Animal Farm 'Dedicated Follower of Fashion', *The Ultimate Collection*, Sanctuary, 2004.

——*The Kinks Are The Village Green Preservation Society*, Sanctuary, 1968, 2005.

——'Village Green', *The Kinks Are the Village Green Preservation Society*, Sanctuary, 2005.

The Beatles, 'Being for the Benefit of Mr Kite!', *Sergeant Pepper's Lonely Hearts Club Band*, Parlophone, 1992.

——'Sergeant Pepper's Lonely Hearts Club Band', *Sergeant Pepper's Lonely Hearts Club Band*, Parlophone, 1992.

——'Strawberry Fields Forever', *The Beatles 1967–1970*, Parlophone, 1993.

Bedford, Harry and Terry Sullivan, 'It's A Bit of A Ruin', London: B. Feldman, 1920.

Bowie, David, 'There is a Happy Land', *The Deram Anthology*, Decca, 1997.

——'Uncle Arthur', *The Deram Anthology*, Decca, 1997.

——'When I'm Five', *The Deram Anthology*, Decca, 1997.

Cream, 'Mother's Lament', *Disraeli Gears*, Lilith, 2007.

The Incredible String Band, *The Hangman's Beautiful Daughter*, Warner, 1992.

The Kinks, 'Apeman', *The Ultimate Collection*, Sanctuary, 2004.

Lloyd Webber, Andrew, David Zippel and Charlotte Jones, *The Woman in White*, Original London Cast Recording, CD, EMI Classics, 2004.

The Scaffold, 'Lily the Pink', *The Very Best of the Scaffold*, Disky, 1998.
The Small Faces, 'Lazy Sunday Afternoon', *Ogden's Nut Gone Flake*, Sanctuary, 2008.
——'Rene', *Ogden's Nut Gone Flake*, Sanctuary, 2008.

Books and articles

'£7m Rescues Brunel's Rusting Ship', *BBC News*, 31 Jan 2002, accessed 8 Apr 2008, http://news.bbc.co.uk/1/hi/england/1794300.stm.
Ackroyd, Peter, *Dan Leno and the Limehouse Golem*, London: Minerva, 1995.
Addison, Paul, *No Turning Back: The Peacetime Revolutions of Post-War Britain*, Oxford: Oxford University Press, 2010.
'Aims and Scope', *Neo Victorian Studies*, ed. Marie-Louise Kohlke, 2008, accessed 5 Jul 2008, http://www.neovictorianstudies.com.
'Alec McCowen', *ImdB*, 2006, *Internet Movie Database*, 2006, accessed 28 Aug 2006, http://imdb.com/name/nm0566680.
Alfreds, Mike, 'A Shared Experience: The Actor as Story-Teller', *Theatre Papers*, Dartington, third series: 1979–80.
Armstrong, Nancy, *Fiction in the Age of Photography: The Legacy of British Realism*, Cambridge, MA: Harvard, 1999.
Atkinson, Kate, *Abandonment*, London: Nick Hern, 2000.
Barber, Benjamin R., *Consumed: How Markets Corrupt Children, Infantilize Adults and Swallow Citizens Whole*, New York: Norton, 2007.
Barber, Stephen, *Weapons of Liberation*, London: Faber, 1996.
Barnes, Peter, *The Ruling Class: A Baroque Comedy*, London: Heinemann, 1969.
Bartlett, Neil, *A Vision of Love Revealed in Sleep*, *Gay Plays: Four*, ed. Michael Wilcox, London: Methuen, 1990, 81–112.
——*Charles Dickens' Oliver Twist*, London: Oberon, 2004.
——*Great Expectations*, London: Oberon, 2007.
Basu, Paul, *Highland Homecomings: Genealogy and Heritage Tourism in the Scottish Diaspora*, Abingdon: Routledge, 2007.
Bauerlein, Mark, 'Social Constructionism: Philosophy for the Academic Workplace', Patai and Corral, 341–53.
Bauman, Zygmunt, *Consuming Life*, London: Polity, 2007.
'BBC Consumer: TV and Radio', *bbc.co.uk*, 7 Aug 2008, http://www.bbc.co.uk/consumer/tv_and_radio/points_of_view/viewersoncamera.shtml.
Belsey, Catherine, *Culture and the Real*, Abingdon: Routledge, 2004.
——*Desire*, Oxford: Blackwell, 1994.
Berger, Peter, Brigitte Berger and Hansfried Kellner, *The Homeless Mind*, Harmondsworth: Penguin, 1974.
Bignell, Jonathan, *An Introduction to Television Studies*, London: Routledge, 2004.
Billington, Michael, *State of the Nation: British Theatre since 1945*, London: Faber, 2007.
Birkenhead, Frederick, *Rudyard Kipling*, London: Weidenfeld and Nicolson, 1978.
'*Bleak House* to Become BBC "Soap"', 19 Dec 2003, *bbc.co.uk*, accessed 20 Feb 2007, http://news.bbc.co.uk/1/hi/entertainment/tv_and_radio/3333511.stm.

Bond, C.G., *Sweeney Todd: The Demon Barber of Fleet Street*, London: Samuel French, 1974.

Bond, Edward, 'Author's Preface', *Lear, Plays 2*, London: Methuen, 1978, 3–12.

———*Early Morning, Plays 1*, London: Methuen, 1997, 135–233.

———*Narrow Road to the Deep North, Plays 2*, London: Methuen, 1978, 171–225.

———*Passion, Plays 2*, London: Methuen, 1978, 237–53.

———*Saved*, London: Methuen, 2000.

———*Selections from the Notebooks of Edward Bond*, Vol. 1, ed. Ian Stuart, London: Methuen, 2000.

———*The Bundle*, London: Methuen, 1978.

Booker, Christopher, *The Neophiliacs: A Study of the Revolution in English Life in the Fifties and Sixties*, London: Fontana, 1970.

Bowen, John, *Florence Nightingale*, London: Samuel French, 1976.

Bowie-Sell, Daisy, 'Arts Cuts: Winners and Losers', *Daily Telegraph*, 30 Mar 2011, accessed 15 May 2011, http://www.telegraph.co.uk/culture/theatre/8416336/Arts-cuts-winners-and-losers.html.

Brantlinger, Patrick, 'Let's Post-Post-Post "Victorientalism": A Response to Erin O'Connor', *Victorian Studies*, 2003, 46(3): 97–105.

Bratton, Jacky, *New Readings in Theatre History*, Cambridge: Cambridge University Press, 2003.

Brecht, Bertolt, 'The Popular and the Realistic', *Brecht on Theatre: The Development of an Aesthetic*, ed. John Willett, London: Methuen, 2001, 107–15.

Briggs, Asa, *A Social History of England*, London: Weidenfeld and Nicolson, reprint 1994.

Bristow, Joseph (ed.), *Oscar Wilde and Modern Culture: The Making of a Legend*, Athens, OH: Ohio University Press, 2008.

Brontë, Anne, *The Tenant of Wildfell Hall*, Oxford: Oxford University Press, 1993.

Brontë, Charlotte, *Jane Eyre*, Oxford: Oxford University Press, 2000.

———*Villette*, Harmondsworth: Penguin, 1979.

———*The Professor*, Oxford: Clarendon, 1987.

Brontë, Emily, *Wuthering Heights*, Trumpington: Cambridge University Press, 1998.

Brooks, Peter, *Realist Vision*, New Haven: Yale University Press, 2005.

Brown, Ian, 'Plugged into History: The Sense of the Past in Scottish Theatre', *Scottish Theatre since the Seventies*, eds Randall Stevenson and Gavin Wallace, Edinburgh: Edinburgh University Press, 1996.

Buffini, Moira, *Loveplay*, London: Faber, 2001.

Burton, Graeme, *Talking Television: An Introduction to the Study of Television*, London: Arnold, 2000.

Byatt, A.S., *Possession: A Romance*, London: Vintage, 1991.

Callow, Simon, *Being An Actor*, London: Methuen, 1984.

Cardus, Neville, 'A Little of What we Fancied', *Guardian*, 23 Dec 1972, 9.

Cardwell, Sarah, *Adaptation Revisited: Television and the Classic Novel*, Manchester: Manchester University Press, 2002.

Carpenter, Humphrey, *That Was Satire That Was: The Satire Boom of the 1960s*, London: Phoenix, 2000.

Carrington, Charles, *Rudyard Kipling*, London: Macmillan, 1978.

Carroll, Lewis, *Alice's Adventures in Wonderland*, Harmondsworth: Puffin, 2008.

Caughie, John, *Television Drama: Realism, Modernism and British Culture*, Oxford: Oxford University Press, 2000.

Cheeseman, Peter, *The Knotty: A Musical Documentary*, Introduction, London: Methuen, 1970.

Churchill, Caryl, *Cloud Nine, Plays: 1*, London: Methuen, 1996, 243–320.

Clarke, Micael M., 'Brontë's 'Jane Eyre' and the Grimms' Cinderella', *Studies in English Literature, 1500–1900*, 2000, 40, 4, 695–710.

'Clarkson Backs Brunel as Top Briton', *BBC News*, 21 Oct 2002, accessed 2 Apr 2008, http://news.bbc.co.uk/1/hi/england/2345837.stm.

Clifford, John, *Great Expectations: Adapted from Charles Dickens, Frontline Drama 4: Adapting Classics*, London: Methuen, 1996, 183–246.

Cohen, Ed, *Talk on the Wilde Side*, London: Routledge, 1993.

Cohen, Josh, *How to Read Freud*, London: Granta, 2005.

Collins, Philip (ed.), *The Public Readings of Charles Dickens*, Oxford: Clarendon, 1975.

Conrad, Joseph, *Heart of Darkness*, Harmondsworth: Penguin, 2007.

Cooper, David (ed.), 'Beyond Words', Cooper, *Dialectics* 193–202.

——*The Dialectics of Liberation*, Harmondsworth: Pelican, 1967.

——'Introduction', Cooper, *Dialectics* 1–12.

Counsell, Colin, *Signs of Performance: An Introduction to Twentieth Century Theatre*, London: Routledge, 1996.

Coveney, Michael, *The Citz: 21 Years of the Glasgow Citizens Theatre*, London: Nick Hern, 1990.

'The Curse of Steptoe', BBC, 19 Mar 2008, accessed 26 Sep 2008, http://www.bbc.co.uk/drama/curseofsteptoe/.

'Dame Judi Dench to Star in BBC One Drama Cranford Chronicles', 31 Jan 2007, BBC, accessed 20 Feb 2007, http://www.bbc.co.uk/pressoffice/pressreleases/stories/2007/01_january/31/dench.shtml.

Daniels, Sarah, *Gut Girls, Plays: 2*, London: Methuen, 1994, 1–94.

Davis, Geoffrey V. and Anne Fuchs (eds), *Staging New Britain: Aspects of Black and South Asian British Theatre Practice*, Brussels: P.I.E. – Peter Lang, 2006.

Dawson, Helen, 'Honeymoon Leftovers', *Observer*, 5 Nov 1967, 24.

De Angelis, April, *Ironmistress, Plays: 1*, London: Faber, 1989, 1–68.

De Jongh, Nicholas, 'The Human Jungle', *Guardian*, 13 Jan 1970, 6.

——*Politics, Prudery and Perversions: The Censoring of the English Stage 1901–1968*, London: Methuen, 2001.

Debord, Guy, *The Society of the Spectacle*, translated by Donald Nicholson-Smith, New York: Zone Books, 2004.

Derrida, Jacques, *Of Grammatology*, Baltimore: Johns Hopkins University Press, 1997.

Dewhurst, Keith, *Lark Rise to Candleford*, London: Samuel French, 1995.

Dickens, Charles, *Bleak House*, New York: Norton, 1977.

——*A Christmas Carol and Other Christmas Books*, Oxford: Oxford University Press, 2006.

——*Our Mutual Friend*, Oxford: Oxford University Press, 1952.

——*A Tale of Two Cities*, Oxford: Oxford University Press, 1998.

'The Director in Rep', *The Best of Plays and Players*, ed. Peter Roberts, London: Methuen, 1989, 20–22.

Dollimore, Jonathan, *Sexual Dissidence: Augustine to Wilde: Freud to Foucault*, Oxford: Oxford University Press, 1991.

Donnellan, Declan, *Great Expectations* by Charles Dickens, London: Nick Hern, 2005.

Douglas, Christopher and Nigel Planer, *Nicolas Craig: I, an Actor*, 2nd edn, London: Methuen, 2001.

Downie, John, *Mary Ann: An Elegy*, Bristol: July Fox, 1979.

Edgar, David, 'Adapting Nickleby', Edgar, *The Second Time*, 143–159.

——*Entertaining Strangers, Plays: 2*, London: Methuen, 1990, 387–502.

——'Festivals of the Oppressed', Edgar, *The Second Time* 226–46.

——*The Life and Adventures of Nicholas Nickleby, Plays: 2*, London: Methuen, 1994, 41–386.

——'Provocative Acts: British Playwriting in the Post-War Era and Beyond', *State of Play: Playwrights on Playwriting*, ed. David Edgar, London: Faber, 1999, 1–36.

——*The Second Time as Farce: Reflections on the Drama of Mean Times*, London: Lawrence and Wishart, 1988.

——*The Strange Case of Dr Jekyll and Mr Hyde*, London: Nick Hern, 1992.

——'Ten Years of Political Theatre, 1968–1978, *The Second Time* 24–47.

Edmundson, Helen, *George Eliot's 'The Mill on the Floss', Frontline Drama 4: Adapting Classics*, ed. Michael Fry, London: Methuen, 1996, 247–340.

Ellis, John M, 'Is Theory to Blame?', Patai and Corral, 92–109.

Evans, Lisa, *East Lynne*, London: Oberon, 2005.

——*Villette*, London: Oberon, 2005.

Evans, Richard J., 'The Wonderfulness of Us (the Tory Interpretation of History), *London Review of Books*, 17 Mar 2011, 9–12.

Faber, Michel, *The Crimson Petal and the White*, Edinburgh: Canongate, 2003.

Farson, Daniel, *Marie Lloyd and Music Hall,* London: Tom Stacey, 1972.

Feay, Suzi, 'Suzi Feay: At the Sharp End', *The Independent*, 8 Jun 2008, accessed 24 Jul 2008, http://www.independent.co.uk/opinion/columnists/suzi-feay-at-the-sharp-end-838054.html.

Flannery, Peter, *Our Friends in the North: A History Play*, London: Methuen, 1982.

Flint, Kate, 'Why "Victorian"?: Response', *Victorian Studies*, 2005, 47, 2, 230–9.

Foucault, Michel, 'Questions of Method', *The Foucault Effect: Studies in Governmentality*, eds Graham Burchell, Colin Gordon and Peter Miller, Chicago: University of Chicago Press, 1991.

——*The Use of Pleasure: The History of Sexuality: 2*, Harmondsworth: Penguin, 1992.

——*The Will to Knowledge: The History of Sexuality: 1*, Harmondsworth: Penguin, 1998.

Fowles, John, *The French Lieutenant's Woman*, London: Vintage, 2004.

Freud, Sigmund, *Introductory Lectures on Psychoanalysis (Parts I and II)*, London: Vintage, 2001.

Friel, Brian, *The Home Place,* London: Faber, 2005.

Fromm, Erich, *The Essential Fromm: Life between Having and Being*, London: Constable, 1995.

Fry, Michael, *Emma: Adapted from Jane Austen, Frontline Drama 4: Adapting Classics*, London: Methuen, 1996, 1–97.

——*Tess of the D'Urbervilles*, London: Samuel French, 1997.

Furedi, Frank, *Culture of Fear: Risk-Taking and the Morality of Low Expectation*, London: Continuum, 1997.

Galgani, Riccardo, *The Found Man*, London: Methuen, 2005.

Gardiner, John, 'Theme-Park Victoriana', Taylor and Wolff, 167–80.

———*The Victorians: An Age in Retrospect*, London: Hambledon Continuum, 2006.

Gaskell, Elizabeth, *The Life of Charlotte Bronte*, Harmondsworth: Penguin, 1997.

Gearing, Nigel, *Dickens in America*, London: Oberon, 1998.

Gee, Shirley, *Ask for the Moon*, London: Faber, 1987.

Gems, Pam, *Mrs. Pat*, London: Oberon, 2006.

Gibson, Janine, 'Style Bible of the 80s Defined Ripping Era', *Guardian*, 2 Jul 1999, accessed 24 Jul 2008, http://www.guardian.co.uk/media/1999/jul/02/pressandpublishing.business.

Giddings, Robert, Keith Selby and Chris Wensley, *Screening the Novel: The Theory and Practice of Literary Dramatization*, Basingstoke: Macmillan, 1990.

Gilbert, William Schwenck and Arthur Seymour Sullivan, *The Complete Plays of Gilbert and Sullivan*, new edn, New York: Norton, 1997 [1941].

Gitlin, Todd, 'The Cant of Identity', Patai and Corral, 400–11.

———*Letters to a Young Activist*, New York: Basic, 2003.

Glavin, John, *After Dickens: Reading, Adaptation and Performance*, Cambridge: Cambridge University Press, 1999.

Glover, Sue, *Bondagers* and *The Straw Chair*, London: Methuen, 1997.

Gow, Gordon, 'One Man and His Script', *Plays and Players*, Jun 1984, 10.

Grady, Hugh, 'Shakespeare Studies, 2005: A Situated Overview', *Shakespeare*, 1.1&2, 2005, 102–20.

Gray, Robert, 'The Falkland Factor', *The Politics of Thatcherism*, ed. Stuart Hall and Martin Jacques, London: Laurence and Wishart, 1983, 271–80.

Gray, Simon, *The Rear Column*, London: Methuen, 1978.

'Great Response to Great Britons', *BBC News*, 23 Oct 2002, accessed 2 Apr 2008, http://news.bbc.co.uk/1/hi/entertainment/tv_and_radio/2353803.stm.

Green, Jonathon, *All Dressed Up: The Sixties and the Counterculture*, London: Pimlico, 1999.

Greenblatt, Stephen J., *Learning to Curse*, New York: Routledge, 1990.

Greig, Noel, *The Dear Love of Comrades*, *Two Gay Sweatshop Plays*, London: Gay Men's Press, 1981, 71–142.

Hadley, Louisa, *Neo-Victorian Fiction and Historical Narrative: The Victorians and Us*, Basingstoke: Palgrave Macmillan, 2010.

Hall, Stuart, *The Hard Road to Renewal: Thatcherism and the Crisis of the Left*, London: Verso, 1988.

———Chas Critcher, Tony Jefferson, John Clarke and Brian Roberts, *Policing the Crisis: Mugging, the State, and Law and Order*, Basingstoke: Macmillan, 1978.

Harben, Niloufer, *Twentieth Century English History Plays*, Basingstoke: Macmillan, 1987.

Hare, David, 'David Hare on *Enemies*', theatre programme, Almeida Theatre, London, 24 Jun 2006, 15.

———*Obedience, Struggle and Revolt*, London: Faber, 2005.

Harris, John, *The Last Party: Britpop, Blair and the Demise of English Rock*, London: Harper Perennial, 2004.

Harris, Jonathan Gill, 'Materialist Criticisms', *Shakespeare: An Oxford Guide*, ed. Stanley Wells and Lena Cowen Orlin, Oxford: Oxford University Press, 2003, 472–84.

Harrison, Tony, *The Mysteries*, London: Faber, 1985.

——*Phaedra Britannica*, *Plays 2*, London: Faber, 2002, 111–208.

——*Poetry or Bust*, *Plays*, London: Faber, 1996, 1–59.

——*The Prince's Play*, *Plays 2*, London: Faber, 2002, 209–345.

Hart-Davis, Adam, *What the Victorians Did for Us*, London: Headline, 2001.

Havergal, Giles (adapt.), *David Copperfield* by Charles Dickens, London: Oberon, 2005.

Hayward, Jennifer, *Consuming Pleasures: Active Audiences and Serial Fictions from Dickens to Soap Opera*, Lexington: University Press of Kentucky, 1997.

Heilmann, Ann and Mark Llewellyn, *Neo-Victorianism: The Victorians in the Twenty-First Century, 1999–2009*, Basingstoke: Palgrave Macmillan, 2010.

Herbert, Ian, Christine Baxter and Robert E. Finlay (eds), *Who's Who in the Theatre*, Detroit: Gale, 1981.

——*Who's Who in the Theatre: Playbills*, 1976–79, Detroit: Gale, 1980.

Hewison, Robert, *The Heritage Industry: Britain in a Climate of Decline*, London: Methuen, 1987.

——*Too Much: Art and Society in the Sixties, 1960–75*, London: Paladin, 1988.

Hewitt, Martin, 'Why the Notion of Victorian Britain *Does* Make Sense', *Victorian Studies*, 2006, 48, 3, 395–438.

Higgins, John, *The Raymond Williams Reader*, Oxford: Blackwell, 2001.

Hingorani, Dominic, 'Tara Arts and Tamasha: Producing Asian Performance – Two Approaches', *Alternatives within the Mainstream: British Black and Asian Theatres*, ed. Dimple Godiwala, Newcastle: Cambridge Scholars Press, 2006, 174–200.

'Historical Archive', *The National Theatre of Brent*, 2008, accessed 3 Oct 2008, http://www.nationaltheatreofbrent.com.

Hobsbawm, Eric, 'Falklands Fallout', *The Politics of Thatcherism*, ed. Stuart Hall and Martin Jacques, London: Lawrence and Wishart, 1983, 250–70.

Holmes, Richard, *Something of Myself* by Rudyard Kipling, Introduction, Harmondsworth: Penguin, 1987, 7–26.

'Ian McKellen Stage: June 1994–June 1997: A Knight Out', *Sir Ian McKellen*, 2006, accessed 22 Aug 2006, http://www.mckellen.com/stage/index12.htm.

Inglis, Fred, *Raymond Williams*, New York: Routledge, 1995.

Itzin, Catherine, *Stages in the Revolution*, London: Methuen, 1980.

Jackson, Bruce, *The Story Is True*, Philadelphia: Temple University Press, 2007.

Jane Eyre by Polly Teale, theatre programme, Richmond Theatre, 3 Feb 2006.

Jarvis, Adrian, *Samuel Smiles and the Construction of Victorian Values*, London: Sutton, 1997.

Jeffreys, Stephen, *Charles Dickens's 'Hard Times': Adapted for the Stage by Stephen Jeffreys*, London: Samuel French, 1987.

Joyce, Simon, 'The Victorians in the Rear View Mirror', *Functions of Victorian Culture at the Present Time*, ed. Christine L. Krueger, Athens, OH: Ohio University Press, 2002, 3–15.

Kaplan, Cora, *Victoriana: Histories, Fictions, Criticism*, Edinburgh: Edinburgh University Press, 2007.

Kaye, Richard A., 'The Wilde Moment', *Victorian Literature and Culture*, 2002 , 30, 1, 347–52.

Kellner, Douglas, *Herbert Marcuse and the Crisis of Marxism*, Basingstoke: Macmillan, 1984.

Kipling, Rudyard, *Rudyard Kipling's Verse*, London: Hodder and Stoughton, 1940.

Kuti, Elizabeth, *The Sugar Wife*, London: Oberon, 2005.

Laing, R.D., 'The Obvious', Cooper, *The Dialectics of Liberation*, 13–33.

Lane, Richard J., *Jean Baudrillard*, Abingdon: Routledge, 2000.

Leigh, Mike, 'Topsy-Turvy: A Personal Journey', *The Cambridge Companion to Gilbert and Sullivan*, ed. David Eden and Meinhardt Saremba, Cambridge: Cambridge University Press, 2009, 153–76.

Leigh, Spencer, 'Pat Kirkwood: "Britain's Betty Grable" ', *Independent*, 27 Dec 2007, accessed 3 Oct 2008, http://www.independent.co.uk/news/obituaries/pat-kirkwood-britains-betty-grable-766892.html.

Letwin, Shirley Robin, *The Anatomy of Thatcherism*, London: Fontana, 1992.

Levin, Bernard, *The Pendulum Years: Britain and the Sixties*, London: Cape, 1970.

Lewis, Lisa, 'Welsh-Language Production/Welsh-Language Performance: The Resistant Body', *Studies in Theatre and Performance*, 2004, 24, 3, 163–76.

Little, Ruth and Emily McLaughlin, *The Royal Court Theatre Inside Out*, London: Oberon, 2007.

MacDonald, Ian, *Revolution in the Head: The Beatles' Records and the Sixties*, New York: Henry Holt, 1994.

Mackie, Lindsay, 'Scot's Gist', *Guardian*, 15 Apr 1974, 6.

McCowen, Alec, *Personal Mark,* London: Hamish Hamilton, 1984.

———*Young Gemini*, London: Elm Tree Books, 1979.

McGrath, John, *The Cheviot, the Stag and the Black, Black Oil*, London: Methuen, 1981.

McGuiness, Frank, *Mary and Lizzie*, London: Faber, 1989.

McHardy, Anne and Richard Norton-Taylor, 'Kinnock's Gibe Reopens Row over Falklands', *Guardian*, 7 Jun 1983, accessed 22 Aug 2006, http://politics.guardian.co.uk/politicspast/story/0,,874718,00.html.

McLauren, Allen, 'Reworking "Work" in some Victorian Writing and Visual Art', *In Search of Victorian Values*, ed. Eric M. Sigsworth, Manchester: Manchester University Press, 1988, 27–42.

McLuhan, Marshall, *Understanding Media: The Extensions of Man*, London: Routledge, 2002.

McMillan, Joyce, *The Traverse Theatre Story 1963–1988*, London: Methuen, 1988.

McMillan, Michael, 'Rebaptizing the World in Our Own Terms: Black Theatre and Live Arts in Britain', Davis and Fuchs, 47–64.

Mallatratt, Stephen, *The Woman in Black*, London: Samuel French, 1989.

Malvern, Jack, 'Pthpthpthphp! Spike Milligan Script Reveals the Truth about Two Ronnies' Raspberry Rogue', *The Times*, 16 Dec 2010, 17.

Marcus, Steven, *The Other Victorians: A Study of Sexuality and Pornography in Mid-Nineteenth-Century England*, London: Weidenfeld and Nicolson, 1966.

Marcuse, Herbert, *Counterrevolution and Revolt*, London: Beacon, 1992.

———*An Essay on Liberation*, Harmondsworth: Penguin, 1972.

———'Liberation from the Affluent Society', *The Dialectics of Liberation*, 175–92.

Marx, Karl, 'The British Rule in India', *Marxists.org*, 2005, accessed 30 Nov 2005, http://www.marxists.org/archive/marx/works/1853/06/25.htm.

———*Capital: An Abridged Edition*, ed. David McLellan, Oxford: Oxford University Press, 1999.

————'Estranged Labour', *Marxists.org*, 2008, accessed 9 Apr 2008, http://www.marxists.org/archive/marx/works/1844/manuscripts/labour.html.

————'The Future Results of British Rule in India', *Marxists.org*, 2005, accessed 30 Nov 2005, http://www.marxists.org/archive/marx/works/1853/07/22.htm.

Mead, Kathryn, review of *Oliver Twist* by Jeremy Brock, *Theatre Record*, 1989, 19, 1747.

Meyers, D.G., 'Bad Writing', Patai and Corral, 354–9.

Millard, Rosie, 'Notebook', *New Statesman*, 12 Dec 2005, 42.

Miller, Lucasta, *The Brontë Myth*, London: Vintage, 2002.

Mills, Sara, *Michel Foucault*, Abingdon: Routledge, 2003.

'Miss Marie Lloyd: Queen of the Music Hall', *BBC*, 26 Feb 2007, http://www.bbc.co.uk/bbcfour/cinema/features/marie-lloyd.shtml.

Montgomery, John, 'King's Jester', *Guardian*, 29 Oct 1974, 16.

Moorhouse, Geoffrey, 'No Laughing Matter', *Guardian*, 14 Sep 1967, 5.

Morris, Keith (ed.), *Theatre in Wales*, 2008, accessed 15 Aug 2008, http://www.theatre-wales.co.uk/index.asp.

Munro, Rona, *The Maiden Stone*, London: Nick Hern, 1995.

Nagel, Thomas, 'The Sleep of Reason', Patai and Corral, 541–52.

Neilson, Anthony, *Edward Gant's Amazing Feats of Loneliness*, London: Methuen, 2009.

Nelson, Richard, *Two Shakespearean Actors*, London: Faber, 1990.

Nichols, Peter, *Poppy*, London: Methuen, 1982.

'Not Just Another Rail Station...' BBC London, 2007, accessed 5 Dec 2007, http://www.bbc.co.uk/london/content/articles/2007/04/12/stpancras_feature.shtml.

Nunnery, Lizzie, *Intemperance*, London: Faber, 2007.

O'Connor, Erin, 'Preface for a Post-Postcolonial Criticism', *Victorian Studies*, 2003, 45(2), 217–46.

Orel, Harold (ed.), *Kipling: Interviews and Recollections*, 2 vols, Basingstoke: Macmillan, 1983.

Ormerod, Nick and Declan Donnellan, *Great Expectations*, London: Nick Hern, 2005.

Orwell, George, 'The Lion and the Unicorn: Socialism and the English Genius', *Penguin Essays*, 144–94.

————*The Penguin Essays of George Orwell*, Harmondsworth: Penguin, 1984.

————'Rudyard Kipling', *Penguin Essays*, 209–21.

Osborne, John, *The Picture of Dorian Gray*, London: Faber, 1973.

Owen, Michael, 'How Alec Hit the Road to Mandalay', *Evening Standard*, 18 May 1984, 26.

Palmer, Richard H., *The Contemporary British History Play*, Westport, CT: Greenwood Press, 1998.

Parker, John, *Who's Who in the Theatre*, 15th edn, Bath: Pitman, 1972.

Parker, Stewart, *Heavenly Bodies*, *Plays: 2*, London: Methuen, 2000, 83–168.

Parkin, Michael, 'Music Hall hath Charms', *Guardian*, 4 Jul 1974, 13.

Patai, Daphne and Will H. Corral (eds), *Theory's Empire*, New York: Columbia University Press, 2005.

Patterson, Michael, '*Early Morning*', *The Oxford Dictionary of Plays*, Oxford: Oxford University Press, 2006, 129–30.

Philips, Caryl, 'I Could Have Been a Playwright', Davis and Fuchs, 37–46.

Pickering, David, 'The Forsyte Saga', *The Museum of Broadcast Communications*, MBC, 2008, accessed 25 Jul 2008, http://www.museum.tv/archives/etv/F/htmlF/forsytesaga/forsytesaga.htm.

Plant, Sadie, *Cornelia Parker: Never Endings*, Exhibition catalogue, Introduction, Birmingham: Ikon Gallery, 2007.

Plater, Alan, Sid Chaplin and Glasgow, Alex, *Close the Coalhouse Door*, London: Methuen, 1969.

Pomerance, Bernard, *The Elephant Man*, New York: Grove, 1979.

Poole, Steven, *Unspeak*, London: Little, Brown, 2006.

Pownall, David, *Livingstone and Sechele*, *Plays One*, London: Oberon, 2000, 71–130.

Procter, James, *Stuart Hall*, London: Routledge, 2004.

Red Ladder, *Taking our Time*, London: Pluto, 1979.

Rees, Roland (ed.), *Fringe First: Pioneers of Fringe Theatre on Record*, London: Oberon, 1992.

Rego, Paula, *Jane Eyre*, London: Enitharmon, 2003.

Rhys, Jean and Angela Smith, *Wide Sargasso Sea*, Harmondsworth: Penguin, 1997.

Rice, Jenny and Carol Saunders, 'Consuming *Middlemarch*: The Construction and Consumption of Nostalgia in Stamford', *Pulping Fictions*, ed. Deborah Cartmell, I.Q. Hunter, Heidi Kaye and Imelda Whelehan, London: Pluto, 1996, 85–98.

Richards, Jeffrey, 'Dickens – Our Contemporary', *Films and British National Identity: From Dickens to Dads' Army*, Manchester: Manchester University Press, 1997.

Ridout, Nicholas, *Stage Fright, Animals, and Other Theatrical Problems*, Cambridge: Cambridge University Press, 2006.

Roms, Heike, 'Performing *Polis*: Theatre, Nationness and Civic Identity in Post-Devolution Wales', *Studies in Theatre and Performance*, 2004, 24, 3, 177–92.

Ros, Nic, 'Leaving the Twentieth Century: New Writing on the Welsh-Language Mainstage 1979–1995', Taylor, *Staging Wales*, 18–32.

Rowlinson, Matthew, 'Theory of Victorian Studies: Anachronism and Self-Reflexivity', *Victorian Studies*, 2005, 47, 2, 241–52.

Royle, Nicholas, *Jacques Derrida*, Abingdon: Routledge, 2003.

Rutherford, Andrew, *Mrs Bathurst and Other Stories* by Kipling, ed. Lisa Lewis, Select Bibliography, World's Classics, Oxford: Oxford University Press, 1991, xxvi–xxviii.

Ryton, Royce, *The Royal Baccarat Scandal*, London: Samuel French, 1990.

'St Pancras Case Study', Dent, 2011, accessed 22 May 2011, http://www.dentlondon.com/dent-architectural/st-pancras.php.

Said, Edward W., *Orientalism: Western Conceptions of the Orient*, Harmondsworth: Penguin, 2003.

Samuel, Raphael, *Island Stories: Unravelling Britain: Theatres of Memory, Volume II*, London: Verso, 1999.

——'Mrs Thatcher and Victorian Values', *Island Stories: Unravelling Britain: Theatres of Memory, Volume II*, 330–48.

——'Mrs Thatcher's Return to Victorian Values', *Victorian Values: A Joint Symposium of the Royal Society of Edinburgh and the British Academy: December 1990*, ed. T.C. Smont, Oxford: Oxford University Press, 1992, 9–29.

——*Theatres of Memory: Past and Present in Contemporary Culture*, London: Verso, 1994.

Sandbrook, Dominic, *White Heat: A History of Britain in the Swinging Sixties*. London: Little, Brown, 2006.

Sanders, Andrew, *Charles Dickens*, Oxford: Oxford University Press, 2003.

Savage, Jon, *England's Dreaming: The Sex Pistols and Punk Rock*, London: Faber, 2005.

Savill, Charmian C., 'Brith Gof', Taylor, *Staging Wales*, 100–10.

Schafer, Elizabeth, *Lilian Bayliss: A Biography*, Hatfield: University of Hertfordshire Press/Society for Theatre Research, 2006.

Sedgwick, Eve Kosofsky, *Tendencies*, London: Routledge, 1994.

Selby, Keith, Chris Wensley and Robert Giddings, *Screening the Novel*, London: Macmillan, 1990.

Shakespeare, Tom, 'Stickin' up for Dickens', 14 Dec 2006, *Ouch! – It's a Disability Thing, BBC*, accessed 20 Feb 2007, http://www.bbc.co.uk/ouch/columnists/tom/141206_index.shtml.

'Shared Experience', *Arts Council England*, 2011, accessed 15 May 2011, http://www.artscouncil.org.uk/rfo/shared-experience/.

Shellard, Dominic, Steven Nicholson and Miriam Handley, *The Lord Chamberlain Regrets ...: A History of British Theatre Censorship*, London: British Library, 2004.

Shepherd, Jack, *Holding Fire!*, London: Nick Hern, 2007.

Sher, Antony, *Year of the King*, 2nd edn, London: Methuen, 1990.

Sondheim, Stephen and Hugh Wheeler, *Sweeney Todd: The Demon Barber of Fleet Street*, New York: Applause, 1991.

Spivak, Gayatri Chakravorty, 'Three Women's Texts and a Critique of Imperialism', *Critical Enquiry*, 1985, 12, 1, 243–61.

Spurling, John, *The British Empire Part One*, London: Marion Boyars, 1982.

———*Shades of Heathcliff and Death of Captain Doughty*, London: Marion Boyars, 1975.

Stafford, Nick. *Luminosity*, London: Faber, 2001.

Stewart, Ian, 'Marching Orders', review of *Kipling – East and West, Country Life*, 21 Jun 1984, 1782.

Stone, Laurie, 'Why Charlotte Dissed Emily', *Literary Review*, 2006, 49.3, 63–70.

Stoneman, Patsy, *Brontë Transformations: Cultural Dissemination of Jane Eyre and Wuthering Heights*, Hemel Hempstead: Prentice Hall/Harvester Wheatsheaf, 1996.

Stoppard, Tom, *The Invention of Love*, London: Faber, 1997.

Styan, J.L., *Modern Drama in Theory and Practice 1: Realism and Naturalism*, Cambridge: Cambridge University Press, 1981.

Sutherland, Ruth, 'A Victorian Value We Couldn't Afford to Lose', *Observer*, 29 Jun 2008, accessed 24 Jul 2008, http://www.guardian.co.uk/business/2008/jun/29/creditcrunch.housingmarket.

Sweet, Matthew, *Inventing the Victorians*, London: Faber, 2001.

Tanitch, Robert, *Oscar Wilde on Stage and Screen*, London: Methuen, 1999.

Taylor, Anne-Marie, *Staging Wales: Welsh Theatre 1979–1997*, Cardiff: University of Wales Press, 1997.

———'Welsh Theatre and the World', *Staging Wales*, 111–9.

Taylor, D.J., *Kept: A Victorian Mystery*, London: Vintage, 2007.

Taylor, Miles, Introduction, Taylor and Wolff, 1–16.

———and Michael Wolff (eds), *The Victorians since 1901: Histories, Representations and Revisions*, Manchester: Manchester University Press, 2004.

Teale, Polly, *Brontë*, London: Nick Hern, 2005.

———*Jane Eyre*, London: Nick Hern, 1998.

Terson, Peter, *The 1861 Whitby Lifeboat Disaster*, Todmorden: Woodhouse, 1979.

Thatcher, Margaret, 'Speech on Women in a Changing World (1st Dame Margery Corbett-Ashby Memorial Lecture)', Margaret Thatcher Foundation, 2005, accessed 22 Aug 2006, http://www.margaretthatcher.org/speeches/displaydocument.asp?docid=105007.

———'Speech to Conservative Party Conference', *Margaret Thatcher Foundation*, 2005, accessed 22 Aug 2006, http://www.margaretthatcher.org/speeches/displaydocument.asp?docid=106941.

———'Speech to Glasgow Chamber of Commerce (Bicentenary)', Margaret Thatcher Foundation, 2005, accessed 22 Aug 2006, http://margaretthatcher.org/speeches/displaydocument.asp?docid=105244.

———'Speech to Greater London Young Conservatives (Iain Macleod Memorial Lecture – "Dimensions of Conservatism")', Margaret Thatcher Foundation, 2005, accessed 22 Aug 2006, http://www.margaretthatcher.org/speeches/displaydocument.asp?docid=103411.

———'Speech to Zurich Economic Society ("The New Renaissance")', Margaret Thatcher Foundation, 2005, accessed 22 Aug 2006, http://www.margaretthatcher.org/speeches/displaydocument.asp?docid=103336.

———and Peter Allen, 'Radio Interview for IRN programme *The Decision Makers*', transcript, Margaret Thatcher Foundation, 2005, accessed 22 Aug 2006, http://www.margaretthatcher.org/speeches/displaydocument.asp?docid=105291.

———and Brian Walden, 'TV Interview for London Weekend Television *Weekend World* ("Victorian Values")', transcript, Margaret Thatcher Foundation, 2005, accessed 22 Aug 2006, http://www.margaretthatcher.org/speeches/displaydocument.asp?docid=105087.

Thomas, Ronald R., 'Detection in the Victorian Novel', *The Cambridge Companion to the Victorian Novel*, ed. Deidre Davis, Cambridge: Cambridge University Press, 2001, 169–91.

Thompson, James, 'The BBC and the Victorians', Taylor and Wolff, 150–66.

'*Upstairs, Downstairs* – The TV Series', *h2g2*, 5 Oct 2005, accessed 6 Oct 2008, http://www.bbc.co.uk/dna/h2g2/A5403629.

Vanden Bossche, Chris R., 'What Did *Jane Eyre* Do? Ideology, Agency, Class and the Novel', *Narrative*, 2005, 13, 1, 46–66.

Waldrep, Shelton, 'The Uses and Misuses of Oscar Wilde', *Victorian Afterlife: Postmodern Culture Rewrites the Nineteenth Century*, ed. John Kucich and Diane F. Sadoff, Minneapolis: University of Minnesota Press, 2000, 49–63.

Walvin, James, *Victorian Values*, London: Andre Deutsch, 1987.

Ward, Maryanne C., 'Romancing the Ending: Adaptations in Nineteenth-Century Closure', *Journal of the Midwest Modern Language Association*, 1996, 29(1) 15–31.

Waters, Sarah, *Affinity*, London: Virago, 2000.

———*Fingersmith*, London: Virago, 2003.

———*Tipping the Velvet*, London: Virago, 1999.

Wells, H.G., 'The Door in the Wall', *Selected Short Stories*, Harmondsworth: Penguin, 1958, 106–22.

———'The New Accelerator', *Selected Short Stories*, Harmondsworth: Penguin, 1958, 339–52.

———'The Remarkable Case of Davidson's Eyes', *Selected Short Stories*, Harmondsworth: Penguin, 1958, 174–83.

Whelan, Peter, *The Earthly Paradise*, London: Faber, 2004.

Whittell, Crispin, *Darwin in Malibu*, London: Methuen, 2003.

Williams, Nigel, *Country Dancing*, London: Faber, 1987.

Williams, Raymond, 'The Bloomsbury Fraction', Higgins, 229–48.

———*The Country and the City*, Oxford: Oxford University Press, 1975.

———'Crisis in English Studies', Higgins, 249–65.

———*Keywords: A Vocabulary of Culture and Society*, London: Fontana, 1988.

———*Raymond Williams on Television*, ed. Alan O' Connor, London: Routledge, 1988.

———*Television: Technology and Cultural Form*, Hanover, New England: Wesleyan University Press, 1992.

———'The Writer: Commitment and Alignment', Higgins, 208–20.

Wilson, Angus, *The Strange Ride of Rudyard Kipling*, London: Secker and Warburg, 1977.

Wilson, Snoo, *Vampire, Plays: 2*, London: Methuen, 2000, 5–59.

Wolff, Jonathan, *Why Read Marx Today?*, Oxford: Oxford University Press, 2002.

Wood, Charles, *H; Being Monologues at Front of Burning Cities*, London: Methuen, 1969.

Wood, Ellen, *East Lynne*, Oxford: Oxford University Press, 2005.

Woolland, Brian, *Dark Attractions: The Theatre of Peter Barnes*, London: Methuen, 2004.

Wright, Nicholas, *Vincent in Brixton*, London: Nick Hern, 2002.

Index

Note: The letter 'n' followed by the locators refers to endnotes.

Heritage, Nostalgia and Modern British Theatre

THE UNIVERSITY OF
WINCHESTER

Martial Rose Library
Tel: 01962 827306

To be returned on or before the day marked above, subject to recall.